Clyde

LOST IN THE HORSE LATITUDES

For people who like this kind of a book,
this is the kind of a book those people will like.
ABRAHAM LINCOLN.

BOOKS BY
H. ALLEN SMITH

Lost in the Horse Latitudes
Life in a Putty Knife Factory
Low Man on a Totem Pole

H. ALLEN SMITH

Lost in the Horse Latitudes

ILLUSTRATED BY LEO HERSHFIELD

Doubleday, Doran & Company, Inc.

GARDEN CITY, NEW YORK

1944

Dedicated to
THE COMMISSIONER OF SANITATION
CITY OF NEW YORK

★ **IMPORTANT** ★

THIS **EDITION** IS **COMPLETE** AND **UNABRIDGED**

THIS IS A FULL-LENGTH BOOK PRINTED IN A
SPECIAL FORMAT DESIGNED TO SAVE
MATERIALS AND MANPOWER

The publishers, in accordance with government regulations, have reduced bulk by the use of lightweight
paper throughout, and have used smaller margins to
allow for more words on each page. You, the reader,
are thus provided with a complete, unabridged text,
and better assured of a continuing supply of books.

Contents

Principal Characters

ABRAHAM LINCOLN, *a book reviewer.*
NOAH WEBSTER, *a speller.*
ULYSSES S. GRANT, *a joker; also a statue.*
HEDDA HOPPER, *a columnist.*
BENJAMIN FRANKLIN, *a wastrel.*
VITO, *a machine-hater.*
JOHN KELCH, *who wanted a new suit.*
HUBERT HIPSKIND, *a debater.*
IRVIN S. COBB, *an after-dinner speaker.*
MAXWELL BODENHEIM, *a poet.*
KNUTE ROCKNE, *who always said something.*
JOE ALEX MORRIS, *an international traveler.*
JOHN D. ROCKEFELLER, *a 20-per-cent tipper.*
SAM DABNEY, *who gets killed off.*
LUCY STREET, *who objects.*
SAM BALLARD, *a St. Louis booster.*
JAMES IRWIN, *who knows an aspirin-maker.*
CHARLES DAGGETT, *who is careful about pencils.*
THE TAGGER WOMAN, *a secretary.*
JAMES FRANCIS CAGNEY, *a farmer.*
BILL CAGNEY, *a pigeon-fancier.*
ED McNAMARA, *who never made an arrest.*
DEEMS TAYLOR, *a son.*
JIM MORAN, *a beam-thrower.*
OSSIP MORAN, *an unborn ostrich.*
BERT ALLENBERG, *an agent.*
JOAN FONTAINE, *a lap-leaper.*
BETTY HUTTON, *who needs no introduction.*
SAM GOLDWYN, *who asked for a promise.*
BUDDY DeSYLVA, *an audience.*
MISS BALLANTINE, *a dish, not a beverage.*
ANDY HARDY, *who gets an ailment.*
DR. GILLESPIE, *who cures it.*

WHITE EAGLE, *a large bird.*
BARNEY BALABAN, *president of Paramount.*
JIMMY WALKER, *a cornerstone-layer.*
EMILY KIMBROUGH, *who wrote a book.*
MISS BEAUTY REST, *a watched pot.*
SIDNEY RESNICK, *a writer.*
ROBERT BENCHLEY, *a support for a derby hat.*
GENE FOWLER, *a lap-runner.*
HARRY BRAND, *a funeral-rigger.*
SIDNEY SKOLSKY, *who bit an arm.*
LOUELLA O. PARSONS, *owner of the arm.*
CHESTER GREENWOOD, *an inventor.*
AL WILKIE, *a good man.*
MR. COMMA-CRAZY, *a boss.*
WILLIAM SHAKESPEARE, *a questionable character.*
DWIGHT MITCHELL WILEY, *who wore a leash.*
FRANK PARTOS, *an amateur lawyer.*
CECIL B. DeMILLE, *God.*
HECHT AND MACARTHUR, *who had a secretary.*
IRENE, *a martyr.*
SETON I. MILLER, *a producer.*
THE SWEDISH ANGEL, *a wrestler.*
FRANK BUTLER, *who taunts elevators.*
RAYMOND CHANDLER, *a detective-story writer.*
JACK WAGNER, *who carries wood.*
BOBBY WATSON, *a Führer.*
FRANK WALDMAN, *a friend to womankind.*
GRANTLAND RICE, *an unwitting race-track tout.*
HAROLD MATSON, *who believes in tailing.*
NEBRASKA, *a treacherous horse.*
Y. FRANK FREEMAN, *a dog owner.*
OBLATH'S, *a resort.*
GENEVIEVE, *printer to the Word Game.*
ORPH GIBBERSON, *who got shot.*
PAUL JONES, *a tangent-talker.*
JOHN P. MEDBURY, *an apprentice druggist.*
WALDO PEIRCE, *a turtle-fancier.*
LEON KAY, *a scalp doctor.*
LUCEY'S, *where the author worked.*
RUFUS BLAIR, *who is tense and nervous.*

José Maniah, *who spoke his piece.*
Dick Carlson, *a voice from the grave.*
Dinah Shore, *who has an unlisted number.*
Joaquin Miller, *whose spirit was in a jar.*
George, *a potted copyreader.*
Dr. Rockwell, *translator of Kokomcar.*
Ben Serkowich, *intimate of Buffalo Bill.*
Lieutenant Beale, *a camel-lover.*
Don Antonio Feliz, *whose head nodded.*
Colonel Griffith J. Griffith, *heir to a curse.*
Frank Lloyd Wright, *who likes nice neighbors.*
Junior, *who was in duck.*
Donald MacBride, *who had two dollars.*
Wild Red Barry, *an athlete.*
Tony Ross, *a superb sportsman.*
Margaret Ettinger, *a bibliophile.*
Edgar Bergen, *a hobby lobby.*
Charlie McCarthy, *who has a woodpecker on his door.*
John Barrymore, *a good judge of books.*
W. C. Fields, *a tank car.*
Gerard Darrow, *a thirsty Quiz Kid.*
Gregory La Cava, *a golfer.*
Mack Sennett, *who chews tobacco.*
Dud, *a dead dog.*
Sidney Whipple, *a shopper.*
Butch, *who needs a Seeing Eye man.*
Bob Burns, *a luncheon guest.*
Chet Lauck, *a Lum.*
Norris Goff, *an Abner.*
Paw Gasper, *a liberator of man.*
Paulette Goddard, *whose navel is discussed.*
Havelock Ellis, *an expert on things.*
Alva Johnston, *a biographer.*
Mrs. Whistler, *a mother.*
William Tecumseh Sherman, *whose wagon turned over.*
Fiorello H. LaGuardia, *foe of pinball machines.*
Basil Rathbone, *who was booted but not spurred.*
Russel Crouse, *an autographer.*
Grover Cleveland, *who is favored for a third term.*

Introduction

THE AUTHOR of this book has recently been under contract to Paramount Pictures in Hollywood.

Perhaps you remember a magnificent sequence in that motion picture *The Good Earth*. A swarm of locusts appears like a black cloud, swoops down on the Chinese farm, and in no time at all leaves the place a shambles.

Now, for "farm" read "Paramount Studio." For the old Chinaman, B. G. DeSylva. And for the swarm of locusts, H. Allen Smith. However cockeyed the parable, you get the idea.

In the early part of 1943 Smith condescended to visit my office where I asked him if he would like to take a crack at writing for the movies. He looked at me as though I were crazy. I now know that I was.

He rose from his chair without a word and, casting a reproachful glance over his shoulder, departed. I later learned from my secretary that he stopped in the outer office, bent over, and whispered to her: "Is that guy in there dependable?"

A month later I received a telegram from New York. It said, "Okay."

When the contract was signed I was understandably elated. I knew Smith to be one of the top humorists of the day and I was delighted that at last he was mine, all mine! That's what *I* thought. I lived to learn that Smith isn't anybody's —at any rate, not for long.

Reporting to the studio, he was given an office and a secretary. The secretary is still in a sanitarium at Palm Springs and the latest word from her is that she will be as good as new in a couple of months. The office has been redecorated.

When Smith and I had our first conference he asked for a collaborator, remarking that he had never written a scenario

9

and didn't know how to start. I told him that it wasn't necessary for him to know. I wanted to get his brand of humor on the screen untainted by any collaboration. We later could put whatever he wrote into script form. I suggested that he do something on the order of Chapter Two in *Life in a Putty Knife Factory,* which concerns Smith, Senior, and other lusty personalities.

"Go on back to your office," I said, "and sit down and write me a movie."

"Where is it?" he asked.

"Where is what?"

"The office," he said. "I've forgotten where it is."

I suppose he found it though I'm not quite sure. I saw so little of him after that. Not that I didn't try. I'd telephone his office and usually I'd get the same answer: "Have you tried Oblath's?" Oblath's is the saloon nearest the studio. "Well, then, have you tried Lucey's?" Lucey's is the bar nearest Oblath's. "What about the Melrose Grotto?" The bar nearest Lucey's. And so on, all the way to Santa Monica.

I recall trapping him one day in the commissary after he had walked past me without speaking. I jockeyed him into a corner and asked him if he was sore about something. He just looked at me awhile and then said:

"One side, scum!"

I pressed him for an explanation.

"How much," he asked, "do you draw down a week?"

I wanted to know what difference that made.

"Listen," he said. "I know all about the Hollywood caste system and I intend to adhere to it. A man who makes $1,500 a week doesn't speak to a man who makes $1,000. A man who makes $2,000 doesn't speak to a man who makes $1,500. I don't know what *you* make. If you want to bring me some of your canceled checks and show me how much you're getting paid, maybe we can do business. I won't have anything to do with you until I find out."

I didn't show him any canceled checks but I guess he discovered I was drawing a big enough salary because he stopped by my office a couple of times. Once he entered unannounced. I looked up and saw him standing in the doorway.

"Oh, I beg your pardon," he said. "I was looking for the gents' room."

He was gone before I could say a word. Another time he came in, face beaming, plopped himself down opposite me, and announced that he had finally come up with a tremendous idea.

"Ah!" I said, rubbing my hands together. "I knew it. I knew you'd come through."

"Out there in the studio park," he said, "I just noticed that the grass is getting a little long. Where's the lawnmower department? I want to get to work."

The rest of the time we communicated by interoffice memos. Those memos of his were extremely readable but unfortunately cannot be printed, even in this book. They might be issued privately under the general heading, "Sex— Indoors and Out," except that they no longer exist. Some were burned on arrival. Others were smuggled out to the back lot and buried in quicklime.

One day, a bit resentful at having received no story or script or word from Smith, I decided to pretend that a long memo from him was actually the story he had been working on and was submitting for approval. This particular memo was concerned chiefly with one of Paramount's most beautiful and shapely actresses. With deep sarcasm I sent a note to Smith saying that I thought the plot was adequate though there was much in his synopsis that needed cleaning up, and that he should proceed with the screen play. I received an immediate reply:

"Get someone else to write the screen play. In *this* one, I want to *ACT!*"

Smith found other ways to amuse himself during his stay with us. He spent one afternoon at the studio's main gate with an autograph book and pen. Each time one of our stars passed in or out he'd approach the performer, open the book, write his own autograph, tear out the sheet, hand it over, and say, "There you are. Thanks very much for asking." On another occasion I heard that he had asked the studio manager for permission to bring an air rifle to his office, but I never knew why he wanted it. I hate to think.

Late one afternoon another studio executive remarked

to me that he didn't feel Smith was contributing much to the dignity of Paramount. He said that whenever Smith answered the telephone in his office it was his custom to sing out: "Smith's house of ill fame!" I thought about it for a while, then put on my hat and walked to Lucey's. I always succeed in finding some daily frustration or confusion that will drive me into Lucey's charming bar. Smith was there ahead of me. He was surrounded by a happy group of extras and bit players. I walked up, but before I could say a word Smith was introducing me around.

"This is Bing Crosby's brother," he told them all.

I got him loose from his friends and we settled into a corner booth.

"Working on your script, I see," I began. "How's it going?"

"What script?" he said. "I gave that up long ago. I thought you knew."

"What, pray tell, are you doing now?"

"Working with Bing and Bob on *Road to Utopia*," he said, "and, brother, I love it!"

As much as I hate to admit it some of the best gags in the latest of the *Road* pictures were written by H. Allen Smith. I hate to admit it because I had given him the wrong assignment and he had found the right one by himself. Paramount got its money's worth out of H. Allen even though he did manage to violate all the rules.

Since his departure we have succeeded in getting the studio back into a semblance of normal operation. I find pleasure in one reflection. I remember that when he first came to work he told me he thought I might make a nuisance of myself by pestering him from day to day. He said he had a wrestler friend named the Swedish Angel and that he would like to engage this man as his secretary. I talked him out of it. Thank God. I have since seen a picture of the Swedish Angel. I shudder to think what might have happened to Paramount if Smith *and* the Swedish Angel were with us as a team.

I have had no glimpse of the book that is to follow. If, in its pages, there is any mention of me, I want you to know that in all likelihood it is a downright lie. I am *not* Bing Crosby's brother.   B. G. DeSylva.

Concerning the Sex Life of Chickens

THIS is the last chapter. I have yanked it out of its proper place and installed it here at the beginning because it was written before any of the others; because the book is so disorganized that nobody would ever notice the difference; but chiefly because a great many people always read the last chapter of a book first, even in mystery stories.

The lilting prose contained in this last chapter is being carpentered in an upstairs room of a farmhouse. Below the window at my right a man is standing in a wagon scattering some stuff over a field by means of a pitchfork. I'm not sure what he is scattering, but I can guess. I have seen stuff thrown with a pitchfork before but never have I seen a man throw it as this man does. He can throw stuff faster and farther than any person I know outside of Hollywood. He creates a fitting atmosphere for the beginning of this project; he inspires me to prodigious effort.

The reason I am sitting in a farmhouse is none of your business. If it were any of your business I might tell you that just recently I returned to New York City from Hollywood. I spent six months in the town Rufus Blair calls Double Dubuque and came pretty close to catching a disease known as the Beverly Hills botts—an affliction characterized by gastro-intestinal disturbances, skin eruptions that would frighten a barbecued ham, and whirring noises in the head. Along toward the end of my visit I found myself scanning the real estate ads and looking covetously at convertible coupés. If it hadn't been for the dove I think I might have taken up permanent residence in that lovely town.

One morning I got out of bed earlier than usual. I had intended sleeping late but outside the window of my apartment a dove was making dove noises. I shaved and dressed and all the while that maniacal bird kept up its melancholy hooting. I've always been under the impression that a dove had some association with tender feelings—that the cooing of a dove was somehow romantic and inspirational, causing the gonads to vibrate. Now I know better. I stood it as long as I could, then flung open a window, poked out my head, and screamed;

"SHUDDUPPP!"

It didn't shut up, so I threw a copy of *The Gay Illiterate* at it and it went away for a while. Then I sat down and

considered my conduct. "Heavens to betsy," I said to myself. "I'm probably the only person in the world who ever screamed in anger at a dove. It's time I got out of this place."

And so I came back to New York City, fairly eager for work. At once a new crisis arose. A squirrel laid siege to my apartment. This squirrel apparently loves the sound of a typewriter and whenever he hears it he arrives on the run, plants himself on the window sill, and just sits there looking at me. It was amusing for a while but not a very long while. On the day that I found myself saying mean, spiteful things to a squirrel, even making passes at the beast with an old mashie, I decided I had better go to some quiet place in the country and get this book rolling. And here I am. Sure wish you could see that guy throw that stuff with that pitchfork!

This is a regulation farm in all details save one. The man who runs it has accommodations for weary, squirrel-ridden city folks who would like to get away from it all, drink gallons of milk, walk in the fields, investigate the behavior of hogs, read detective stories, or just sit.

A few miles away is the place where Noah Webster once taught school. As a pedagogue in these parts he grew dissatisfied with the spelling book then in use. I don't know whether he was unhappy over the way the words in it were spelled, or whether the binding struck him as unlovely, or what. In any event, Noah set to work and wrote his Blue-Backed Speller which sold twenty-five million copies. This income made it possible for him to give up teaching, go back to Connecticut and assemble his dictionary. I sometimes catch myself wondering how a man would go about writing a speller. I suppose old Noah employed his spare time and recess periods wandering around the countryside looking at things, spelling them, writing them down. He sees a cat. "Cat," he says. "C-A-T. Cat. Reckon I'll use that one."

Off to the west within sight of this farm is a big house where Ulysses S. Grant smoked his last cigar. His doctor told him to stop, so he came up to this place and had his last smoke. I don't know the details and I bring the matter up simply because I have a story about Grant and a cigar. Back in the 1860s a man named Horace Norton, founder of Norton College, met Grant, and the general gave him a cigar. Dr. Norton didn't smoke it but cherished and preserved it as a memento of the meeting. In 1932 a big Norton reunion was held in Chicago and Dr. Norton's grandson, Winstead Norton, brought out the stogie, now aged seventy-five. Winstead Norton stood up before the assemblage and delivered a sentimental oration. During his speech he lit the cigar and declaimed between puffs:

"And as I light this cigar with trembling hand it is not alone a tribute to him whom you call founder, but also to that Titan among statesmen who was never too exalted to be a friend, who was . . ."

Bang!

After seventy-five years a Ulysses S. Grant joke paid off.

There are several other visitors here at the farm—city guys who have come up to rest and sit around and tell lies to one another. It has been fun watching some of these slickers react before the wonders of Nature.

The traditional ignorance of New Yorkers in agricultural lore and the deportment of livestock has been bandied in many a joke. Usually the joke involves a cow. Cows have been installed in the city zoos because many New York kids had never seen one and didn't even know which section of the cow the milk came from. Those that did know couldn't understand how a big, clumsy animal with no hands could ever squirt straight enough to get the milk in bottles.

At this farm, however, the chief interest of the metropolitan minds seems to be in chickens. A few days ago one of the men from New York asked the farm manager if he might gather eggs at the henhouse. He soon came back with a pail full.

"John," he said to the manager, "I got them all but one. I left it down there because it didn't have time to harden yet."

It appears that he actually had come upon one egg with a soft shell, a consequence of the hen's having not taken enough bromo seltzer or some such thing. The city feller quickly concluded that all eggs are soft-shelled when they are laid and that the shells turn hard only after exposure to the air. He couldn't believe that a hen, with her somewhat delicate construction, could extrude an egg with a hard shell around it. The very thought of such a thing was horrifying to him.

Last summer there was a society guy from Park Avenue visiting here. He needed some exercise, so the farm manager took him into the fields and showed him how to pitch hay onto a rack. The society guy sweated and coughed and scratched and complained and finally threw down his fork in disgust.

"This," he said, "is the biggest god-damn piece of nonsense I ever heard of. What do you want to come out here and pitch this hay for? All you got to do is get on the phone and they'll bring a whole bale of it around to your door."

This very morning I was walking toward the barn with a *soigné* gentleman out of Greenwich Village. He is a native New Yorker and thinks hay is something a hot singer says twice. Off to our left I happened to see a rooster performing a biological uproar on a hen. I pointed out this interesting though commonplace manifestation of nature to my friend. He stood and looked at it until it was over and then said:

"Well, maybe I shouldn't admit it, but this is the first time in my life I've ever seen that done and I'm past forty."

He scratched his chin and ruminated for a few moments. Then he observed:

"I don't imagine it'd be much fun."

I don't either.

CHAPTER II *The Horse Latitudes*

THE SUMMER OF 1943 was the period in which I got lost in the horse latitudes. For a while I thought maybe I was going through the change of life. This sort of thing happens to men nowadays; I mean the doctors recognize it nowadays as occurring among males, whereas the women used to have it all to themselves and welcome to it. In Hollywood I was told about a certain gentleman known around the studios as a competent screen writer who took down with the change of life and like to drove everybody daffy before he finished with it.

This man began showing signs of mild eccentricity before his case had been properly diagnosed. He set up a makeshift chemical laboratory in his basement and then launched a sort of crusade to reduce the weight of every woman he knew. He considered that his mission in life was to make every girl slender and willowy. Well, not exactly willowy—that word is misused in describing girls. To say a girl is willowy seems to suggest that you could pick her up by the ankles and whip a horse with her. I have never known but one girl who answered such a description and she was of no earthly use except, perhaps, as an emergency buggy whip. At any rate, this poor menopause-ridden guy began appearing in public with a leather case containing several vials. In the vials, he said, were rare potions of his own brewing. Blended properly, he explained, his medicine would take a stated amount of beef off any female almost immediately. He boasted that he could stir up a draught that would fetch Kate Smith down to the size of Frances Langford.

The man's wife was understandably worried for a time. She would be having a hen party when her husband would emerge from his basement laboratory. He'd go quietly, professionally, from one to another of the guests, feeling them for fat. A terrible thing. His wife tried to get her girl friends to humor him along until the spell passed.

"I'll humor his nasty hands off at the wrists," said one lady, "if he ever puts them there again."

The wife eventually got hold of the leather case and found out that the medicines were harmless, confected of Worcestershire sauce, ammonia, coffee, and tarragon vinegar. Out of love for her husband she continued to take the stuff, even though it would gag a buzzard, and in time he lost interest in weight reduction, though he wasn't altogether a well man.

She came home one afternoon to find him in his study with a young mountain lion. A friend of his had trapped the beast up in the hills and the afflicted writer got possession of it by promising to make a pet of it. When his wife arrived home she found he had the mountain lion trussed up and was pulling out the animal's toenails with a pair of pliers. He'd take hold of a claw, give it a yank, and yell: "Take that, you inhuman bastard!" It took quite a bit of effort and several doctors to get the guy straightened out after the mountain-lion incident, but I understand he eventually passed through the climacteric and is now working steadily at Warner Brothers.

As for myself, I didn't put on any shows like that. I was simply restless—wandering in the horse latitudes. The horse latitudes are certain zones in the ocean which used to be the despair of sailing vessels. They are characterized by dead calms and light, baffling winds. They got their name, I understand, back in the days when cargoes of horses were being sent from Europe to the West Indies. A ship would come along with a load of horses and get involved in one of those dead calms. If it lasted very long they'd run out of drinking water and the horses would go berserk and start kicking the ship to pieces, whereupon the sailors would throw them overboard.

I'm giving you this explanation of horse latitudes with a purpose in mind. I've got to have *some* explanation for the title of this book. I had planned originally to call it *Like Elephants, I Remember*. Hedda Hopper ran a piece in her column while I was in Hollywood saying that was the title. Back East the editors of Doubleday, Doran read it and promptly wired me: ELEPHANT TITLE NO GOOD. IT MAKES SENSE.

In my own opinion the horse latitudes title makes more sense than the elephant line. I doubt very seriously if an elephant remembers anything more than the fact that it is fun to look at people who are looking at elephants. Elephant memory is probably a myth, just as so many other popular beliefs are myths. Clean as a hound's tooth? A prominent veterinarian spent years examining the teeth of hounds to prove that they are the dirtiest teeth on earth. Benjamin Franklin was a model of thriftiness? In 1940 someone dug into the records of the Pennsylvania Company, oldest bank in the country, and discovered that Ben was overdrawn at least three days out of every week.

The dead calms and light, baffling winds of that summer led to a lot of aimless wandering. Sometimes I'd go up to get a haircut when I didn't need a haircut. I simply enjoyed the company of a barber named Vito. He knew things and he had opinions, this Vito. Once he asked me if I wanted a singe and I told him I didn't. Then I asked him the reason for people getting their hair singed.

"They gotta idea," he explained, "that they gotta holes insidea hair. If holesa open, air goesa insidea hair, blow away alla roots. So, if getta singe, closea up holes, air don't getta in."

One day I walked into the shop and Vito wasn't there. The boss said he was off sick. A week later I was back and found Vito still absent. I asked the boss about him.

"He'sa no sick," said the boss. "He'sa mad."

Beyond that he wouldn't go, but he did tell me that I might find Vito loafing in a cigar store around the corner.

Sure enough, there he was, dressed in his Sunday clothes, unhappiness written all over his face. He was glad to see me but as soon as I asked about his troubles he went into a tantrum. He speaks what someone has aptly described as broken broken English and all I could make out of his discourse was that his boss was a dope.

I soothed him a little and told him I'd like to have him go back to the shop and cut my hair.

"You go back," he said, "tella boss Vito no usea tam machine."

I returned to the shop and told the boss that Vito seemed upset about a machine. The boss seized me by the arm and led me across the room.

"Look," he said. "Looka fine machine."

Against the wall was a small black metal contrivance—a machine for making lather. The boss showed me how it worked. He flipped back a sliding cover, a motor hummed, and creamy lather poured out of a hole into his hand.

"Costa me plenty, thisa machine," said the boss. "But Vito getsa mad, says machinea no good. I tell Vito he usea machine or losea job."

Well, I didn't want to see Vito losea his job so I talked the boss into letting him come back, at least long enough to cut my hair, suggesting that perhaps another appeal would convince Vito the machine was okay.

Vito came back with me, grumbling against the machine, entered the shop without speaking to the boss or anyone else, and carefully avoided glancing at the infernal lather factory as he passed it. He got into his white jacket and went to work on my thatch.

Nobody bothered him and at last he reached that part of the operation involving shaving my neck. He picked up a shaving mug, got some warm water in it, and started whipping up some old-style lather. Immediately the boss was at his side.

"Vito," he said. "Vito, pleasea usea machine."

What Vito said to him is not known to me for it was uttered in Italian, and while I understand no Italian I certainly recognize unprintable stuff when I hear it in any language. By the time Vito's eruption was half finished he had on his coat and hat and was storming through the door making noises like Caruso with a bone stuck in his throat. The boss shrugged and came over to finish shaving my neck. He was quite upset, as indicated by the fact that he picked up the shaving mug and got his lather out of it, forgetting all about the machine.

Vito finally came back but on his own terms. No tam machine. I never found out why he hated that machine—why he insisted on using the old shaving mug. I don't think he was a Republican. I assume it was a pure case of invincible stubbornness. I dislike stubborn people when they are being stubborn toward me but when they're working on somebody else I enjoy their perversity. I have a clipping about a boy named John Kelch of Glassport, Pennsylvania, who is capable of being obstinate. Back in 1930, when John was eighteen years old, he asked his parents to buy him a new suit of clothes. They said no, his old suit was good for a while longer. John got so mad about it that he announced he would never, as long as he drew breath, set foot outside the house.

Ten years later the Selective Service Law was passed and some of the Kelch neighbors happened to remember about John and got to wondering what had happened to him. This neighborhood speculation reached the ears of local draft officials and a man was sent around to check up.

The investigator found John Kelch in his room. John was by now twenty-eight but he looked like a prophet of yore, with long, tangled hair and a beard in which you could have easily hidden a crate of cantaloupes. They forced him to leave the house and register for the draft and that's the last news I heard of him. If he actually was inducted, I suppose he took it with good grace. Induction would, in a sense, have meant victory for his principles—he'd get that new suit of clothes.

CHAPTER III   *On Public Speaking*

A COUPLE of years ago somebody sent me a clipping from the *Herald-Press* of Huntington, Indiana. The clipping was headed, "Items of Yesteryear Culled from the Files," and in the era when I had the job of culling items of yesteryear from the files of the same paper I never suspected I'd be culled myself someday. Yet here it was, under the subhead, "Twenty Years Ago Today, Saturday, March 11, 1922"—an account of a debate at St. Mary's School. The subject of the debate was, "Moving Pictures Are Detrimental to Our American Youth." The pertinent paragraph was this:

"The affirmative debaters were Allen Smith, Dolores Shinkle, Hubert Hipskind, Isabelle Eckert, and Florence Zahm. The affirmative side was the winner."

That's me, without the *H*. I suspect that I wrote the original newspaper item myself, since my name was not exactly last on the list. Yet I can't remember a single thing about that debate. I have a faint recollection of Hubert Hipskind; but I doubt if the debate ever actually took place. I can't picture myself getting up and busting loose with a speech without killing my team's chance for victory. Shinkle, Hipskind, Eckert, and Zahm must have been hot that day.

Since I became a book author people have been telephoning and writing me asking me to make speeches. For some mysterious reason an author is considered to be, by the very nature of things, an accomplished orator. He writes a book, perhaps a novel about a girl who is pure in heart, a girl whose nobility forbids her climbing in the hay with anybody making less than $5,000 a year. He writes this book and immediately he is called upon to deliver speeches on postwar planning, how egg-beater handles are made from the soybean, of facts about our national debt. Why should he be an authority on these things? If any person asked me to discuss the public debt I would promptly knock him down provided he was no bigger than Yvonne Dionne. Not that I don't know all about it.

I did make one speech a few years back. The Journalism

Club of New York University wore me down and finally I agreed to address its members. Irvin Cobb once said that when he started out trying to make speeches each performance was an ordeal involving cold sweat, hot flashes, trembles, dry tongue, and general physical collapse. He decided that he might conquer the thing by going around to small neighborhood meetings and giving talks. After a couple of years of such practice he was ready to appear before more important gatherings and he wound up as one of the best after-dinner speakers in the country. I thought maybe I ought to try some such system, and that's why I accepted the invitation at the university.

I didn't write a speech and try to memorize it for I'm not capable of memorizing my own telephone number. I did jot down a few notes but all they did was worry me for two days. I remembered a passage in Mark Twain where he discussed his early difficulties as a lecturer. He was unable to keep his lecture organized so he broke it up into ten parts just as though it were written in ten long paragraphs. All he needed to do was to remember the beginning of each paragraph and he would be able to give the whole thing proper flow and continuity. He took a pen and wrote the opening word of each section on a fingernail. It was his plan to glance casually at the first fingernail, start off with the word written on it, proceed until he had exhausted that section or paragraph of the speech, then pick up his cue from the word written on the next fingernail, and so on through the ten. Right away he ran into trouble. He began getting the fingers mixed up because he couldn't remember which fingernail he had looked at last and which was the next in sequence. Moreover, after the lectures people from the audience would come around and ask him if anything was wrong with his hands. For a while he thought he'd try licking the ink off each fingernail as he came to it—boldly sticking the finger into his mouth and sucking it off and disposing of it—but then he decided that that would not look very dignified.

I found no solution to my own problem there. I just went up to New York University and faced the thing. A young fellow got up to introduce me. He let go with a quotation from Santayana which didn't make a bit of sense to me and threw me ten miles into a state of confusion. I thought he was comparing me to the siege of the Alamo. At last I was on the platform. I gulped and stammered and dropped my notes all over the place and finally got going, and actually I wasn't doing so badly when the door opened and a cross-eyed man came in.

As it turned out the boys on the newspaper where I worked, knowing that I was nervous over making this speech, had decided to have their little jest. They sent this cross-eyed guy and he walked in, sat down in the front row, tilted his head over to one side and stared at me, or in my direction, until I had finished. I tried not to look at him but couldn't keep from doing it. Knowing my newspaper friends, I figured that sooner or later he would start tossing roses at me, or turn loose a chipmunk in the room, but he did nothing of the kind—just sat there and stared cross-eyed at me.

What I said to those journalism students remains lost in a pea soup as thick as fog. That cross-eyed guy had me so numb that when it was over somebody came up and said something and I said yes and they had me trapped again. They wanted to present me with a scroll and in order to get it I had to attend their Junior Prom at one of New York's fancier hotels.

I had never been to a Junior Prom in my life, or to any other kind of a prom, so it was quite an event. My wife went down to Union Square to buy an evening gown. There's always a hot scramble for the choice items in the store she picked—an establishment where ladies' garments are sold at perhaps a third of what they cost on Madison Avenue. In this Union Square store a woman stands a fair chance of getting herself locked in mortal combat before she is finished with her commerce there. The mammoth Glyptodon, which backed up to its enemies and beat them to death with its horny spiked tail is long extinct but the lady bargain hunter still abounds on our planet.

My wife, an expert catch-as-catch-can bargain wrestler, picked three gowns from a rack and took them into a small booth. The booths are minus doors in order that the customers may be observed hiding dresses under their dresses and trying to walk out with them, such being the quality of the clientele. My wife began trying on one of the gowns and suddenly a hand came around a corner, snatching one of the other two dresses away. It was a black flowered taffeta contrivance and my wife favored it over the other two, especially since somebody else seemed to favor it, so she went flying out of the booth in pursuit of the snatcher. She found the miscreant to be an attractive young girl who was accompanied by her mother—a large, muscular lady who appeared capable of whipping her weight in women.

There was a ladylike squabble with much pulling and yanking at the dress, and finally my wife surrendered in the face of superior forces.

That night we arrived at the Junior Prom and were escorted to a table up front. Everything was as solemn as the swearing in of an inspector of weights and measures. And in the midst of it all something happened to cause my wife's eyes to bug out. Approaching our table was the president of the class and with him was his girl. Out of perhaps five hundred girls in that ballroom here came, to be sure, the black flowered taffeta.

The college girl tried to carry the thing off by saying hodja do and likewise I'm sure. I rather fancied my wife's reaction. She is unalloyed woman. She smiled sweetly and said, "I'll bet you're the one voted most likely to succeed."

A little after that they called me up to the microphone and handed me the scroll and left me standing there. I muttered something into the mike, whereupon a screw came loose and the thing dropped about two feet. I jackknifed myself over and started talking into it before I thought of telescoping it back to its proper height and by the time I *had* thought of that everybody was laughing like mad and I dropped the scroll and in trying to pick it up knocked the microphone over on the floor, whereupon I made a clumsy little bow, walked back to my table, got my wife, and went out and got orry-eyed. Sometimes I think that I'm the Smith for whom smithereens were named. On that evening I did highly resolve that I would never again respond to a call for oratory.

Whenever I turn down such invitations the people extending them occasionally get sore at me. They won't accept my explanation—that I look upon speechmaking with abhorrence and would vastly prefer having a baby to delivering a speech. Instead they say, "Who the hell does he think he is anyway?" and "It'll be a month of Sundays before I ever buy that stinker's book."

So I've had to figure out some more convincing excuse. I've prepared a little form letter and handed it over to my publishers with instructions to mail it to any and all individuals or organizations soliciting my services as a speaker.

Here is the letter:

Dear (Sir) (Madam):

We regret to inform you that Mr. Smith will be unable to address the＿＿＿＿＿＿＿＿＿＿＿＿＿＿＿＿＿＿＿＿ at＿＿＿＿＿＿＿＿＿ on＿＿＿＿＿＿＿ .

Mr. Smith informs us that he recently has acquired a skin disease called impetigo which requires periodic and vigorous scratching. Up to now he has been able to do his own scratching, but he finds it impossible to concentrate on anything else when that duty is before him. He feels that if he appeared before you as a speaker, the impetigo itch would come upon him and, in order to continue his talk, it would be necessary for someone else to stand alongside him and claw him. He has no valet to perform this service and his wife bites her fingernails and therefore is not competent in that direction. Therefore, *you* might have to scratch him while he lectured.

Mr. Smith has had his affliction for six months. I'm sure you would be interested to know that during those six months he has found it impossible to take a bath. At the present writing he smells like an old gymnasium.

Yours very truly,

ABNER DOUBLEDAY

DOUBLEDAY, DORAN & CO.

Keeping up with correspondence is a labor that to me is restful and relaxing, holding none of the terrors of speechmaking. I get at least a half dozen letters a day from strangers, the great majority being from servicemen scattered all over the globe. These letters from the war fronts are gratifying but so are some of those from civilians. Just recently I got a letter signed by three girls attending a college in Texas. They had read *Low Man on a Totem Pole* and they had a question to ask. What is a chastity belt? They couldn't find any mention of it in their dictionary and would I please send them a definition and description? I tried answering it several ways, but it can't be done, not in a letter to three coeds.

In another book, *Life in a Putty Knife Factory,* I told of a man who has the unique ambition of wanting to collect enough belly-button lint to stuff a pillow. Readers of that book must have thought *I* was the man because for months the mail brought belly-button lint. An executive in a Rockefeller Center organization wrote me that all the secretaries employed by the firm had formed a Belly-Button Lint Club and were pooling their harvestings with the intention of getting enough for a pillow and sending it to me. People are essentially kind and considerate and helpful, all right. I never heard from the club and assume that the skyrocket rise of Sinatra killed the project. I didn't want belly-button lint. Those people who sent it to me were motivated by brotherly love and the good-neighbor policy but I must inform them that I didn't keep the stuff. I simply put it out on the window sill and the birds came along and got it and took it away to make nests. I earnestly hope that the lint-senders will not be offended, particularly the man and wife in Virginia who kept their winter underwear on two months longer than was customary just to increase their yield.

There is one more letter worth mentioning—from a Mrs. Virginia Tackett of Little Rock, Arkansas. Mrs. Tackett said she got a copy of *Life in a Putty Knife Factory* from the Little Rock Public Library. When she reached home she opened it by chance at the chapter headed "Dissertation on Strong Drink." Someone had inserted a piece of printed matter. It was a cheap grade of orange paper and bore the title, "A Liquor Tragedy." Beneath this title was a picture of a bum, obviously suffering from the shakes and trying to chatter the neck off a bottle of redeye. I consider the text that followed as having a rightful place in a book and therefore am including it here. Attend!

In a Northwestern city a preacher sat at his breakfast table one morning. The doorbell rang; he answered it, and there stood a boy about twelve years of age. He was on crutches, his right leg off about the knee, shivering with cold, and he said,

"Please, sir, will you go up to the jail with me and talk and pray with Papa? He murdered Mama. Papa was good and kind —but whisky did it! Will you come and be with me and my three little sisters when they bring him back? The governor says we can have his body after they hang him."

The minister hurried to the jail, and talked and prayed with the unfortunate man. He had no knowledge of what he had done. He said, "I don't blame the law—but it breaks my heart to think that my poor children must be left in a cold, heartless world. Oh, sir, whisky did it!"

The minister was at the hovel when the undertaker's wagon drove up with the body. They carried the pine casket into the little house. They led the little boy up to the casket; he leaned over, kissed his father, sobbed, and said to his little sisters:

"Come on, sisters; kiss poor Papa's cheeks before they grow cold," and the hungry, ragged, whisky orphans hurried to the casket, shrieking in agony. Police, whose hearts were adamant, buried their faces in their hands and rushed from the house. The minister fell on his knees, lifted his clenched fists and tear-stained face toward heaven, and took an oath before God that he would fight the cursed business until the undertaker should carry his body out in a casket.

Young folk, many terrible things are brought on by drinking liquor, and let me say to you now: be careful how you vote, or you may be responsible in the eyes of God at the judgment day for causing someone to be lost over strong drink.

Yes, my friends, take heed. Take heed as I took heed the first time I read the thing. I lifted my clenched fists and tear-stained face toward heaven, then buried my face in my hands, and rushed from the house. Guess where I rushed to.

CHAPTER IV *Social Notes for Posterity*

It's ABOUT TIME we put down another Time Capsule. Perhaps you have forgotten about the first one. It was rigged up by the Westinghouse Electric and Manufacturing Company at the New York World's Fair in 1939— back in the pale era of the unstickered windshield.

They dug a hole fifty feet deep and put the Time Capsule, which was seven and a half feet long, at the bottom of it. During 1939 visitors at the Fair could step up, aim their eyes down the hole, and say good-by to the capsule. Then in 1940 the Westinghouse people poured in a porridge of grease to seal the thing up. Detailed instructions were prepared and deposited in libraries all over the world. The Time Capsule is to stay down there five thousand years, until 6939, and then whoever happens to be around may dig it up and have a look.

Among the items they salted away in the capsule were a woman's hat, a can opener, a fountain pen, a safety razor, some dictionaries, lipstick, a pair of spectacles, a tobacco pouch with zipper, a toothbrush, and, for all I know, a whirling douche. I remember that day in 1940 when a lot of people stood around with bared heads, a bugler sounded taps, and the Westinghouse people sealed 'er up.

Five years have gone by and the capsule has been all but forgotten. I have a feeling they ought to dig it up now and throw it away, or at least clean it out, discard that old-fashioned junk, and refill it, getting in some ration books, Eleanor's Pullman stubs, a bottle of that Canadian hangover cure made of half tomato juice and half beer, a pair of bobby socks, a frozen chicken gizzard, a still life of Westbrook Pegler, an Eversharp pencil that is guaranteed forever, sales figures on *The Robe*, and an adequate report on a social gathering, or party, as of the 1940s. I am prepared to furnish the last-named item even though I'm convinced that the people of 6939 won't be people at all, but probably corn borers.

If 4995 years from now the world has been taken over by corn borers or thrips or gall gnats or earwigs, it is unlikely that they would know how to dig up a Time Capsule or that they would be interested in reading about any haps that happened back in the 1940s. Nevertheless, I'm going to give them descriptions of not one but three different parties of the period.

The first was an arty affair in Greenwich Village. The Bohemian traditions of the Village reached a pretty sorry state as of the fifth decade of the twentieth century. Yet that section of Manhattan continues to lure the flaming intellects from the hinterland. In my occasional prowlings through the district I have encountered little evidence of the fabled Greenwich Village. One night I was introduced to Maxwell Bodenheim in a Village groggery. I bought him a drink whereupon he threw back his head and recited a hand-wrought poem for me. As I recall it was something about Love.

The party was one of those intellectual affairs given by a couple who moved East from Ohio a few years back. They were bookish and arty, don't allow a radio in their home, and if you should mention Paulette Goddard to them, they would furrow up their brows and then say, "Oh, to be sure—the lady who's a close friend of Diego Rivera."

At this party the conversation dwelt on esoteric matters, most of the talk being three light-years over my head, and at last the hostess, a girl named Chloe, addressed herself to a young couple seated on the floor.

"Miriam," said the hostess, "how about you and Fred singing the Detroit song now?"

Miriam and Fred proved to be a young married pair fresh out of Detroit. They were hefty, bouncy, healthy-looking kids. When Chloe asked them to sing the song they bridled and blushed and said, "Aw, no, you don't wanna hear that old thing again."

But Chloe, who was a jump and two gin rickeys ahead of everyone else, insisted, and some of the other people got polite and joined in the aw-come-ons and the next thing anybody knew Miriam was saying:

"Now, before we start I better explain that you really ought to know Detroit real well to understand this song. Fred and I wrote it and it won't mean a darn thing to you if you don't know all about Detroit. Well, anyway, here we go."

She looked at Fred and wagged her hand three times and off they went in a patter duet. As singers they were no pellets of fire, but if you paid close attention you could make out the drift of their song, which went on and on.

They sang of Mr. Cadillac and Hamtramck and the State Fair Grounds and River Rouge Park and Hudson's store as well as Himelhoch's. They sang of re-tooling and Station WXYZ and Hank Greenberg and the D&C line.

Chloe the hostess sat in a corner beaming upon them. At the point where the singers touched on the career of Mayor Jeffries she interrupted them. Miriam and Fred stopped long enough for Chloe to assure the rest of the company:

"Isn't it a scream! If you only knew Detroit! I mean you've really got to know Detroit to see how clever it is! Go ahead, kids."

They sang of Woodward Avenue and the Common Council, of the fire of 1805 and the Pere Marquette Railroad, of the Free Press and Water Works Park and the RKO Uptown. They went on with Jefferson Beach and Fyfe's and Father Coughlin and the Book-Cadillac and Briggs Stadium and William S. Knudsen and the Grosse Pointe Club and Fisher Bodies, ad infinitum, ad nauseum, ad wolgast.

At last it was finished. There was a patter of applause and Fred spoke up eagerly.

"Glad you liked it, folks. You might be interested to know we're writing another one. It's about Cleveland and we got it about two thirds done."

"Oh, good!" cried Chloe. "Sing it. Go on, now, sing it!"

Miriam looked at Fred and Fred looked at Miriam and Miriam raised her hand again and I quickly found my hat and said Jim Howard was expecting me around on Eleventh Street. That e.e. cummings life is too strenuous for me.

Note: Just got the two-volume edition of *Studies in the Psychology of Sex*, by Havelock Ellis. Wow.

The second social gathering on which I want to report might be termed a collarbone party because most of the ladies wore dresses designed to expose many of their features from the umbilicus up. This was a Sunday-evening affair featuring cocktails and much learned talk of war and politics. There were thirty or forty guests and they formed into little groups around the house gobbling canapés, drinking martinis, and theorizing over matters foreign and domestic. Things were a little dull for me at the beginning because nobody seemed interested in having me talk about myself and my heroic exploits. Then new life came into the party with the arrival of a young man whose identity I never learned. He was plastered and he got plastereder. He was dressed in what appeared to be a big-league umpire's working clothes. He fastened himself onto a large highball and started the rounds. He'd insert himself into a group of people who were arguing, say, about what should we do with the Germans. He'd listen a while, then lean forward, raise his index finger, and say:

"Know what Rockne always said?"

They'd murmur politely that they didn't know what Rockne always said, whereupon the young man would throw back his head and roar at the top of his voice:

"When in doubt—PUNT!"

All evening he kept it up, moving from group to group, and every ten or fifteen minutes I'd hear that voice raised above the buzz and babble of the others, crying, "When in doubt—PUNT!" I rather enjoyed it.

As for myself, I couldn't get settled into any groove. The people, all but the disciple of Rockne, were being polite and cultured. I do remember standing alongside a man who had on a dinner jacket and who was trying to amuse a girl by talking a trifle risqué. The thing that struck me funny about him was his precise grammar. He employed the verb "lain" when he meant "laid." He was spreading it on thick for this lady and she seemed to be enjoying it, when all of a sudden another female came up. It became apparent at once that the newcomer considered the grammarian to be her property; he may even have been her husband. At any rate she ignored the girl and addressed herself to him.

"Do you," she said, "know where heaven is?"

"I believe I do," said the dinner jacket.

"Do you know where high heaven is?"

"Yes, certainly," he replied.

"Well," she said haughtily, "I'm glad you do because *that's* where you stink to."

She turned and started away, then thought of something else and came back, addressing the dinner jacket again.

"Do you know what water is?" she asked.

"Certainly," he answered. He appeared to be enjoying the little game.

"Do you know what the *first* water is?"

"I do."

"Good," she said. "That's what you're a son of a bitch of." Such behavior!

Over in a corner I saw an old friend of mine named Joe Alex Morris who had just come home from London. He was

surrounded by a dozen people, mostly pretty girls, and they were eagerly asking him questions about the state of affairs abroad. I walked over and stood near Joe for a while and then I got jealous of him. I had known him for years and he wasn't so much, yet here he sat, surrounded by beautiful babes, all gushing over him and pawing him and making a hero out of him. I went away, found a corner that was fairly quiet, and sat down to sulk. Next to me sat a tall man with a black mustache, a stranger to me. We got to talking about domestic affairs such as Veronica Lake, Nick Kenny's poetry, and chili-bean nail polish.

None of those pretty girls came to listen. Oh, no! There they were, still swarming over that blabbermouth of a Joe just because he had been on a puny little old trip to London, and it made me sore. So I decided to do a little talking of my own about The Situation.

It happens that I don't know much about international affairs but I read the newspapers and can splatter names and localities around, so I cut loose. I began talking big and important-like, after the fashion of Gabriel Heatter. There wasn't a thing about the war I didn't pretend to know.

The man with the mustache let me ramble on. Occasionally he would nod gravely and say, "Yes. Yes. I see. I see." This receptiveness spurred me to greater Kaltenborning. I went up and down the map of the world with all the facility of Mr. Rand and Mr. McNally, and I honestly believe that I was doing a more eloquent and convincing job of it than old Big Mouth across the room. I summed up the Situation in Russia and the man with the mustache murmured:

"Indeed! I'm glad to hear you say that. Now, about . . ."

But I wouldn't let him talk. I scurried across the steppes, knocked off China, and was giving Japan's internal situation a going over when I heard the mustache say:

"Yes, as I was saying in one of my classes only last week . . ."

I stopped in the middle of a sentence and stared at him.

"In one of your what?" I finally asked.

"In one of my classes," he repeated.

"Where?"

"Up at Columbia University," he said.

"You . . . you have a . . . you teach a class?" I faltered.

"Oh, to be sure," he answered. "Several of them."

"You're . . . a . . . professor?"

"Oh yes," he said. "I thought you knew."

"Professor . . . professor of what?" I asked in a small voice.

"Political science," he said.

I blinked a couple of times. I didn't say another word. I didn't want ever to say another word. I just sat there, wishing deep in my heart that we didn't have this ridiculous freedom of speech so somebody could compel me to keep my big trap shut. Since that evening, whenever I encounter a conversation involving world affairs, I content myself with spreading the gospel of Knute Rockne, advising anyone who cares to listen:

"When in doubt—PUNT!"

☆   ☆   ☆

My report on the third party may be a trifle confused because it concerns a social event, or events, which took place on New Year's Eve. I am able to write about it only because I took notes during its progress. The report was written, in fact, the morning after, when I struggled out of bed, groped my way to a typewriter, and made an effort to get it on paper. I have that essay before me now and even though I appear to be the person who went to the party, I'm not certain about some of the details. Here's the way it goes:

Now, let's see. Ouch. Where are those notes? I can remember taking notes at Tom's house, and someplace else. Wait a minute. Here they are. In my hip pocket. First time I ever put notes in my hip pocket.

Now, let's have a look. Seems like a panther had been trying to eat this wad of paper. Somebody walked on it, that's certain. Here's a heel mark, and this second sheet must have been rolled up and used for stirring something. Boiling molasses, by the looks of it.

Now, it says here . . .

redhead stub toe vinegar on popcorn w. 44th

It's my writing, all right. That must have been in that place on Forty-fourth Street. No, that was later. Let's see. We were at Tom's first. Oh yes. Sure. That's it. That red-headed girl. But what's that "w. 44th" doing in there? Tom's place is uptown. Oh, now I get it. The redhead told us about the place on West Forty-fourth. Vinegar on popcorn. Don't seem to be able to place that one. Something she said, probably, but, well . . .

Think I'll skip that notation. Probably just showing off at Tom's. Whipping out paper and pencil and taking notes in front of everybody. Show 'em I'm a writer. Show 'em I'm observant, never miss a thing. Showing off. Never again. Never, never, never.

Now, what's this? It says . . .

newsie Bryant pk pigeon shines shoes says choffuge giriff

That last part gets me. What in the hell do they want to have a New Year's Eve for anyway? Look at that! "says choffuge giriff." Might have something to do with a giraffe. Somehow we must have got from Tom's to Bryant Park. "shines shoes." That certainly wasn't me. If ever I saw shoes that hadn't been shined, mine are them. No, I almost believe that somebody picked my pockets and got my notepaper and wrote that stuff on it. Except that it's my writing. Sort of. Think I'll go lie down awhile and see if I can't think. Can think, I mean. Maybe it'll come back. No, I'd better not. Might go to sleep and never wake up again. Hey, back there! Turn that damn radio down!

Got to get on with these notes. After all, even though it was New Year's Eve, I know I ran into some good stories. Should have, anyway. Went so many places. Now I'm beginning to remember. Harry's Palace Bar and Grill. That must have been around two. Let's see. Here it is. It says . . .

harry sailor lex ky no tell hoe corn

Sure. That sailor from Lexington, Kentucky. Throwing his money around like a drunken civilian. I can see him clearly now. He was redheaded. Say! Could he be the redhead? No, that was the girl at Tom's house. This was much later. The sailor. Maybe *he's* the one got his shoes shined. No, we didn't go to Bryant Park after that. It was before. Before Tom's. But the sailor, I know damn well he gave me a good story, else I wouldn't have put it down. He was at Harry's. Now I remember. Came over to our booth. Throwing his money around. Redheaded. Let's try to figure this out. "no tell hoe corn."

Nope. Can't do it. Doesn't make a bit of sense. "no tell

hoe corn." When I wrote it down I had a wonderful idea for a magazine article or a book chapter or something. That's certain. But who can make a magazine article out of "no tell hoe corn"? Not me. Not today anyway. Never again.

There's one more page with notes on it. Maybe that'll explain everything. This is the one somebody stepped on. It says . . .

morris gairowski cap backwards fat woman 23rd st taking nubbolk stub toe

Godamighty! Stub toe again. This time a fat woman. Or maybe it was me. Maybe that's the answer. Maybe I was stubbing my fool toe all evening and every time I stubbed it I made a note of it. No, that would be silly. Well, all right, maybe I *was* silly. But who, in the name of time, was "taking nubbolk"?

Maybe that was me too. Well, if it was, I'll never take it again as long as I live. No more nubbolk for me. Never, never, never.

CHAPTER V *Feet Have Their Good Points*

THE UNWRITTEN LAW in Hollywood has nothing whatever to do with sex. It prohibits walking. Even in these days of crumbling motors and empty gas tanks the people of southern California refuse to walk. If they find it necessary to travel more than half a block, they drive, or spend twenty minutes waiting for a taxi which may never arrive. When sheer desperation compels them to walk a quarter of a mile, they boast about it in public as though they had pushed a peanut with their nose from Seattle to San Diego.

A girl from New York went to Hollywood to work for an advertising agency. She was accustomed to regular walks in Manhattan and she tried to continue these in Hollywood. She told me how she was walking on the slopes north of Hollywood Boulevard when a police car came along, circled the block, then pulled in to the curb alongside her. A cop got out and asked her what she was doing.

"I'm taking a walk," she said.

"Where to?" demanded the cop.

"No place in particular," she said. "I'm just walking for exercise."

The cop glared at her and told her to wait right where she was. Then he went over and held a long conference with his partner in the car. He returned and resumed questioning the girl. He couldn't understand why anyone would indulge in aimless walking. She wasn't armed, had clothes on, and hadn't been soliciting any men, so there was nothing he could do about it beyond shaking his head in wonderment over her eccentric behavior.

One evening I walked from my Hollywood apartment to the home of a friend about a mile away. A party was in progress and when I remarked that I had hoofed it all the way, I was immediately surrounded by people as though I had just flown non-stop around the world, upside down. These people laughed and grinned and made much over the thing, and some of them said, "What a screwball!"

Though I am endowed with a pair of the flattest feet outside of duckdom, walking is one of my favorite pre-occupations. Not heel-and-toe walking. I have seen these heel-and-toe walkers engaged in competition at track meets and I see them sometimes practicing around Central Park. A heel-and-toe walker is the most graceless spectacle on earth and I can get along the rest of my life without looking at one, unless it could be Elsa Maxwell.

Riding taxicabs can be as pleasurable as walking. Much slop has been written about the nobility of the New York cabdriver. He is supposed to be a friend in need, a source of wise sayings, and, above all, as honest as a Burroughs adding machine. I've had dealings with many honest drivers but I've also run into a few who were not altogether trustworthy.

One of my favorite taxicab stories concerns a businessman from the Middle West who arrived one day at Grand Central Terminal. He had a room reserved at the Hotel Roosevelt which adjoins the station. All he had to do was walk from his train, through an underpass, and up a flight of steps into the Roosevelt's lobby. Instead of that he went to the street and got into a cab.

"Hotel Roosevelt," he said, trying to make it sound city-like.

The driver hesitated a moment. The Hotel Roosevelt was just a few steps away. Well, he decided, if he had trapped a yokel, he had trapped a yokel. He lit out for Brooklyn. He drove all over that borough, worked his way into Queens County, crossed the Whitestone Bridge into the Bronx, and rambled around there for half an hour. Not a word from the man in the back seat.

At last the cab came down into Manhattan and pulled up at the entrance to the Roosevelt.

"How much?" said the passenger.

"That'll be twenty-six dollars and forty cents," said the driver.

"Oh no you don't!" exclaimed the visitor. "You think you've got a country boy on the string but you haven't. Listen, brother, you don't get any twenty-six dollars and forty cents outa *me*. The last time it was only eighteen dollars and twenty-five cents and that's every penny you get!"

It is now my intention to demonstrate how walking can be profitable to a writer. First, however, I want to tell about having lunch with John D. Rockefeller because I started out from there. I don't mean to say that I sat at the same table with John D. Rockefeller. He was two tables away from me and we didn't speak, but we had the same waiter, and by the time I was through I knew all I wanted to know.

Mr. Rockefeller was lunching alone in his own restaurant —a place with large windows looking out on the Rockefeller Center skating rink. He finished eating ahead of me and then left. The next time the waiter came along I asked him if Mr. Rockefeller had paid his check.

"Sure," he said. "Sure he pays. Every time."

"It's his restaurant, isn't it?" I asked.

"Absolutely."

"Well," I went on, "you don't ordinarily find a restaurant owner paying for his own meals in his own restaurant, do you?"

"Maybe not," said the waiter, "but this is different. That

man's got so much of what it takes that he would probly feel silly if he didn't pay. Get what I mean?"

"Sure," I said. "But how about the tip? Does he tip well?"

"He always leaves a percentage tip," said the waiter.

"Ten per cent?"

"Twenty per cent," he assured me. "Twenty per cent— two-buck meal, forty-cent tip."

"Did he have a cocktail?"

"Never," said the waiter. "Always has milk."

"Does he usually eat alone?"

"Most always," he said. "I suppose there's lots of big shots he could eat with, but he has to do his writing. Look at this pencil."

The waiter produced his own pencil, an ordinary wooden instrument whittled down to the halfway mark.

"Listen," he went on, "Rockefeller uses a pencil much worse than this one. Just a plain little old pencil with some tooth marks on it. And all the time he's in here he just sets there and writes little notes."

"What about?" I asked him.

"Money matters," he said. "What else?"

"How do you know he writes about money matters?"

"What else has a Rockefeller got to write about?" he demanded. "And anyway, I can see. It's always arithmetic and figuring on the paper."

"Does he ever leave any of the notes on the table?"

"No *sir!* Gathers them all up and puts them in his coat pocket. A man like that has got to have a system. Got to be systematic."

A lady signaled the waiter, wanting more coffee, and while he was gone I watched the skaters tearing around the ice and occasionally doing spectacular flops. I thought about the peculiar pursuits of humankind—fastening chunks of iron on their feet and sliding around to nowhere, now and then falling down and breaking their arms. Pretty soon the waiter was back—a man happy in having an audience. He reopened the conversation.

"It's not for me," he said, employing a confidential manner. "Maybe for him, but not for me."

"What's not for you?"

"Money matters," he said. "I mean big money matters like Rockefeller has got on his mind all the time. He looks calm and cool about it but underneath I bet it is almost driving him crazy. If I was in his shoes I would blow my top. You take the big shots like that. Can't even set down to lunch without figuring, figuring, figuring. Go back upstairs to his office and figure some more. Worry, worry, worry. Go home at night and probly have a pencil and paper at the dinner table. Figure some more. Go out to a picture show. Don't enjoy a bit of it because they always got to be worrying their heads about money matters. Go home and go to bed. Toss around half the night, bite the pilla, fight the blanket, worrying about money matters for the next day.

"Nope. It's not for me. Don't want any part of it. I get my few bucks a day. I put it in my pocket and go out and buy me a nice meal. I eat it without no pencils in my hand. I enjoy it. I go to a picture show. I look at it and enjoy it. Then I go home and fall into bed and go to sleep. He can have it. Not me."

Now you know all about how frightful it must be to be John D. Rockefeller. Time to head for home. Let's walk to Forty-second Street first.

Opposite the Public Library stands a man and beside him is a large telescope. Let's ease back against the wall and watch him a moment. Whenever I see him I enjoy looking at him and his telescope. He is engaged in a remarkable commercial enterprise.

The telescope points at the observation tower of the Empire State Building. The man charges a dime a look. For ten cents you may step up and ogle the people who are on top of the tallest building in the world. When they built the Empire State Building they added the observation tower not altogether for decorative effect. They stuck it up there to make money. A big tobacco company wanted to have a concrete cigarette two hundred feet high mounted on top of the building instead of the present tower but somebody vetoed the deal. The tower does all right as a tourist attraction. The management charges something over a dollar for a grown person to visit the observation tower and since the structure was erected more than ten million customers have gone up there for the purpose of looking down at the people on the ground. And here, on Forty-second Street, are people down on the ground paying ten cents to look up at the people who are looking down at them looking up. This thing could cost me a lot of sleep. I leave it, abandon it, and refuse to think about it any longer.

Back in suburbia I decided to stop by the home of James Street. (Note that I'm changing the past participle or indicative tense of this stuff.) I was walking from the subway when I found myself immediately behind an old man. I was on the point of passing him when I heard him talking. He was talking to himself. He was God-damning and Jesus Christing and a couple of times I heard him mention the name "Grover." I snooped along behind him but couldn't make any sense out of his monologue. I have seen him several times since and he is always talking to himself—a pursuit that is by no means uncommon among New Yorkers. I've eavesdropped on him, trying to catch what he is talking about. Finally a neighborhood druggist told me about him.

It appears that the old man is a trifle daft on the subject of Grover Cleveland. He believes Grover Cleveland is still alive and favors him for a third term in the White House. The old man's bitterness, expressed in his profane conversations with himself, is directed against political enemies of Grover Cleveland who once charged the statesman with seducing a woman named Maria, rendering her with child, and then running out on her. The druggist told me that this accusation weighs on the old man's mind, and he denounces it as smear propaganda against his hero, declaring that the gossip about this Maria woman is the only thing keeping Cleveland out of his rightful place in the White House.

So, at last, I arrived at the abode of James Street and learned of the death of Sam Dabney.

Sam Dabney is a fictional character, a man in a book. He made his appearance four years ago as the chief character in a thick historical novel called *Oh, Promised Land*. The book had a large success and most people who read it developed an affection for its hero. Sam Dabney was a strapping, handsome guy who galloped and fought and loved through eight hundred-odd pages of Jim Street's book.

Jim was now at work on a sequel to his novel, a book called *Tap Roots*. Came a day when, secluded in his study, a crisis arrived. He got up from his work, went into the living room, lit a cigarette, and sat staring at the floor for half an hour. Then he went out and walked around the block a couple of times. There was no way out of it, he at last concluded. He had to kill off Big Sam Dabney.

Quite likely you cannot imagine what it meant to him, what a shocking job it was for him to go back to his desk and do the unhappy deed. Sam Dabney was as close to him, as real to him, as any human being on earth. Around the Street house they had talked about Sam for years just as though he were a member of the family. And a good deal of that feeling about Big Sam had been transmitted to the friends of the Street family.

Jim kept quiet about the job he had to do and went grimly ahead with it. He killed Big Sam Dabney there at his typewriter around eleven-thirty at night when the house was quiet. He got the whole business, the whole deathbed scene, out of the way and then he went out and sat down in the living room. Lucy, his wife, kept watching him. She rather suspected from his behavior that he was about to take down with a fever or a case of author's pip. At length she said to him:

"Jimmie, what on earth is the matter with you? Are you sick?"

"I just killed Big Sam," he said.

"Jimmie!"

Well, you never saw the beat of it after that. Lucy said later that her first impulse was to send off a telegram to the two Street boys who were away at school. There were ructions. She told her husband that she wouldn't stand for it, that he could march right back in to that typewriter and revive Big Sam.

The house virtually went into mourning for a week. Lucy telephoned family friends and gave them the sad news. People called to find out all the facts. One girl, particularly hipped on the passing of Big Sam, drove in fifteen miles from Long Island, walked into the house, and said:

"How did it happen?"

Jim assured her that Sam Dabney died quietly.

"What was it?" she demanded.

"Cancer," said Jim. "He had a cancer. You knew that." The young woman almost flung a conniption.

"You simply can't do it to him that way," she said. "That's too painful. You ought to be ashamed of yourself. You've got to change it to something else."

"Listen," said Jim, "I'm not going through it again. He's dead. He couldn't live forever, and that's the way he had to die."

"Well," snapped the young lady, "all I can say, Jim Street, is that you're a mean, hateful person . . . and a *murderer!*"

CHAPTER VI *General Grant and the Present War*

ON THE morning of Saturday, December 6, 1941, I had a telephone call from two men with whom I had formerly worked on newspapers. They were Sam Ballard and James Irwin, and they were in town from St. Louis, stopping at the Waldorf-Astoria. They wanted me to join them for lunch.

It was noon when I reached their hotel suite for the reunion and it was five minutes past noon when we ordered the first trayload of toasting equipment. At that time I was writing a daily column and these two men, both in business in St. Louis, began telling me things about their city. By all means, they said, I should go to St. Louis and write a series of columns about the town and its marvelous personalities. I had first known Irwin on the Denver *Post* but now he was a big business executive, assistant to the president of the Monsanto Chemical Company.

"If you'll come out to St. Louis," he said, "I'll fix it up for you to interview a man who makes a barrel of aspirin tablets every day."

Then Sam Ballard, who was my city editor long ages ago, began reciting ideas for snappy columns. The second tray of saluting material arrived. The waiter asked if we wanted to order lunch and we ran him half a block down the corridor.

"Then there's General Grant," said Sam Ballard. "General Grant would make you a dandy column."

"Good old General Grant!" I said. "Here's to General Grant!"

"Furthermore," put in Jim Irwin, "St. Louis *loves* you."

"I love St. Louis," I responded. I had never been in St. Louis in my life although I was born one hundred and fifty miles from the place.

"You don't love St. Louis one tenth as much as St. Louis loves you," said Sam Ballard.

"The hell I don't," I insisted. "I *worship* St. Louis."

"There's this statue of General Grant," said Sam Ballard. "It stands in front of the City Hall in St. Louis. Out in South St. Louis there is a grivic soup—a civic group, that has been agitating to get that statue moved. They want General Grant in South St. Louis and they have a good argument to put forward. They say that whenever General Grant was in town he spent all his time in a tavern in South St. Louis. They say that if St. Louis is to honor General Grant with a statue, that statue ought to be right in front of the old saloon. They're moving heaven and earth to get it there."

"Fellas, old pals," I said, "that is the most wonderful story I ever heard. I've *got* to go to St. Louis. I've just *got* to see General Grant."

"Why don't you come out right away?" suggested Jim Irwin.

"That's exactly what I intend to do," I said. "When you leaving?"

Sam Ballard consulted his wrist.

"In an hour and a half on the Spirit of St. Louis from Penn Station," he said.

"So am I," I said.

At six o'clock then I was on the Spirit of St. Louis with Ballard and Irwin. I had no baggage, no pajamas, no toothbrush, very little cash, and no brains.

We reached St. Louis around noontime the next day, scurried out to Webster Grove where my friends lived, and were all settled down in the Ballard living room when somebody telephoned and said to turn on the radio, that the Japs had bombed Pearl Harbor. We turned on the radio and a dance band was playing, so we turned it off. Then somebody else called and said to turn on the radio. We did, and in a few moments there was a break for more bulletins.

It was Tuesday noon before I managed to get on a train and head back to New York, and during the forty-eight hours I spent in St. Louis I caught only the faintest, foggiest glimpse of General Grant. When I did reach Penn Station and came up to the street I found New York City gone haywire over a false air-raid alarm.

I believe that I can truthfully say that when war came to the United States I was the first citizen to black out.

CHAPTER VII   *McNamara's Band*

CHARLES DAGGETT is a chunky ex-newspaperman of large capabilities now serving as head press agent for Cagney Productions, Inc., in Hollywood. Mr. Daggett is an amiable and entertaining man whose secretary is known as "The Tagger Woman." The secretary won a contest some years back when the movies were searching for a girl to play the part of a "tiger woman." She was transported to Hollywood along with other tiger-women contest winners, but another girl clawed her way to victory in the finals and Chuck Daggett's Tagger Woman took to secretarial work.

Mr. Daggett comes from the Missouri Ozark country and is quite handy at telling stories of that region. His grandfather is one of his best characters. Grandpa Daggett went through World War I convinced that he was surrounded by German spies. One day he summoned his grandson, peered around a few corners to make sure no alien snakes were eavesdropping, and then said:

"Chuck, they's a new German spy in town. He's got a hull trunkload of pencils, so if anybody offers you a pencil don't take it. These here are German spy pencils. You know how everybody takes a pencil when they get ready to write something, and first off they lick the point with their tongues so it will write good. Well, this here German spy hands you a pencil and says for you to write something. So you stick the point in your mouth and lick it and—IT BLOWS THE WHOLE TOP OF YORE HEAD OFF!"

Chuck Daggett began writing me teaser letters about Jim Cagney and various other Cagneys a couple of years ago. These letters included anecdotes about Ed McNamara, who is perhaps the Cagneys' closest friend. Before long I was convinced that I should head for Hollywood and undertake a magazine article on the Cagney clan. I got the approval of the *Saturday Evening Post* and took up temporary residence in the movie city. The Cagneys were shooting their first independent picture and I spent a month hanging around them. It was a happy month.

After years of quarreling with Warner Brothers Jim Cagney walked off the company's lot the day he finished with *Yankee Doodle Dandy*—the picture that later brought him the Academy Award. It was the fourth time he had told the Warners where to kiss and he swore a decorative oath that it was the last. In August of 1942 the new Cagney corporation was formed and the old cry went up in Hollywood: Cagney had grown too big for his britches; he'd come crawling back to Burbank crying: "Please, Mister Warner, can I have another chance?"

The Hollywood hooters may have overlooked one significant point in the Cagney apostasy. To be precise about it Jim Cagney was not setting himself up in business. When he walked away from Warners' an outsize duplicate of himself walked at his side. Bill Cagney, younger brother of the actor, is the financial tactician of the family. He is president of Cagney Productions, Inc. Jim's talent is the company's chief asset, yet if Cagney Productions, Inc., turns out successful, Brother Bill's way with a dollar surely will have been a large factor in that success.

Bill's modest office on the United Artists lot is a scant twenty feet from the private quarters of Samuel Goldwyn, the master bargainer. Mr. Goldwyn has been known to hurl himself into a swoon as a method of expressing shock over the salary demands of an actor. Notwithstanding his reputation, there are people who would bet good money that Bill Cagney could out-haggle Goldwyn two falls out of three.

Ninety per cent of the business transacted in Hollywood consists of two men sitting down and trying to out-connive each other. The biggest of the film bosses take inordinate pride in their genius for high-class horse trading and, quite naturally, when those men come unsuspectingly against an opponent who pins their ears back and leaves them bleeding on the floor, they resent it bitterly. That may well have been the basic trouble between the Warners and the Cagneys. Stubbornness is a prime characteristic of the Cagneys, and they can make stubbornness look like pure insolence. They don't know the meaning of the word surrender and they have no truck with the institution of compromise. "We love everybody," says Bill, "and we don't give a damn for anybody."

Bill and Jim are the only members of the clan involved in motion pictures. Two other brothers, Harry and Ed, are doctors in Hollywood while the sister Jeanne travels back and forth between Hollywood and New York, her chief interest being the Broadway stage.

Carrie Cagney, mother to this remarkable brood, brought up her boys under a novel code. Her children describe her as having been one of the best stand-up fighters of her time. She taught them to slug with their fists because that was the best method, she believed, of developing sportsmanship. The father, for whom Jim was named, died in 1918, six months before Jeanne was born.

Jim grew up as an odd-jobs boy in New York. His first theatrical experience was in a two-act drama staged at the Lenox Hill Settlement House. It was called *The Faun*.

"I was the faun," says Jim. "I had my hair in ringlets and a goatskin around my middle and I pranced around the stage speaking lines like these: 'Nay, sweet, give it me,' and 'Spring is running through the fields chased by the wynd,' 'The wayward wynd ran its fingers through the pine tree's hair.'" He got into vaudeville as a song-and-dance man and finally made the grade in a couple of Broadway plays. Al Jolson was largely responsible for Jim's going to Hollywood.

Under the new independent setup the Cagneys are giving themselves the things they always claimed they couldn't get from the Warners. Jim won't have to make four or five pictures a year. And he and Bill take their sweet time choosing stories. They looked at more than 400 scripts before they chose their first production. They go about their business with pleasant informality and there's a minimum of hair-tearing and screaming on the Cagney sets. The long days are broken up with little practical jokes, quip-tossing, and good side-line talk. Bill seldom lets a day pass without introducing a gag of one kind or another. In the first Cagney production there was a reproduction of a village square with a grassy park in the center. Standing on the edge of this park was a statue of the town's Civil War hero. Bill rented a flock of live pigeons and turned them loose in the park, explaining that he couldn't trust the make-up men to give the statue a natural decorative effect—that only live pigeons could make a bronze statue look authentic.

The two doctor brothers visit the set almost every day. Dr. Harry always fetches his bag and hustles about distributing free pills to members of the company, checking blood pressures, examining scratches and bruises, and administering shots of Vitamin B to such individuals as appear to need them.

Jim is one of the most energetic, hard-working individuals in Hollywood. He is vice-president of the new company. He is its chief actor. He is a top man in the Screen Actors' Guild (which he helped organize). He is involved in the direction of half a dozen Hollywood war groups. No one of these jobs is nominal—he works with the diligence of a donkey engine at each of them. It may also be mentioned that he is a home-loving husband, father of two adopted children; that he is a farmer both in Beverly Hills and Martha's Vineyard, and that he is a charter member of the Wednesday Night Irish Club—a group that includes Pat O'Brien, Spencer Tracy, Frank McHugh, and George Murphy.

These are his major activities and he breezes through them without recourse to vitamin pills or rash retarders. Since the war brought a multitude of new duties to most of the stars, shingles has become the occupational disease in Hollywood. Many of the actors suffer from standing-up nervous breakdowns. Gallons and gallons of pink calamine lotion pass over the Hollywood drug counters, and the gobbling of vitamin pills has succeeded gin rummy as the town's chief preoccupation.

Jim Cagney is past forty but he has the physical stamina of a pack mule and the nervous system of a fire plug. He is out of bed before seven o'clock. He spends half an hour fussing around the garden, feeding his ducks and chickens. He's on the set wearing make-up by nine o'clock. Whether acting or clowning on the side lines, he seems to be forever in motion. Before the camera he enjoys a self-confidence that is transmitted to other performers and puts them at ease. He is small in stature but he has to watch his diet carefully. All the Cagneys have a tendency to fatten up, but Jim keeps his weight stabilized at around one hundred and sixty. At lunchtime on the set he often forgoes food, puts on a rubber shirt, and spends half an hour in vigorous hoofing. Dancing is a hobby with him as well as a method of exercise.

He has neither the time nor the inclination for social life. On those evenings when he's free he enjoys staying home with his wife, who was his vaudeville partner years ago, and the two kids. The children, a boy and a girl, were adopted some years back, and Jim permits no extensive publicity about them. This is a common precaution taken by the many Hollywood people who have adopted children. You won't often see photographs of those kids, and for good reason. Suppose Herpes Zoster, wealthy movie star, adopts a child out of some institution. Photographs of that child appear in newspapers and magazines. There is nothing to fear from the real parents because they signed documents assuring the new owner that they will keep their distance and hold their tongues. But maybe a second cousin of the real father or mother will spot the pictures, turn up in Hollywood, and start making a nuisance of himself until he is bought off. Such a person should be subjected to defenestration—killing by throwing out of a window—yet he must be dealt with, since he is a bona-fide member of the human race and probably reads a verse of the Bible every night before going to sleep.

Jim and Billie Cagney prefer staying home to nightclubbing. Jim likes to practice on his guitar or read a good book. He reads serious things and has accumulated a first-rate library. His house is small but a dandy. Both Jim and Billie knew hunger and shabbiness in the days when they trouped in vaudeville and they both appreciate the good living they have now. They insist, however, that they'd be just as happy living on their Martha's Vineyard farm and doing all the manual labor that goes with farming.

Jim, as everybody knows, is an outspoken liberal in his social attitude but in his personal life and habits he is thoroughly conservative. He demonstrated this conservativeness on the night he received the Academy Award.

Sensible people who attended the Academy dinner say Hollywood reached a new height in flatulence that night. Actresses wept unconvincingly and pushed other actresses around when those other actresses, also weeping, tried to hog the stage. It was a night of speeches in which some of the biggest people in motion pictures behaved as though they were slobbering apes. One Los Angeles reporter chose to ignore the whole sorry spectacle, found a seat at the rear of the room, and devoted his newspaper article to a description of each lady who headed in haste for the powder room. Only two speakers seemed to retain a sense of balance. One was Irving Berlin and the other was James Cagney. When Gary Cooper handed the "Oscar" to Cagney the audience applauded and settled back for another long-winded oration. Jim stepped to the microphone and said:

"I've always maintained that in this business you are only as good as the other fellow thinks you are. It's nice to know that you people thought I did a good job. And don't forget that it was a good part too. Thank you very much."

Then he sat down.

It was one of the most impressive performances ever turned in at an Academy dinner.

Jim's mother hadn't known that he was to get the award. She was in her apartment that night with Dr. Ed Cagney and they were listening to the Academy proceedings on the radio. When the award was announced they were understandably thrilled. They sat and talked about it awhile and then Dr. Ed told his mother it was past her bedtime. Her health had been bad for a long time.

"I'm not going to bed yet," she said. "Jim'll be coming by to show it to me."

Dr. Ed assured her that Jim wouldn't come by the apartment—that Jim knew it was after midnight, that he wouldn't dream of coming by, that he'd probably be over in the morning with his Oscar. "Now, Mom," he insisted, "you go on to bed."

"No," said Carrie. "Jim'll come by tonight, and when he gets here I intend to be waiting for him. I'm sure he'll come. I'll bet you ten bucks he comes."

Dr. Ed sighed and shook his head. "All right, Mom," he said. "I'll take the bet. He won't come by."

An hour went by and then another. Down on Sunset Boulevard a car was heading out toward Beverly Hills. In it were Mr. and Mrs. James Cagney and Mr. and Mrs. Bill Cagney. Bill was driving and they had entered Beverly Hills when Jim spoke.

"Hey," he said, "hold it. Let's go by and show it to Mom."

Bill argued with him. Look at the time—after two o'clock.

Mom would have been asleep long ago. Jim could go over in the morning.

"No," said Jim. "I want Mom to see it tonight. Turn around."

And so the four of them trooped into Mom's apartment and found her sitting there with Dr. Ed, fully dressed and waiting. She didn't jump up and throw her arms around the Academy Award winner. She simply looked across at Ed and grinned and said:

"Okay, Ed. Hand over the ten-spot."

The Cagneys appear to have been created by William Saroyan, who contends that nearly everybody on earth has a beautiful soul and is bloated with human juices. I searched high and low trying to find someone who would knock the Cagneys. No luck. Finally I went to James Francis Cagney himself and put my cards on the table.

"Listen," I said, "I'm faced with the prospect of writing a piece that has nothing but compliments in it for you. It's not fashionable nowadays to write an article about a guy and say he is just pure all-around wonderful. Search back through your experience," I said, "and try to remember somebody who called you an ingrate or a son of a bitch or something like that."

He tried hard to be helpful. He searched back through his experience and finally said:

"Once when I was working at Warners' they notified me that I had to contribute two days' pay to the Merriam-for-Governor campaign fund, that every employee on the lot had to do it. I said nuts. So Jack Warner told somebody that I was a professional againster."

There, then, is the sordid side of Cagney. Of course you might recall the great Hollywood Red Scare of 1940. James Cagney figured prominently in it along with several other actors who were accused of contributing to organizations which followed the Communist party line. Cagney spoke for his fellow actors when he said:

"We are accused of contributing to radical causes. When you are told a person is sick or in need, you don't ask him his religion, nationality, or politics."

At the height of the Hollywood Red Scare Jim went to

Washington to attend the President's Birthday Ball. Mr. Roosevelt gave him a wide smile and said:

"Jimmy, I see by the papers you've been a bad boy."

Jim grinned back.

"All I did, Mr. President," he said, "was believe in the things you believe."

"Attaboy, Jimmy!" said the President.

Of his "radical" activities Jim says today: "I've always felt sorry for poor people. We never had any spare money in the house when I grew up and we were usually surrounded by people poorer than ourselves. A man can't forget those things. And as far as the union question is concerned, it's natural that I should be a union man. My father was a staunch union man. He was a union bartender."

Jim's closest friend outside his family is Ed McNamara. It had been my intention to write extensively about McNamara. Recently I went to see him at The Players in New York and found out that he is thinking of doing a book himself.

"I'm the heavyweight champion failure of the world," he explained. "I've had greater opportunities than any man alive—one right after another, year after year, and yet every God-damned one of them has blown up in my face."

McNamara was a policeman in Paterson, New Jersey, before Mme. Schumann-Heink discovered his singing voice. He was a cop for seven years and never made an arrest. He was too tenderhearted to pinch anyone, and it was his custom whenever a lawbreaker hove in view to run and hide in a dark alley.

The closest he ever came to making an arrest, he says, was one night on a Paterson side street. Officer McNamara was walking along in front of a cathouse when he noticed a man emerge from the establishment and stagger to an automobile at the curb. The man got into the car and started fumbling with the controls but couldn't get it started. He was yelling and cursing and finally Officer McNamara approached him.

"Why don't you let me call you a taxi?" suggested the kindly cop.

The drunk spattered him with profane shrieks, heaping obscenities on the entire police department. McNamara remained placid. He asked the drunk to move over in the seat and he, McNamara, would start the car for him. The drunk continued to abuse him, however, and McNamara took note of the fact that the car's battery had run down and the starter wouldn't work. He was husky enough for it, so he decided to give the guy a push and get him started. Just then the drunk's wrath took a new direction. He began denouncing McNamara for being a so-and-so Irishman. That was too much. But did McNamara spoil his record by arresting the guy? Certainly not. He just glared in anger at him for a moment, then said:

"All right, you son of a bitch. I was gonna give you a push and get you started, but now you can go straight to hell. You can stay right here all night for all I care, and in the morning people will see you and know you've been in a whorehouse."

With that Officer McNamara turned and strode off down the street, his record unspoiled.

He was the only singer ever taken as a pupil by Enrico Caruso. His close friends have been Heywood Broun, Harold Ross, Joel Sayre, Alva Johnston, Deems Taylor, and many other unique personalities.

Among my favorite McNamara stories is the one which finds him spending a week end in the home of Deems Taylor. McNamara had just got out of bed and wandered into Taylor's study. The ex-cop had a hangover and was restless. It had been sleeting and outside the apartment window a huge Sanitation Department truck was stalled. Another truck of equal size had come up behind it and was trying to push it out of the frozen rut. The big motors would roar and there would be the clash of metal and the shriek of spinning wheels on the ice. Taylor had been working at his desk but he got up and went to the window to see what was making all that unholy racket. He stood and looked at the straining trucks a bit, then remarked:

"What a strange time of year for those things to be mating."

He went back to his desk and McNamara continued his pacing. He was passing behind Taylor when he noticed a photograph of an elderly woman on the desk. McNamara was in an unhappy state of mind. He gestured at the picture and said:

"Who's that dopey-looking old harridan?"

Deems Taylor didn't answer immediately, nor did he move. He sat without turning his head then, at last, replied in precise accents:

"That happens to be a photograph of my mother."

Another long silence. Then McNamara's voice:

"Is there a revolver in the house?"

CHAPTER VIII *Sex Life of the Date Palm*

IF YOU are a cultured, civilized, well-informed person, versed in the niceties of gentle living and possessed of a strong streak of vulgarity, you have read *Low Man on a Totem Pole* and therefore know all about Jim Moran.

When I got to Hollywood I found Jim living in a lovely patio giving on a little house. He had become a small-scale country gentleman in the San Fernando Valley. He had gone West hoping to favor the population of southern California with a new radio program called the *Slo-Gro Hour*. The population of southern California, being made up of screwballs, was not impressed with Mr. Moran's antic screwiness, so he retired to his patio, sat in the sun, and dreamed of the time he refought the Battle of Bunker Hill.

Jim was the sole performer on the *Slo-Gro Hour,* writing the script and playing the role of Professor Rhinelander Briggs. The show was sponsored by the Slo-Gro Corporation, which was engaged in not selling Slo-Gro. Slo-Gro was a preparation for rubbing on the head. It retards the growth of hair so that a person using it regularly will need only two haircuts a year instead of, say, forty.

"Slo-Gro," Jim explained to me once in New York, "is a salve of my own devising. We would never attempt to sell it, for it would put the barbers out of business and the world could ill afford to have a million or so barbers running around with nothing to do. Actually I have perfected Slo-Gro to such a degree that it stops the growth of hair altogether. The only reason I allow for a slight growth is to replace the hair that wears out from the putting on and taking off of hats and caps or the erosion brought about by the caressing fingers of hot women."

This Professor Briggs was a man of many attainments, a practical man if there ever was one, and the world's foremost authority on turban-wrapping. When he was on the radio in New York he dedicated odd moments of the program to civic betterment. During the heaviest snowstorm of that winter the professor came on the air with a scientific suggestion. He first called attention to the cruel problem created by a snowstorm in New York City. Then he cited some statistics. He had figured out the total snowfall on the streets and sidewalks of the city. He determined the precise area thus affected and he divided that figure by the population of New York.

"It works out," he told his listeners, if he had any, "to one handful of snow per person. Now, we can solve this problem in five minutes. Right this moment I want everyone to run out in the street and get a handful of snow. Bring it in the house and put it in the sink and run hot water on it. Every person in the city must get a handful. Wake up the children and send them out too. Go wake up your neighbors if they are not listening to this program. If everybody gets a handful of snow the streets and sidewalks will be as clean as a whistle in five minutes."

Before he left New York to conquer the West Jim happened to call at a book publishing house to see a friend. On the friend's desk was a neatly bound book, a volume with maroon binding and the title stamped in gold. Jim picked it up, opened it, and found that there was nothing inside it but blank pages. It was a publisher's dummy* containing a couple of hundred pages on which no single word was printed. Jim quickly talked his friend into giving him this book.

He rode the Chief of the Sante Fe lines from Chicago to Los Angeles and it was his custom to stroll into the club car with the book under his arm, order a drink, and settle into an easy chair. He'd station himself so that other occupants of the car could see the blank pages of the book

*Not to be confused with an author.

when he had it open. Then he'd sit there pretending to read it. He'd go through emotional upheavals, sometimes bursting into fits of laughter, sometimes scowling, as he turned the pages. The other people in the car would look at him, then glance at the book, and see blank pages. Jim would concentrate on his reading for a while, let the book drop into his lap wide open, and pretend to think, shaking his head slowly from side to side as though he had just come upon the most remarkable statement ever printed. He kept up this little game throughout the trip and for some reason the other passengers left him strictly to himself, even refusing to sit at the same table with him in the diner.

When I found him in Hollywood he had just taken a job operating a turret lathe in a war plant. He didn't have an automobile but his patio was near the highway which runs into Hollywood by way of Cahuenga Pass. Jim had worked out a technique for hitchhiking.

"Through long experiment," he explained, "I've developed a method of controlling thought waves. These waves emanate from the brain and, unless you know how to govern them, they simply fly off in haphazard directions, hit a tree, and explode. I have reached a point where I can control my own waves, converting them into a sort of beam. I can stand at the side of the highway and watch a car approaching. In that car may be a man who never picked up a hitchhiker in his life. He cannot resist *me*. I put the beam on him and he slams on the brakes. I can make the beam weak or strong. I practiced with it at home—practiced first on my electric refrigerator. I can sit there in the kitchen and turn the beam loose and slow down the refrigerator. After I got so I could kill insects at a distance of thirty feet I knew I could make a driver stop and give me a ride. The other night I was standing by the road when a car came along hitting about fifty. I wasn't concentrating on my job, and as this car came up I didn't have the beam strong enough. There was a little bit of a drag on the car but it went on by. That made me sore and I turned on the juice full strength. I wish you could have seen that car. It was a hundred feet past me when it stopped so abruptly that the hind wheels bucked two feet off the pavement. I let that guy have the works, and his car began backing up almost as fast as it had been going forward. Oh yes, I can jam zippers with it too."

One evening Jim was visiting my apartment. He was trying out two new lectures. One was on termites. He had virtually memorized Maeterlinck's book *The Life of the White Ant,* and his monologue on the subject was delightful. The other lecture was on "The Sex Life of the Date Palm." The date center of the nation is in the Coachella Valley, not far from Los Angeles, and somewhere out there is an institute where a man delivers regular lectures on the same topic. Jim has improved on the professional's material, though his entire discourse is scientifically accurate.

The male and female date palms lead a pretty dull life except for a couple of weeks in February, when they settle down to the business of mating. They have no sense of shame, and it is recorded that the Prophet Mahomet once prohibited their carryings on. Soon after the prohibition the date crop failed and Mahomet had to let the trees go back to their old habits, no matter how revolting they appeared to him.

The usual date garden has three or four male trees to each hundred females. Why is this? Why is it that date palms and chickens and gnus and sultans get all the breaks in life? Never mind. There are other points about the date-palm thing that are not quite clear to me. I do remember that all the trees bloom in mid-February. When the male blossom reaches maturity it begins to make a rustling noise. It has, so to speak, a date with a date. Since it is attached to a tree and the tree is attached to the ground and the female trees are maybe half a block away, it just can't climb down and walk over to them. It rustles, so somebody with legs will come along and take pity. Meanwhile, over on the female tree the lady blossom, anticipating action, produces a drop of moisture. Isn't this interesting?

In the old days, when the male blossoms began rustling and the female let go with that drop of moisture, the date grower would take a knife and cut off the male blossom. Then he'd take it over to the female tree and tie it to the female blossom. It couldn't happen in Boston.

Nowadays science has improved on this technique. Improved, that is, so far as the production of dates is concerned. I don't think, however, that the blossoms would consider it an improvement. Especially the male blossom. What they do now is hop on that male blossom the minute he begins to rustle. They cut off the blossom when it is in the very prime of life and lay it away someplace and let it dry out. Then the dustlike pollen is shaken on puffs of cotton and the cotton is tied to the female blossom. Sometimes they just gather up all the boy dust and put it in a spraying machine and squirt it at the girls. On behalf of all male date-palm blossoms, I wish to say God damn human beings.

After Jim had finished his lectures it was time for him to go out and put the beam on an automobile driver. I walked with him as far as Cahuenga, where the cars were whipping upgrade toward the Pass. Jim wanted to demonstrate the functions of his beam. We stood there at the curb and as each car passed Jim would execute a sweeping gesture with his arm. The motorists all ignored him.

"Now," he said, "I'll turn on the beam. Quiet, please."

A big sedan was whizzing toward us. Jim furrowed his forehead, set his jaw, and scowled at the oncoming car. This time he made no dramatic waving motion. He stuck his arm out in a casual gesture. The tires screeched on the pavement and the car stopped beside us. There were seven or eight people in it already. The rear door opened and a voice sang out, "Hop in!"

Jim turned to me and grinned.

"Good night," he said. "Thanks for the chopped-egg sandwich."

One night he went with me to Jim Cagney's house. The two Jims got along fine, both being addicted to the classical guitar and both being talkers. Moran gave his lecture on diversified toilet flushes and Cagney told some Hollywood stories. Cagney's top performance that evening was an impersonation of a nance. Moran's was a tale of a newspaperman he had known in his Washington days.

This newspaperman sold a short story to a magazine one day and got a check for something over $1,000. He promptly, and logically, went on a bender. He got himself a classy babe, a girl with beauty and poise and lovely clothes and no morals to speak of. He took a suite in a good hotel and the two of them sort of kept house for a few days.

Thus the binge began, on a more or less elevated plane. Day by day, as the consumption of liquor increased and the working capital decreased, the scale of living descended. The classy dame gave way to a cheaper trull. The fancy suite became a room in a lesser hotel.

At the end of three weeks we find our hero at the bottom of the ladder, almost ready to be salvaged and restored to his job. He is in a flea bag, a shabby room with an iron bed and a washbasin fastened against the wall. His companion by now is a street girl of the lowest order. He is unshaven and red-eyed and shaky, and the last bottle of gin is at his side. He is asleep on the bed.

The girl gets up and goes to the washbasin, hoists herself up, and sits on it. This basin is against the wall at the foot of the bed. Our friend sleeps on. Suddenly there is a rending noise and a crash. The basin, under the weight of the lady, is torn from the wall and crashes to the floor along with its burden. Two sharp streams of water shoot out from the wall. One stream is boiling hot, the other is icy cold, and they strike our sleeping hero full in the face. He comes out of his coma screaming.

Jim Moran got the trouble straightened out for the poor guy by greasing the palm of the hotel manager. After the manager got his money he was inclined to forgive and forget and to regard the incident with humor. He said to Moran:

"When the two streams of water hit him . . . Well, I tell you, in my time I've heard all kinds of screams, but this one belonged strictly in the middle of a zoo."

The last I heard from Jim he had just returned to Hollywood from a ten-thousand-mile automobile trip during which he sold goggles to war-plant workers. He reported that the hours and hours of driving bored him and he had to find some way of amusing himself.

One day he stopped in a novelty shop in a Midwestern city. He bought one of those rubber false faces that come in realistic variations. Jim's mask made him look a trifle like Mortimer Snerd. Driving along the highway he would have the mask on with the face looking backward over his left shoulder. Then Jim, his own vision unobstructed, would wait for some driver to start passing him. As the other car came up Jim would lean just a bit to the left. The effect on the approaching motorist would be quite startling. He'd see this leering goon, sitting at the wheel of a speeding car but leaning out, staring back and paying no attention to the road ahead. Jim said nobody got killed that he knows about.

He has two projects in the back of his mind, to be undertaken when the world is restored to a condition which will permit a Moran to operate according to his natural bent.

He wants to become the father of a baby ostrich. Several years ago in New York he came out to my house full of enthusiasm for this project. As usual he had made a careful investigation of the difficulties involved. A zoologist in Philadelphia had promised that he would provide Jim with an ostrich egg and Jim's idea was to hatch this egg himself, personally.

"It's not an unreasonable thing," he said. "The male ostrich does most of the hatch work. After the female lays the egg the male plants himself on it and stays there until his fanny gets tired. Then he lets the female take over for a while. I've found out that there's no reason in the world why I couldn't hatch out an ostrich egg. What I want to do is hatch one in public. I'd like to get a window somewhere in Rockefeller Center. I'd bring the egg up from Philadelphia and build a special nest in the window, rig up a contraption so I wouldn't break the thing by setting on it. A male ostrich weighs as much as three hundred pounds, but he's got a lot more give to his bottom than I have, so I'd have to be careful. I'd have a tailor make a pair of hatching pants for me, so I could preserve my modesty and, at the same time, wrap my buttocks around that egg. I'd sit there in the window all day long and most of the night. I could put a sun lamp on it while I was away from it but I figure I could spend about eighteen hours a day on the nest. Incidentally, you have been a good friend of mine, so when I get this thing all organized, I think I'll get a copy of *Low Man on a Totem*

Pole, and while I'm hatching that egg I can be reading the book. Good advertisement, don't you think?"

I asked him about the percentage—where does the Moran pocketbook figure in the project? Would he charge admission?

"Certainly not," he said. "Anybody in the United States could step up and see me on that egg. Think what an educational thing it would be for the little children. I'm surprised that you don't see the payoff. Eventually I'd hatch a baby

ostrich. That baby ostrich would be *mine.* Practically my own flesh and blood. I'd be the only man in the world who could say he was the father of an ostrich. When that ostrich is hatched he gets a birth certificate. He is Little Ossip Moran. He and I will tour the country, appear in vaudeville, get on Fred Allen's program, appear on *We the People,* sign movie contracts. Maybe Little Ossip would go well on *Information, Please!* We'll be in lights—'Jim Moran and His Son Ossip.' I'll make a fortune, provided Ossip doesn't grow too fast. If he gets too big, he's likely to end up by kicking his papa to death."

One other thing is stirring around in the Moran brainpan. "One of these days," he told me, "I'm heading South. I've been reading quite a bit recently on the Civil War. You are aware of the fact that many people are still fighting that war. One thing has impressed itself on my mind. I've been unable to find, anywhere in the histories, a word about the last shot of the Civil War being fired. It is my belief that the last shot of the Civil War was never fired. If it was, the historians know nothing about it, for they never mention it. This is a terrible state of affairs. I've decided to rectify it and set history straight. I'm going to fire the last shot of the Civil War. I'm going to take a musket and go down to Mason and Dixon's line and stand on the line and fire a shot into the air. That will be the last shot of the Civil War. It'll be over and done with. I don't want to hear any more about it."

CHAPTER IX   *Theft of the Statue of Liberty*

A TALL, grim, humorless man named Bert Allenberg was put in charge of my destiny in Hollywood. Allenberg is one of Hollywood's leading agents, and while most of the animals in his stable are actors and actresses, he is not above dirtying his firm's good name by taking on a few writers.

He summoned me to Lucey's one day for lunch and we got into a booth. A waiter came along with a plug-in telephone and Allenberg went to work making calls like mad. He has magnificent offices in Beverly Hills but he operates his business, for the most part, on the run.

He had just finished a call when something came flying through the air and landed in his lap. It was a girl. She planted a juicy kiss on Mr. Allenberg's face, mussed up his hair, hugged him, and cried out: "Bert, darling! How are you, darling!" She had on a loose-fitting blouse and tight-fitting slacks. She continued to bounce around and make actress noises and suddenly I noticed that the tight-fitting part of her slacks was about to settle down into Mr. Allenberg's shrimp cocktail. I started to reach over and put my hand on the tight part of the slacks and push it away but I restrained myself, thinking someone might misinterpret the gesture as constituting a feel. They would have been right. At any rate, I'm sorry I restrained myself because it turned out that the girl was Miss Joan Fontaine. She was one of Mr. Allenberg's clients, and while I was a little startled at her vigorous mode of greeting her agent, I soon learned that such methods are normal among actresses. Betty Hutton, for example. Miss Hutton rarely enters a restaurant without hurling herself into the arms of a man or men. I got the treatment myself one day in the Paramount commissary. I was sitting there minding my own Salisbury steak when Miss Hutton came around a corner and did a jack-knife dive all over me. For a moment I thought I had been attacked by a jaguar and in trying to get squared away I planted my right hand squarely in Rufus Blair's plate of Boston baked beans. Meanwhile, Miss Hutton had secured a triple stranglehold on me and was whooping and yelling "Darling!" and so on, and there I was, trying to claw her off with my left hand and snapping baked beans onto the floor with my right. I was embarrassed as all hell, though I shouldn't have been, because people were paying no attention to us. Finally Miss Hutton quieted down and leaned back off my lap, looking at my face which was red with the rush of blood and redder with splotches of lipstick.

"Darling!" she yipped. "What was the name again?"

I had never met her in my life. A few months after that somebody asked me to autograph a book for her, which I did, inscribing a tender vulgarity in it. The next day I was walking along in front of the bank near the Paramount Studio. A dozen studio workmen were loafing around the bank entrance and just as I got up to them I heard a yell from the middle of the street:

"Hey! H. Allen!"

I looked up, and there she was at the wheel of her car.

The car was moving in brisk traffic on Melrose Avenue but she was leaning out of the window looking at me, paying no heed to the cars swishing past her on both sides.

"Oh, you lambie pie!" she screamed loud enough to be heard in El Paso, Texas. I put on a sickly grin and just then she pushed out her lips and started making loud kissing gestures. She turned away just in time to avoid a head-on crash with a Pepsi-Cola truck. I was sorry she avoided it. The workmen all around me were snickering and heh-heh-heh-ing, and I ducked into the bank and wrote a check for three times what I had on deposit before I knew what I was doing. If I could have had that dame alone right then I'd have kicked her pratt off.

Bert Allenberg gave me a small shock that day in Lucey's by telling me that Sam Goldwyn wanted to see me and maybe hire me. We made a date and a couple of days later were at the Goldwyn studio. It turned out that Mr. Goldwyn was getting ready to produce a Bob Hope picture and thought perhaps I could do some writing on it.

Mr. Allenberg apparently had reached the conclusion that I am somewhat less than half witted when it comes to business dealings—an evaluation that is on the conservative side—so I was not permitted to attend the session in which money was discussed. I found out later that Mr. Allenberg set a price for my services and Mr. Goldwyn offered half of that. Mr. Allenberg refused to budge and Mr. Goldwyn was equally unbudgeable. Nobody asked me what I thought. I learned that Mr. Goldwyn said:

"Look, Bert. This man knows from nothing about the motion-picture business. So what am I doing? I am offering to bring him in here and give him the bannafitt of all my years' experience in motion pictures. He will learn the business in the best place because I will titching him all I am knowing."

To this Mr. Allenberg answered:

"Listen, Sam. Just how much tuition do you want Mr. Smith to pay for studying under you?"

That ended the discussion. Meanwhile, I was in an outer office listening to a middle-aged secretary worry out loud. She asked me if I had noticed the huge gas-storage tank which stands across from the entrance to the Goldwyn lot. I said I had.

"I tell you," she said, "I can't sleep at night for worry about it. I think it's an outrage to have that tank right here under our nose. I'm a nervous wreck. You know very well that when the Jap planes come over here they're going to aim their bombs straight at that tank." She closed her eyes, bowed her head, and shuddered. "It's awful," she went on. "It will blow this whole studio to bits. They won't even be able to find our bodies. I write letter after letter to the authorities and tell them that tank has just got to be moved away, but they pay no attention to me. I can't stand it much longer. There are better ways to die than . . ."

Mr. Allenberg opened the door and beckoned me into Mr. Goldwyn's room. Mr. Goldwyn stood up and smiled and shook hands. I had no inkling of whether I was now working for him, or what.

"I read the book *Poddy Knife*," said Mr. Goldwyn. Then he laughed. "Fonny," he said. "I read it on the train. It is fonny. But you know something?" He gave me a sly look, cocking his head to one side and grinning. Then he pointed an admonitory finger at me and said:

"I think maybe you putting *me* in the books. I think you write about *me* next time and this I don't want. You make me a promise. Promise you don't put me in the books."

I didn't promise. I'd put him in the books plenty except that Alva Johnston has already put him in the books plenty, and wonderfully well. One thing I can say about him. While he is the butt of many Hollywood jokes, he is universally respected. He knows how to make good movies. He can't get along with his employees, and one of the most common remarks heard in Hollywood is: "I'll never work for that so-and-so again as long as I live."

I met a cameraman, one of the top geniuses of the trade, at a restaurant one night. He said he was just finishing up a picture for Mr. Goldwyn and that he would never work for that so-and-so again as long as he lived. He said that Mr. Goldwyn was continually interfering with his work. That very day the producer had been critical about certain camera angles, and the cameraman had said:

"Mr. Goldwyn, I thought you hired me and offered me a big salary because I'm supposed to know about camera angles. Why don't you leave me alone?"

"I don't care what you say," insisted Mr. Goldwyn. "What I want is close-ups with the feet in!"

Yet the guy knows his business. Idwal Jones reflects the opinion of the industry when he says: "You can always depend upon *quality* in a Goldwyn picture. He knows how to select and hire the best talent and I don't think he's ever made a picture that didn't have quality."

I'm certain Mr. Goldwyn is a smart man. He was altogether correct in my case. No, he wasn't, either. If he had hired me at his own price he'd have been a fool.

A few days after the Goldwyn episode I was at Paramount corrupting the morals of various employees when Blake McVeigh, one of my close friends there, told me Buddy De-Sylva wanted to see me. Mr. DeSylva is a brilliant showman, an artist, a bon vivant, a talented writer, a dynamic diplomatist, a fashion plate, a pool shark, a musician, a genius, and not very tall. In short, Mr. DeSylva is a great man. Any man who thinks what Mr. DeSylva thinks about me is a great man. Take my word for it.

I went to his office and introduced myself to his secretary. She said her name was Miss Ballantine. She was a looker. She told me to sit down and I chose a chair in a corner.

"No," she said, "come over here and sit in this chair." She indicated a place directly in front of her. "I want to look at you awhile," she said.

I sat down in the chair she had indicated and she looked at me a long time. At last she spoke.

"Well, I never!" she said. "I can't believe my eyes. I didn't think you would look human."

I couldn't think of anything to say. I held up my hand and made a circle with thumb and forefinger. I'd seen it done in the beer ads. The gesture is supposed to signify, "I want Ballantine" or "Make mine Ballantine," or some such thing, though I never saw the business done at a bar. If a guy ever pulled that thing in a saloon the bartender would take him for a fairy and go for him with the beer bat. Miss Ballantine didn't seem to catch the symbolism, so I said:

"That means I'll take Ballantine. Back in New York you're a beer, and even a whisky."

She ignored me and started pressing buttons and talking into boxes. Suddenly a door flew open and Mr. DeSylva came bounding out in his shirt sleeves. I am told that this was a precedent—that he never comes all the way out of his private office to greet a visitor—that he wouldn't do it unless the visitor were Saul of Tarsus or Westbrook Pegler.

We went into his playroom, a sunken office about four feet below the level of those surrounding it. Mr. DeSylva came to the point at once.

"You," he said, "are going to work for me. I don't give a damn what you say to the contrary. You might as well make up your mind to it."

"Oh, mott of Cambroney!" I said, showing off my French.

I tried to tell him that I was satisfied to sit back in New York and write occasional books; that I knew nothing about writing for the movies; that everybody I knew told me to beware of the Hollywood pitfalls; that he wasn't gonna make me into any bird in a gilded cage; that he couldn't tempt me with all that gold; that I had loved him ever since the night he had fallen off the chair in Dinty Moore's restaurant in New York, but that *I was not going to work for the movies!*

"The hell you're not," he said. And as I was leaving he laughed like Raymond on the radio and yelled after me, "You'll be back!"

"Sure I'll be back," I said. "I'll be back to sit here and talk to you because you're the best audience I ever met. But not to work."

It's true about his being the best audience on earth. I never met a man who enjoyed laughing as much as Buddy DeSylva. Robert Benchley is his nearest competitor. You can pull the simplest, corniest gag on DeSylva and he'll throw back his head and almost split his duodenum. Later on I heard some of the writers around Paramount complain about it. They said they'd go into his office with a story idea, an outline for a film comedy. They'd tell him the story and all through it he would howl with laughter, fall on the floor, bite the legs of his chair, and gasp through his hysterical cachinnation, "Call the doctor! My God, I'm dying!" Then, when the writer reached the end of his story, Buddy would get back into his chair, sop the tears off his face, and say:

"It stinks."

☆   ☆   ☆

So I went back to New York. I had to write some magazine pieces and that kept me busy for a while and I was happy in the thought that I had been firm in resisting the blandishments of Hollywood. Then I found myself wondering occasionally just how a person would go about writing a movie. I remembered the Statue of Liberty story.

During the last few months of my employment on a New York newspaper my desk was within eavesdropping distance of the desk occupied by the publication's film critic. Normally this gentleman kept irregular hours and sometimes wasn't seen around the shop for a week at a stretch. During the period of which I write, however, he arrived in the office daily at about 2:30 P.M. He'd toss his hat on the desk, run through a stack of mail, and then the story conference would begin.

Two other young men participated in the story conference. One was a Broadway columnist of sorts and the other was a gentleman who, I was told, possessed a certain technical skill in screen-play construction.

These three were engaged in a profound and noisy project aimed at getting some of that Hollywood gravy. They were collaborating on a movie. The collaboration had been launched one evening when the critic and the columnist were sitting with a movie press agent in a Times Square tavern. The movie press agent suggested that the critic and the columnist were pure idiots if they didn't turn out an original story for the screen. All they needed, he said, was a story technician and he knew just the guy for them.

It was agreed that the collaborators should gather each afternoon in the newspaper office and, simply by yelling at one another, work out the plot for their scenario. In the beginning these sessions were horribly distracting to the people who had to work in the immediate vicinity of the critic's desk. They flung situations and gags and fragments of dialogue back and forth across the desk. Sometimes two conferees would be talking simultaneously and sometimes even three. I'd be sitting there trying to write a story, trying to spell childern properly, or seperate, or Fiorella, and the screen-play hullabaloo would go on and on. There was a time when I felt like going to the boss about it, and I might have done that save for one thing. Suddenly I found myself getting interested in their movie.

The plot involved the theft of the Statue of Liberty. The three boys fancied themselves as actors and as each bit of their drama developed it was their custom to act it out. The columnist, for example, took the role of the man who, at the very opening of the story, discovered the theft of the Statue of Liberty. He was a passenger aboard a ferry, inbound from Staten Island, and he was supposed to be leaning against the rail. The columnist would lean an elbow on the back of a chair, an expression of early-morning commuter dopiness on his face. Then suddenly he'd execute a sort of double take, stiffen in amazement, thrust his head forward in a stare of disbelief. After that he'd clap his hand to his forehead, stagger backward a few steps and, with thorough disregard of Hays office restrictions, exclaim:

"Holy jezuss!"

The idea, of course, was that he had just noticed Bedloe Island and there was no Statue of Liberty on Bedloe Island.

That was the way the thing started. Some time during the night somebody had made off with the statue. It had been there at dusk of the previous evening but now it was gone and all that remained was the bare pedestal.

Being a sucker for the under half of double features I soon grew so interested in this remarkable drama that I tried to arrange my schedule so I would be present at the fringe of the afternoon story conferences. The boys didn't know, of course, that I was snooping. There were times when I itched to join them, when I had ideas of my own that I felt would be of use to them. But I held back, fearful of being told to return to my shoddy labors and leave them alone.

They had no great difficulty in setting up the monstrous crime. The critic and the columnist would shout back and forth, describing shot after shot to demonstrate the galvanic effect the theft of the statue had on the nation. There would be a scene in a newspaper city room as the flash came in, shots of police cars skidding around corners, dramatic close-ups of teletype machines thumping out the awful news, carrying it even to the White House where the President, stunned for a moment, would seize a telephone and speak crisply:

"Gimme J. Edgar Hoover of the G-men!"

The theft of Liberty and the confusion wrought in the nation were easy matters for the scenarists but when they came to the problem of motives and methods they were soon in a high sweat. They'd bellow at one another by the hour, and then there'd be long periods of silence during which they thought and thought and thought, broken occasionally by one man exclaiming:

"We could have this guy that . . . I mean this G-man . . . he could of come up through Jersey and found these Nodzies over there . . . this would be back before the statue disappears . . . you gotta do flashback stuff sometimes . . ."

The "Nodzies," to be sure, were the thieves—that was conceded from the beginning—though at one time the boys, bogged down in their own mental morass, tried to struggle out by switching to Japs. That didn't help a bit because the essential problem remained. They went into debate after debate and set up scene after scene, with the technical man speaking learnedly of "dolly" and "pan" and "montage" and other such matters within his purview. They got their Nodzie characters established, including their arch-fiend ("Otto Preminger's the guy! A natural for Preminger!"). They established a hideout for the villains—a suite of rooms reached through a sliding panel in the back wall of a restaurant kitchen. They got a girl and a boy—reporters on rival newspapers. They worked out a comedy role—a dumb soldier stationed on Bedloe Island ("Frank McHugh! Perfect!").

Still they made no real progress. Day by day their plot

grew more complex, acquired more fearfully ragged ends that needed taking up. They'd yammer and quarrel and pound the desk, and the critic, about once in every twenty minutes, would slump back in his chair and say:

"But God damn it, fellas! *How* did they get that statue offa that island in one night? Don't you see we gotta straighten that out before we can go another step."

Along about this time, when they had achieved a virtual stalemate, I resigned from the newspaper. I didn't, however, forget that plot. Months passed, and I watched the movie columns and the trade papers, but never a word appeared about the Statue of Liberty epic. I wanted to know how it came out. I wanted to know where those Nodzies took that statue, and how they were captured. Most of all, I wanted to know how in hell they ever got away with it.

After a period of worrying over the matter I figured out an excuse to telephone the columnist. I had a question to ask him about some Broadway character. He gave me the answer and then, quite casually, I said:

"Hey, what did you fellas ever do about that movie you were writing?"

"You mean that Statue of Liberty thing?" he answered. "Don't mention it to me. Makes me sick to the stummick to even think about it. Remember that guy was working with us? Well, right in the middle of things, right when we were just about to get the thing in shape where we could put it on paper, that bum got himself drafted into the Army. We couldn't go ahead without his technical advice. You gotta have a guy that knows the mechanics."

"But how," I said, "did you finally decide they got away with the statue overnight?"

"That," said the columnist, "was one of the things that bum was supposed to figure out. That's a technical matter. So what does he do? Goes and gets himself drafted, and last I heard he was in Kansas or Texas or somewhere. Now we gotta wait till the war's over to do anything about it."

It's been a long wait, but I'm still curious over how those Nodzies did it.

If those three geniuses ever get together again in an effort to finish their drama, perhaps I can help them by suggesting a new method of procedure.

At the M-G-M Studio in Hollywood two writers finished a screen play and were told to stay close to their offices because a new job was being cooked up for them. The days of waiting stretched into weeks and the two men got restless. Just for fun they decided to write a screen play to suit themselves. Two big money-making properties at Metro were series films: the Andy Hardy pictures with Mickey Rooney and the Dr. Gillespie stories with Lionel Barrymore. The two playful writers thought of merging these stories, which they did, turning out a tenderly beautiful scenario. In it Andy Hardy caught the clap and at the end Dr. Gillespie cured him of it.

The authors of *The Theft of the Statue of Liberty* might conquer their problem by adding the main ingredients of another story to what they already have. And I think I know the story for them.

About ten years ago one of the major studios, inspired by the success of the picture *King Kong*, decided to produce a fantasy every bit as spectacular as the story of the huge ape. The hero of this picture would be an aviator named "Slim" —a character patterned quite definitely after Charles A. Lindbergh.

At the beginning Slim is an army flier, a genius in the cockpit but a reckless lad who violates regulations by stunting and generally defying his superiors. He gets into trouble and is canned out of the Air Corps. But old Slim doesn't worry about that. He has become so famous that he can almost write his own ticket and he gets a nice commercial job immediately. He is engaged by an advertising agency to make a non-stop flight around the world passing over both the North and South poles. The flight is to advertise breakfast food or used cars or old diamonds or underarm deodorant or some such thing.

Slim takes off on his great flight, heading southward. He gets as far as the South Polar region and things are functioning nicely when out of the sky comes a bird as big as a Flying Fortress. This bird is an eagle, a white one, and he sails into Slim's airplane, biting chunks out of the fuselage, clawing off propellers, and generally making a nuisance of himself. Slim manages to land his ship without killing himself and lo! He finds himself in the middle of a Lost Colony. It is a lost colony of Vikings who have been living near the South Pole for years and years.

Slim makes friends with the Vikings and tells them about the colossal bird. "Him White Eagle," they say. They explain that the region is inhabited by hundreds of gigantic eagles, as big as airplanes. They have succeeded in domesticating all the birds except White Eagle. He is the mean one—a Moby Dick with feathers—the biggest and nastiest of the lot.

"I'll fix that scamp," says Slim. "I've got a bone to pick with him anyway."

He doesn't kill White Eagle. It appears that the Vikings use the big eagles for transportation, putting reins on them and riding them through the skies. Slim lures White Eagle to earth with some of the breakfast food or underarm deodorant and soon breaks his spirit. White Eagle becomes the aviator's personal mount.

When Slim's airplane came down it was pretty well smashed up, but he succeeds in salvaging the radio. There are sequences in which he demonstrates radio to the Lost Vikings. He tunes in Eddie Cantor and the Vikings all throw up their fish suppers. Then he gets a short-wave broadcast and learns that a tremendous Nazi fleet is bearing down on the United States.

Slim goes into action. All the big eagles are saddled, including White Eagle, and off they go—hundreds and hundreds of them, with Slim out front waving the flock onward into battle. They soon locate the Nazi armada and descend upon it. I don't know how those Eagles with Vikings on them ever succeeded in sinking warships, but they did it, and then proceeded to Washington where Slim was received as the greatest hero in all history and got put back in the Air Corps.

A trustworthy Hollywood informant told me that story and said that the studio actually spent a million and a half dollars on it, shooting almost all the special effects. Then

Lindbergh lost his great popularity and the whole project had to be put on the shelf.

It seems to me that if the Statue of Liberty boys could take that story and work it into their own plot, they'd come up with a box-office champion. Maybe it could be the Vikings who stole the statue under the impression it was good to eat. Or perhaps the Nazi fleet could be on its way back to Europe with the statue when White Eagle and Slim ride to the rescue. I don't know just how to jigger the thing into a plausible story. If I did know, I'd probably still be working at Paramount.

CHAPTER X　*Miss Beauty Rest*

FROM long experience at reading books, magazines, and newspapers I am in a position to warn you never to believe a single thing you see in print.

You read about the great excellence of Stradivarius and Guarnerius violins, how they are sometimes worth more than a heavy bomber. Then you learn that in 1939 a Harvard physicist conducted a series of tests proving that Stradivarius and Guarnerius violins are no better than violins turned out in our own fiddle factories.

You spend most of your life holding a reverent view of Whistler's Mother. I have a book called *Great Works of Art* which I sometimes use to demonstrate my skill with a golf club. I can lay the book on the ground, put a golf ball on it, take a midiron, and clip the ball off it, never touching the book one time out of five. The top cover is gone, the preface has long since been ripped to shreds, and seventeen pages of the introduction have gashes and deep welts in them, otherwise the book serves me as an excellent reference work. I've had it for ten years and now, at last, I have a chance to use it. The author, F. W. Ruckstull, is talking about Whistler and his work. He quotes somebody named Kobbe as saying the portrait of Whistler's Mother is great "because it expresses with reverence, profound and touching, the spirit and sanctity of motherhood." And Mr. Ruckstull himself says:

"The world which hangs photos of this picture on its walls, as we have done, does not care about its color, which is not beautiful, nor its technique, which is not wonderful, nor its quality of color, which is not superb, but it does so, because it is not mere paint, but is a picture—full of solace and inspiration; it is a monumental suggestion that, in the final analysis, a truly beautiful, lofty, holy mother is the sublimest creation of the cosmic volition."

Well, old Whistler must have been a genius to accomplish all that with the material at hand. A few years ago Albert Parry wrote a book about Whistler's family and brought out some revealing things about the old lady. He proved by her own diary that she was a grasping, sly old gal, avid for power—in other words, a crone you wouldn't trust as far as you could punt Sydney Greenstreet.

That's the way it goes: you can't believe anything and be safe. I suppose several million references have been made to the time William Tecumseh Sherman said that war is hell. In the popular belief Sherman made the crack while watching the burning of Jackson, Mississippi. Almost everyone assumed that he said it while viewing some scene of horror. A few years ago Dr. W. D. McCain of the Mississippi Department of Archives came up with what is thought to be the true story.

Sherman was watching his army cross the Pearl River. Just as the troops got across, one of the wagons loaded with provisions plunged into a swamp and turned over, spilling valuable groceries all over the mucky landscape. Sherman was fit to be tied. He stared at the mess for a minute, shook his head from side to side, and then said:

"War is sure hell."

A long series of such disillusionments has made me a skeptic. When the temptation came to try Hollywood and the movies, I remembered the many stories I had read about the treatment accorded new writers when they sign on with the movie studios. Most of these stories follow a pattern. A writer who has had success back East is hired by a movie company. He reports to the studio and is given an office. He is told to wait there and someone will get in touch with him and tell him what to do. So he plants himself in a chair and waits for weeks, maybe months, until his mind begins to wilt and then, quite likely, he goes out and throws a brickbat or a midget through the window of the executive producer's office. He never writes anything, and he goes away with bitterness in his heart and dashes off an article or a book denouncing the movie bosses for fatheads, cosmic wastrels, illiterates, and weregoats.

Well, I simply refused to believe such stories. In the late summer of 1943 I was in the clear so far as work was concerned. Nobody was pleading with me to write anything for them. Nobody was calling up to find out what radio program I had turned on. Nobody was inviting me to endorse Lux as being essential to the beauty of my underthings. Mayor LaGuardia had seized all the pinball machines in town, depriving me of physical exercise. It was considered illegal to go out and shoot people you don't like, so there I sat; and suddenly I got to thinking about that mad, beautiful, screwball town of Hollywood. I made it to the telegraph office in four minutes flat and sent a wire to DeSylva.

A few weeks later Buddy arrived in New York to be present at the opening of a picture. The date had been set for me to report at the studio but I hadn't started West yet. I was invited to a cocktail party given for Mr. DeSylva. I started right off by getting in solid with Paramount Pictures, Inc. I was sitting at a table with Alton Cook, Kate Cameron, Al Wilkie, Bob Gillham, and Buddy DeSylva. Cook was telling me stories about our friend Doc Rockwell and we were paying no attention to the rest of the people around us. Along came a bald gentleman in a tweed suit and Bob Gillham began introducing him around. Cook and I stood up, said pleased-ta-meetcha, shook hands with the newcomer, failed to catch his name, didn't give a damn, sat back down, and resumed our private conversation. The bald gentleman took a chair and began talking and all present listened attentively to his remarks, except Cook and Smith. We ignored him even when he was talking in our direction and finally he went away. When he was gone I turned to Kate Cameron and said, within hearing of everyone:

"Who was *that* bald-headed old goat?"

"That's Barney Balaban," she said.

Mr. DeSylva was looking at me with some misgiving. So were Messrs. Gillham and Wilkie.

"And who the hell is Barney Balaban?" I demanded. "And why does he want to come sticking his . . ."

"Barney Balaban," said Mr. DeSylva firmly, "is the president of Paramount Pictures."

I was a little glad Barney Balaban hadn't heard what I said. I have been fired many times in my life, but no boss ever fired me a month before I went to work for him. I'm sorry I said what I did and I'm willing to make amends here and now. Recently I picked up a story that should be of great interest to Mr. Balaban. It concerns the cornerstone ceremonies at the Paramount Theater building in Times Square, back in the mid-twenties. I got the story from a reliable informant who says he was present and took part in the affair.

Paramount spent a ton of money to ballyhoo the new theater and building. Supplementing its regular promotion and publicity staffs, the company hired a gang of newspaperman to help create the biggest noise since the island of Krakatao exploded.

On the day of the ceremonies there were bands playing and mobs of people jammed in Times Square and Mayor James J. Walker laid the cornerstone. It was a mighty impressive scene, particularly when a big copper box was lowered into the cornerstone. Mayor Walker spoke eloquently of the wisdom of the men who had made this thing possible; of the unselfish public spirit lying behind this magnificent project; of the beauty and nobility and altruism and brotherly love in the hearts and souls of the men who controlled the destinies of Paramount. He told how the copper box contained a record of our times. There were copies of current newspapers and periodicals, a print of the film which would open the theater, some newsreels and biographical sketches of the men who had been responsible for this edifice, this steel-and-concrete flowering of civilization, so that posterity might know the greatness of those men. Then, mid a solemn hush, the copper box was sealed in the cornerstone, the band lit into some slow anthem music, and it was over.

What Jimmy Walker didn't know and what those noble Paramount big shots didn't know was that certain secret operations had been conducted the night before. Most of the newspapermen who had been hired for the promotion campaign were gathered in the Paramount offices. One of their jobs had been to assemble the articles that were packed in the copper box. And among other things, they had composed the glowing biographical sketches of the Paramount executives.

They were sitting around that evening, swapping drinks out of bootleg bottles, and they got to talking about the Paramount moguls who were their temporary employers and whose sweetened biographical sketches were already packed in the copper box. The box itself stood there in the office, ready for posterity.

These newspapermen didn't like the Paramount executives, didn't believe any of the stuff they had written about them, actually despised them. Somebody had an idea.

"Why don't we write the truth about those big bums?" he suggested.

In no time at all the boys were at their typewriters. They wrote biographical sketches that reflected their true opinions. Under the spell of prohibition rotgut they went to town with the words. They blistered those noble, public-spirited, altruistic gentlemen. They cudgeled them in print as brutally as if they had been working on them with baseball bats.

My informant tells me that after the fresh biographies had been walloped out on the typewriters the boys unpacked the copper box. They removed the eulogistic sketches and substituted the revised versions. And if the story is true, those revised versions are nestled there at this very moment, waiting for posterity. And if, immediately after this book appears, blasting operations are heard in the dead of night at Times Square, you'll know what it means.

I wasn't told the identity of any of the newspapermen who took part in the affair. I rather suspected Gene Fowler had a hand in it, but he says no.

Whenever I think back about it I still consider it somewhat of a miracle that I ever reported for work at Paramount
after that train trip. Whenever I can arrange it I try to
travel on The Chief or The Super Chief of the Sante Fe
between Chicago and Los Angeles. The Super Chief, to my
mind, is the finest riding device invented by man. This time,
however, I booked passage on the Union Pacific out of
Chicago, and within ten minutes of boarding I was home-
steading in a club car the like of which I never imagined
existed. You wouldn't properly call it a car. It was a room,
and it was called, to the best of my memory, The Golden
Nugget. That was the name I think was printed on the
doors though I never bothered much about reading during
that trip.

The Golden Nugget was done in red plush and gilt after
the fashion of old-time sporting houses I have heard about.
There were chandeliers and period engravings on the walls
and, at one end of the car, a little bar. The bartender had
a big mustache, an 1880 hair-do, a gold toothpick, and at-
mospheric clothes. If I could spend the remainder of my
life in that car I'd be happy.

Emily Kimbrough, in the book about her trip to Hollywood, told about her roomette on the train, how she pulled
down the bed, got trapped under it with a hot-water bottle
between herself and the floor, and almost never got loose.
I had one of those roomettes, but the bed in it had a fat
chance of ever pinning me to the floor. It never saw me
long enough. The same was true of about a dozen men and
women who were inclined to stay with The Golden Nugget
to the bitter end. Among these were several Army officers, including a general. Also present was a lovely young lady known
to the company as Miss Beauty Rest. Every man inhabiting
that car, with the sole exception of myself,* was on the
make for Miss Beauty Rest, but there was a formidable obstacle barring the path to ecstasy. The obstacle was Miss
Beauty Rest's mama. She was a woman of fine physical
proportions and she had a nice face save for the fact that
she kept a stern and forbidding look on it. No mother ever

*It says here.

did a better job of chaperoning than she did for Miss Beauty Rest.

Whenever Miss Beauty Rest was in The Golden Nugget her mama was with her. The boys who had dedicated themselves to conquest had to behave themselves. All they could do was just sit and steal clothes-ripping glances at her, wishing the while in their secret hearts that the old lady would go get herself an attack of acute appendicitis.

One hope buoyed their spirits and kept them on the kwee vivvy. Mama always ordered double scotch. She seemed capable of ingesting eight or ten of these at a sitting without ever growing frivolous and without taking her watchful eye off Miss Beauty Rest. Yet there was always the chance that she'd take down with a wet brain.

There were about eight campaigners earnestly bent on despoiling her daughter, and these ranged from twenty-eight waistlines to fifties. Each man talked openly about it whenever Mama was out of earshot. Yet in the presence of Mama they were almost overbearing in their courtliness, buying her double scotches, speaking politely of their adventures here and abroad, accidentally revealing the extent of their estates by speaking intemperately about the income tax, and mentioning their close friendship with this or that movie celebrity in Hollywood. Miss Beauty Rest's mama took it all in, smiling wisely, watching her daughter, and hurling it down the hatch. She knew, of course, what was in their minds but she never let on. She was soft-spoken and there was an aura of culture and refinement about her. Under other circumstances she would have been a popular member of The Golden Nugget group, but as matters stood she was looked upon as a mean, inconsiderate, suspicious old spoilsport.

Through one long and lovely evening that was the way things stood. By nine o'clock in the morning of the following day the members were assembled in their customary places. A few went so far as to waste time eating. Fine stories were told, and the conversation was always pleasant. There was much good laughter.

The general stayed pretty much to himself, sitting in one corner of the car, smoking a pipe and studying documents.

He looked with an affectionate eye on the proceedings but took no active part in them.

Came the last night out. The campaigners had just about abandoned all hope of conquering Miss Beauty Rest. The bartender was as busy as a pointer turned loose in the middle of a Long Island duck farm.

Miss Beauty Rest entered, radiant in a change of costume. Behind her came Mama. Miss Beauty Rest hurried to join the merry throng gathered near the middle of the car. Mama hesitated near the door, then the car lurched and she was thrown to one side almost into the lap of the general. The next thing I noticed she was sitting alongside him and they were talking and drinking together.

Things went along swimmingly with the rest of us. The evening wore on, and it must have been after ten when we saw the general and Mama get out of their chairs and leave The Golden Nugget. The campaigners swung into action—maybe this was the big chance!

It was that way as midnight drew near, and then the door at the end of the car swung open with a bang. There stood Mama. She had an unlovely leer on her face and she was neatly plastered. She advanced into the car, moving like a yawl tacking into the wind, and finally she reached a position where she could hold onto the back of a chair. The general was behind her.

Miss Beauty Rest took one look and cried:

"Mother!"

All eyes were on the swaying lady. Then she spoke—this quiet, refined, cultured, lovely American mother. She spoke so that she could be heard above the rumble and clatter of the wheels on the rails.

She described the gentlemen of the company as a bunch of gutter bums and worse. She said she knew all along of the designs they had on her daughter. She described those designs and used Elizabethan language in the description. She went on for quite a while, piling obscenity on obscenity. Then she wished upon everyone the pleasures of sizzling in hell, turned around, and seized hold of the general.

"Come on!" she yelled. "Come on, you sweet old son of a bitch! Le's go knock off another bottle!"

The general led her out. Miss Beauty Rest sat there, eyes wide, and then she screeched. A long pause, and then she screeched again, burst into tears, and ran blindly from the car.

That's the last we saw of them. I looked around for them when the train reached Union Station in Los Angeles but they were nowhere in sight.

Sidney Reznick, then a writer for Jimmy Durante, was among the survivors of the voyage of The Golden Nugget. A couple of months later he told me that he had been walking on Vine Street in Hollywood when he almost bumped into Miss Beauty Rest's mama. She was with a large member of the United States Marine Corps. She didn't even notice Sidney.

CHAPTER XI *Wherein There Is a Poem*

DURING all the time I was in Hollywood I caught sight of only one stiff gentleman's hat. It was traveling briskly along Marathon Street and holding it up was Robert Benchley. In a way I am a blood brother to that derby hat because one of the things that is holding *me* up is Robert Benchley. The fact that he approves of my cross-purpose strivings . . . Well, the effect on me is something like the salubrious effect obtained by pouring a shot glass of penicillin on a pimple.

Mr. Benchley is partly to blame for my efforts to create a mare's nest in Marathon Street. Marathon Street is the back alley on which the Paramount Studio fronts.

Assuming you are a thorough and methodical person, you have read what Buddy DeSylva had to say up there in the introduction. I thought it was a perfect introduction to a book because (a) it was written many weeks before I ever started this book; (b) it is filled with exaggerations and inaccuracies, and (c) he didn't charge me anything for it.

I'd like to add that Mr. DeSylva wrote it himself. So many people will be asking me who actually wrote it. That's the way it was when Fred Allen wrote the libelous introduction to *Low Man on a Totem Pole*. Scores of human misfits, each afflicted with cirrhosis of the head, accused me of writing it, and when I denied it heatedly, suggested that Mr. Allen's press agent or his wife or his sister-in-law Laston wrote it. The best I could wish on these petty skeptics is that they should have athlete's foot until their toes are split clear up to their knees. Micturate on them! Fred Allen wrote that introduction and Buddy DeSylva wrote this one.

The Fred Allen connection caused me acute embarrassment at least once. This little episode took place on Vine Street in Hollywood. The Satyr bookshop, abaft the Brown Derby, had run out of *Low Man on a Totem Pole* and I needed a copy in a hurry, having promised delivery that day to Hal Bock of NBC. I walked on down Vine Street and entered another bookstore. There was a lady inside, reading a newspaper.

"Do you," I said, "have a book called *Low Man on a Totem Pole?*"

She began saying the title over and over to herself, searching her memory. By and by her face brightened.

"Oh, sure!" she exclaimed. "What's the matter with me today? That book by Fred Allen."

"Yes," I said reluctantly. "That's the one."

She began searching the shelves and I joined the quest. After a while I spotted a copy in a corner of the window and pointed it out to her. In order to reach it she had to climb over a desk which was piled high with old books, and by the time she had got it and come back she had knocked a couple of hundred volumes to the floor. She put the book down before me with a triumphant flourish and asked if I wanted it wrapped. I did.

"He's some guy, this Fred Allen," she said as she began wrapping it.

"He sure is," I agreed.

"For the life of me," she went on, "I don't see how he gets time to write these books like this with all that broadcasting and movies and signing autographs."

"He's a busy man all right," I said, glancing around the store. If I had to hit her I wanted to hit her with a pictorial history of the Civil War.

"You know," she said, biting off the string, "he's written

another book since this one. Fred Allen, I mean. We don't have it because we sold out. Some people say his new one is better than this one. It's about puddy knives."

I snatched the package out of her hand and departed.

Getting back to Robert Benchley. If Mr. DeSylva has reason to resent my attitude during the period I worked for him, let him blame Mr. Benchley. Just before I left New York I encountered Mr. Benchley at the Stork Club. I told him I was going to Hollywood to labor for the cinema.

"Poor boy," he sighed, shaking his hoary head. "You poor, poor boy. Let me feel your brow."

"Aw, now," I said, "it's not as bad as all that."

"Give me your hand," he went on. "Now, let's see how the pulse is behaving. Oh, barkeep! Fetch this patient a double medicinal Johnnie Walker. He has been bitten by snakes."

I demanded that he be more explicit.

"They'll break your heart," he said. "Look at me—a veteran of that debilitating system—old before my time. I've been working in Hollywood off and on since 1926. It took years for me to learn it, but now I know that the only thing for a writer to do in Hollywood is to act, and not write. I was hired originally as a writer. I worked on *fourteen different stories* before a single line of mine ever turned up on the screen. And then it wasn't much of a line. It was nothing more than a policeman walking into a scene and saying, 'Get along with yez now.' The way I had it was, 'Now, get along with yez.' They changed it on me, but the words were mine. They'll kill you!"

"Okay," I said. "They'll kill me. They'll shatter my heart. So what should I do?"

"Don't go," he said, "but if you must go, take the advice of a broken old man. Don't let them scare you. There'll be times when you'll know the blackest despair. There'll be times when you'll start exercising your big toe so you can use it to pull the trigger on a shotgun, the opposite end of which you have in your mouth. You'll sit there in your office and weep, and make howling noises that no sound-effects man could duplicate. You wait and see! You'll be saying that Mother Benchley told you there'd be days like this.

"Now," he went on, "there's one way to beat it. Every time they slug you, every time they knock you down, don't count ten. Just let your mind dwell on one thing. Think of that lovely little man in the cage—the little man you see every Thursday. Thursday is payday. Just conjure up a vision of that delightful little man, and a vision of yourself doing this." Mr. Benchley went through a pantomime as though he were pulling legal tender toward himself across the bar, wetting his thumb between hundred-dollar bills. "It's negotiable," he said. "Just think of that when tragedy overwhelms you and the hell with everything else."

Mr. Benchley's philosophy was helpful. There are some people who pretend that it's shameful for a person to accept the kind of money Hollywood hands out to writers. To point up this point I have now reached the point where I am going to insert a poem in one of my books. Normally I wouldn't dream of such a thing. If it's poetry you want, go buy a book of it. The poem that follows is about Gene Fowler and was written by Gene Fowler and it treats of the attitude of Mr. Fowler's friends on learning that he had hit the Hollywood jackpot. It was written some years ago just

after Mr. Fowler had gone to work for Darryl Zanuck. Mr.
Zanuck got it in the mail one day just as it is here:

HOLLYWOOD HORST WESSEL

The boys are not speaking to Fowler
 Since he's been the wine of the rich;
 The boys are not speaking to Fowler—
 That plutocrat son of a bitch.

For decades he stood with the bourgeois,
 And starved as he fumbled his pen.
 He lived on the cheapest of liquor
 And, aye, was the humblest of men.

And even though women foreswore him
 And laughed when he fell into pails,
 He went over big on the Bow'ry,
 The toast of the vagabond males.

The wrinkles were deep in his belly,
 The meat on his thigh bones was lean.
 Malaria spotted his features;
 The stones that he slept on were mean.

Then Midas sneaked up to the gutter
 Where old Peasant Fowler lay flat,
 And the King of Gelt tickled the victim,
 Who rose with a solid-gold pratt.

Gone! Gone was the fervor for justice,
 And fled was the soul of this man;
 This once fearless child of the shanty
 Was cursed with an 18-K can.

He hankered for costlier raiment
 And butlers who'd served the elite.
 He tore down the old family privy
 And purchased a Haviland seat.

Ah, God, how this parvenu strutted,
And smoked only dollar cigars.
His jock straps were lined with chinchilla,
His drawers were the envy of stars.

Ah, where was the once-valiant spokesman
Who gave not a care nor a damn?
Alas, when they scaled his gray matter
It weighed hardly one epigram.

The boys are not nodding to Fowler
Since he rose from the alms-asking ditch;
The boys do not cotton to Fowler—
That sybarite son of a bitch!

Being both an admirer and friend of Mr. Fowler, Mr. Zanuck was indignant. He telephoned Mr. Fowler at once. He said that some dirty bum, jealous of Mr. Fowler's popularity and success, had written a nasty poem about him. He read it to Mr. Fowler over the phone.

"Good, isn't it?" commented Mr. Fowler.

"Good hell!" replied Mr. Zanuck. "I think it's almost libelous."

"I still think it's good," said Mr. Fowler. "I wrote it myself. I wrote it as spokesman for the general public."

Mr. Zanuck was unutterably confused for a time but, knowing the unpredictable nature of Mr. Fowler, he was soon able to accept the joke in good humor.

One day Sidney Skolsky and I drove out to Twentieth Century-Fox studio for a session with Mr. Fowler and his close friend Harry Brand. Sidney Skolsky is celebrated for two things: his undeniable talent, and his size. If he were hollow and had a strap on him he'd make a good golf bag. His size, however, is deceptive and masks a tempestuous soul. He once picked up a Coca-Cola bottle and chased the editor of a trade paper out of the Brown Derby and the editor of the trade paper didn't go in the place again for three months. On another occasion Mr. Skolsky attended a dinner and found himself seated next to Louella O. Parsons. Mr. Skolsky at that time didn't like Miss Parsons and Miss

Parsons didn't like Mr. Skolsky. She said something that made Mr. Skolsky so furious that he came near exploding. He couldn't bring himself to clout a female, but there was nothing in the rule book about . . . He simply leaned over, seized Miss Parsons' arm with both hands, and *bit* it. He is a man not to be trifled with.

Gene Fowler's magnificent biography of John Barrymore had just been published at the time we went to see him and we spent a lot of time talking about the Monster. Then Harry Brand got to reminiscing over some of Mr. Fowler's personal exploits.

One day a tremendously important meeting was held in an office on the Paramount lot. The meeting had something to do with the United Artists organization. Among those attending were Mary Pickford, Douglas Fairbanks, Charlie Chaplin, Sam Goldwyn, Joseph Schenck, and William Gibbs McAdoo. Mr. Fowler chose that day to show up at the studio. He assembled a few crapulous friends and they adjourned to a near-by groggery. In the course of time Mr. Fowler's spirit burgeoned and oceans of vigor began to crowd into his athletic frame. Someone mentioned the mighty conference then in progress across the street. Mr. Fowler quietly slipped away from his companions.

The meeting was being held in a room attached to one of the big sound stages. It was a hot day and one window stood open. The celebrated participants were hard at work, rendering decisions that would affect the future of the whole movie industry. Suddenly a head appeared at the open window. The head spoke:

"Nurmi. Lap one."

Then it was gone.

Half a minute later it popped in view again.

"Nurmi. Lap two."

This sort of thing went on with distressing and clocklike regularity. Lackeys were sent out to do something about it. Yet nothing was accomplished. That head kept showing up and saying:

"Nurmi. Lap thirty-nine."

The celebrated personalities inside didn't know the identity of the man who was disrupting their earth-shaking ponderings. Someone offered a suggestion that the studio police be notified and instructed to shoot the pest—just wing him, not kill him.

"Nurmi," said the head. "Lap forty-seven."

Then Harry Brand was summoned. The conference demanded what in the hell was going on and why wasn't something being done about it.

"It's Gene Fowler," Mr. Brand told them. "He's just running around the outside of the sound stage—just getting a little exercise. I think he's weakening and if you'll only——"

"Nurmi. Lap fifty-two."

"—if you'll only," continued Mr. Brand, "be a bit patient, he'll wear himself out and fall down."

Mr. Brand was right. Nurmi was on lap sixty-three when he went down. His marathon, though it contributed to the general tone of the historic meeting, was not mentioned in the minutes.

Then there was the time Mr. Fowler found himself at the corner of Hollywood and Vine, and the policeman was blowing his whistle for traffic, and . . . But no. What's the matter with me? I can't tell that one.

One other Fowler-Brand adventure was concerned with the funeral of Tod Sloan in Hollywood. The little man who has been called the greatest jockey in history died broke. Few people knew he was penniless because he had great pride and kept up a front to the end.

Gene Fowler and Harry Brand had been friends of Sloan, and soon after his death they got wind of the fact that the little guy's body was to be dumped in potter's field. They got busy. They knew a prominent undertaker (Fowler *always* seems to know a prominent undertaker) and they talked him into furnishing a proper casket, an adequate chapel for the service, and a respectable burial plot. The eloquence of the two friends was so great that the mortician even threw in the services of a classy preacher.

Gene and Harry now went to work on the promotion job—publicizing the forthcoming funeral of Tod Sloan as an event comparable to the burial of an emperor or a Mason.

Leading screen stars, top sporting figures of the West coast, and funeral-happy politicians sent word that they would attend.

The hour for the services approached and the two promoters arrived ahead of time. One glance around the chapel and they knew something was wrong. There were no flowers —not so much as a single blossom. It was too late to order them now. Gene and Harry, cursing themselves for the oversight, wandered down a corridor. Suddenly they came to a door leading into another chapel. Stretched out in this room was the body of a prominent Los Angeles businessman. His funeral service was scheduled for an hour after the Sloan rites. And his casket was surrounded by several tons of flowers.

Gene and Harry went to work. Piece by piece they lugged the floral devices into the Tod Sloan chapel, and when they had finished, the jockey's room was a botanical sight to see.

So the people came and marveled and during the ceremony Jim Jeffries turned to Bull Montana and remarked:

"Yep, that's old Tod all right. Always went first class."

The service was finished and the crowd prepared to leave for the cemetery. Mr. Fowler and Mr. Brand were just climbing into a limousine when they were interrupted. Their undertaker friend had shown up.

"Come with me, boys," he said. They followed, meekly. And they had to tote every last one of those floral pieces back to the dead businessman. The two men who had saved Tod Sloan from a pauper's grave, who had given him a send-off commensurate with his famous days, didn't get to see the rest of the show at the cemetery. They finished their work and then they went out and got . . . Well, they went out some place.

EXTRA CHAPTER

GOING through a stack of old notebooks and an accumulation of clippings I have found some scraps that ought to be included in this book, but I can't find any place to fit them in. Believing that you are entitled to them, I lump them all together and throw them in right here, free. They are informative and educational and also I want to get rid of them. Here they are:

A man named Sir Clifford Allbutt made certain important discoveries relative to blood pressure.

The ladies of ancient Crete were modest about exposing their necks but let their breasts stick right out in public. I mean hang right out.

The sex life of corn is dull, all the work being done by the wind.

Guy Dailey, a vaudeville actor, was the first man in history to eat a banana under water.

What ever happened to Wilbur Huston? In 1929 he was chosen America's brightest boy in a contest sponsored by Thomas A. Edison. The last I heard he had become a leader in the Oxford Movement.

The people of the United States consume more than five million pounds of aspirin each year.

No matter how beautiful a girl may be, it's an even money bet she's got pimples all over her bottom.

Chester Greenwood of Farmington, Maine, invented the earmuff.

Darwin, to test the effect of music on plants, had a trombonist play to a row of beans several hours each day. Make up your own joke.

My landlord, the Queensboro Corporation, put the first radio commercial on the air in 1922.

Sir Arthur Thomas Quiller-Couch, compiler of the *Oxford Book of English Verse*, lived to be eighty years old, was hit by a jeep, and died.

The Algonquin Indians invented succotash, for which the hell with them.

CHAPTER XII *The Great Comma Crisis*

ON THE MORNING I reported for duty at the Paramount Studio I arrived at nine o'clock and had to sit around for an hour before anyone showed up who could tell me what to do and where to do it. During that hour I remembered something. I remembered that this was the second time I had been on the Paramount pay roll.

Back in 1935 I suddenly found myself unemployed and unmoneyed. Prior to that time I had been a newspaperman in New York and as such I had been a great guy to many characters around Broadway. They invited me to cocktail parties and put their arms around my shoulders and sent me Christmas presents and had me to their houses.

The moment I was out of a job I became as popular as a gonococcus with bad breath. It's always that way. I spent days sitting in the outer offices of men who had courted and flattered me in the past, knowing quite well that those men didn't want to see me now and were using the side entrances to get away from me. Out of dozens and dozens there were only two or three guys who didn't duck across the street to avoid me, and one of these was Al Wilkie of Paramount. He got me a job—not much of a job, but it bought groceries and paid the rent.

I was assigned to the "press-book unit" in the Paramount building. A press book is a thing ordinarily about the size of the *Saturday Evening Post,* and one press book is prepared for each picture before the picture is released. These press books are distributed to theaters where the film is to be shown and are used by the theater people to simplify their advertising and publicity campaigns. There are pages containing ads of various dimensions. There are other pages containing suggestions for promotional stunts, such as tying a horse outside a theater where a Western picture is playing, or hanging an authentic Dorothy Lamour sarong in the lobby when Miss Lamour is on the screen so that male customers may feel it on the way in. And the press book also includes pages containing publicity stories about the picture and its stars.

Suppose we have a picture called *Redheads Are Dangerous,* starring Vilma Piddle and Mayhew Fobb. The proprietor of the Badgergame Theater in Trafllams, Indiana, is going to show *Redheads Are Dangerous.* He receives a copy of the press book for that picture. He cuts out the ads he wants to run and then he cuts out some of the publicity stories. The advertising man for the Trafllams *Daily Membrane* comes around. He is given the ad copy and the publicity stories. It is understood that when the theater takes an ad, it is entitled to some publicity space. The publicity story might start out like this:

THRILLING DRAMA
COMING_____
TO BADGERGAME

Alluring Vilma Piddle, last seen in Paramount's *Ganged in Hawaii*, will return to the screen of the_____
Theater on_____ as star of the inspiring new epic drama, *Redheads Are Dangerous*.
Opposite Miss Piddle will be that romantic . . .

And so on for as much space as the local editor will allow. He simply pencils in the name of his theater and the date of showing. If he doesn't use that publicity matter, the theater owner quite likely will quit buying ads. It is the same principle under which a metropolitan daily will devote space to the doings of the Gimbel's Stamp Club or Macy's toy-boat regatta even if it means throwing out news that a cure for cancer has been discovered. It is the same principle under which a metropolitan daily will devote four times as much space to the obituary of a minor executive in an advertising agency as it would give to the death of a scholar or scientist whose name will be in the history books of the future.

My job at Paramount was to sit all day at a typewriter and wham out the publicity copy for the press books. I wrote it all. In the hypothetical case of *Redheads Are Dangerous* I'd have to write interviews with Miss Piddle and Mr. Fobb, as well as with the producer, the director, and maybe the cameraman. There'd be short items about things that happened during production of the picture. There'd be stories about bit players and extras. The material for these essays would be collected by the publicity men at the studio in California and sent East. Much of it was faked and the guy doing the writing on the New York end was expected to fake up the fakes wherever possible.

I got along fine until the crisis about commas arose. The boss of the press-book unit was a stubborn man with wavy hair who picked his nose with the butt end of his fountain pen. All my copy had to go through his desk and meet with his approval. One day he called me into his office, fastened his hard eyes on me (using a Little Miracle Stapling Machine), and said:

"Do you know you are making me lose sleep at night?"

I said I didn't know it.

"Didn't anybody ever tell you in school how to use a comma?"

"No," I said. "I quit school before we got past the period."

"I suspected as much," he said, ignoring my attempt at levity. Then he picked up a piece of my copy, an interview with an actor which I had made up out of thin air. He pointed to a paragraph which went something like this:

"*I make a point of answering every fan letter I receive,*" *said the noted star.*

"Now," said the boss, "what's wrong with it?"

I didn't know.

"Look at that comma!" he snorted. He rammed his finger against the comma after the word *receive*. That comma, he said, should go *outside* the quotation marks. It should be this way:

"*I make a point of answering every fan letter I receive*", *said the noted star.*

I disagreed with him. I said that if I knew one thing in this world about commas, it was where they go in relation to quotation marks. I said the rightful place for a comma is *inside* the quotation marks, next to the word.

"From now on," he said, "you put the comma *outside* the quotation marks. Every God-damn comma you use goes *outside.*"

I went back to my typewriter and tried it. I had been putting commas inside quotation marks for years and there was simply something revolting about doing it the other way. It was like trying to pat the stomach and rub the head, like buttoning the fly with the left hand. After a day or two of this perverse practice I quietly rebelled and began putting the commas inside. Immediately I was summoned to Mr. Comma-Crazy's office. He was in a cold fury. I took it all and went back to his way of life. The next day I got a copy of the New York *Times* and went all through it, putting penciled rings around the commas that were all inside quotation marks. I put the newspaper on his desk and didn't say anything. It came back to me with one word written large across the front page:

"OUTSIDE!"

The day after that I brought in the complete works of Shakespeare and showed him all the commas inside of quotation marks.

"This guy was wrong," he said, handing the book back to me.

I was working on a picture involving Mae West. I wrote an interview with Miss West and at the very end I had her say:

"If I have learned one thing in this life, it is that commas always go inside quotation marks."

When the boss got that he like to split a gut. He told me that I could resign myself to putting the commas outside quotation marks or I could get the hell out of that office and stay out. By this time I wasn't sleeping nights for worry over the thing. I was in no position to carry the fight further.

The man had already come and taken away the radio and I was two months behind on the rent. But I was so mad that I went to the man who was boss over my boss. He was a flamboyant little guy trying to be dynamic, though ill-equipped for it since he had the appearance of a fugitive from an iron lung. He was opening letters and yelping into a box as I sat down opposite him and started my tale of woe. I went on and on about commas inside of quotation marks and commas outside of quotation marks and the New York *Times* and Shakespeare and I was almost sobbing by the time I was through. He hadn't even looked at me during all that appeal to reason but now he pierced me with his gimlet eyes.

"Commas schmommas!" he said.

That was all I got out of *him*.

I went back to my desk and wrote a note and took it and handed it to old Comma-Crazy. It said:

"You are a horse's ass,,,,,,,,,,,,,,,,,,,,,,,," said Mr. Smith.

I had my hat on and was in the elevator before he could read it and I never went back.

The thing still rankled in my breast after eight years, but I knew nobody at Paramount would tell me where to put my commas now. It makes no difference where you put a comma in a movie script. The actors don't speak them, so the producers don't care where you put them. I must report, however, that I ran into that same guy—old Comma-Crazy—in a Hollywood restaurant one evening. He came over to my table.

"Well, well, well," he said. "Long time no see. You're quite the author now! What're you doing out here?"

"I'm putting commas *inside* of quotation marks," I said, "and *for Paramount*."

So that was the pleasant memory I was enjoying that first morning when a cigarette holder came up to me. Fastened on the end of it was Dwight Mitchell Wiley, the short-story writer, who was also reporting for work at Paramount. After a while we were escorted to the fourth floor of the Writers' Building and shown our offices. The girl who took us up there told us that any time we wanted to see any movies, just to give her a ring and she would have them run for us in one of the projection rooms.

"You mean for nothing?" asked Mr. Wiley. He had never been inside a movie studio before and he was startled to learn that it's considered ethical to look at movies on the company's time. He and I spent that first day together just wandering around. I knew the studio pretty well and a lot of the people who worked there. We adhered to the popular myth about writers and looked upon everything with a cynical eye. We were walking down a studio street when we saw Mr. Basil Rathbone approaching. He was working in a costume picture called *Up Frenchman's Creek* and had on an outfit such as D'Artagnan wears in the books. It was a mighty fancy get-up all the way around, but the thing that attracted our attention first was the boots. They were high boots reaching almost to the hips, flaring out at the top. As Mr. Rathbone came abreast of us I looked him in the eye and said:

"You in pictures?"

He ignored me and passed on. Whereupon Mr. Wiley turned around and yelled after him:

"Goin' wadin'?"

That sort of playful thing went on all day except for those periods in the afternoon when we had to go back to our offices and sign papers. I wrote more that first day than I did during the remainder of the six months, and all I wrote was my name. There was a steady procession of girls bearing documents concerned with wage stabilization and declaration of citizenship and Clause Eight to be initialed by party of the second part and withhold 20 per cent for the government and withhold some more for the state and withhold some more for the Motion Picture Relief Fund and withhold some more for Old Age and withhold some more for unemployment insurance and withhold some more for some other things and who to be notified if suddenly killed.

I was sitting there signing my name right and left when my next-door neighbor called on me. He was Frank Partos, a screen writer who looks somewhat like the late Lew Cody. Mr. Partos came in and introduced himself and said he had something mightily important to tell me.

"I make a practice," he said, "of calling on every new writer and giving him a tip. You have come out here from New York so you are a comparative stranger to Los Angeles. There is one very important thing I must warn you about. Otherwise you'll find yourself in terrible trouble. I hope you'll not consider me bold for walking in here to give you advice, but I do it only because I know it will save you much worry and trouble. Now, just remember this one thing. Never, never, never, as long as you are in this town, never shoot a rabbit from the platform of a trolley car. There is a law here against shooting rabbits from the platforms of trolley cars and if you violate it you'll go to jail. If you *must* shoot rabbits from trolley cars, shoot out the window."

I was grateful for this advice, and Mr. Partos, who is one of the best screen writers in the business, became my friend. Thereafter, every time the impulse came to shoot a rabbit from the platform of a trolley car, I remembered his kindly warning and restrained myself and shot a policeman instead.

After Mr. Partos had returned to his own office I sat alone for a while and then I began to hear yips and snarls and squeals coming from other parts of the building. "Good God!" I thought. "Can that be the writers at work?" Later on I learned that the noises were made by dogs. Several writers in the building make a practice of bringing their dogs to work with them, and for that practice I think those writers should be compelled to undergo some slight penalty, such as being hit on the head with sledge hammers.

My office was not very fancy. Almost all the varnish had been chewed off the front of my desk as well as off the surfaces of my swivel chair. At first I figured this room had formerly been occupied by a dog-owning writer and that the dog, or dogs, had a weakness for the taste of zinc oxide or turpentine. Later on I revised this theory and concluded that the desk and chair had been gnawed by a writer. The walls were scarred and pock-marked as though someone had been trying to shoot ducks in the room. I didn't know how long I'd be staying, so I didn't bother about decorating those walls, except to hang up a picture of Buddy DeSylva in a characteristic pose, tilted back in his chair with his feet on his desk.

The prospect from my window was enchanting. The office overlooked a little park with a fountain full of goldfish in the center. This quadrangular park was known to the writers as The Campus because you could look out the window at any time and see beautiful girls with bobbing fronts and jiggling behinds trotting back and forth with interoffice memos. It was very difficult for me to stay away from that window. Directly across the park were the stars' dressing rooms and their goings and comings became routine.

The Campus was used quite frequently for outdoor scenes and on those days when shooting was in progress I simply planted myself at the window and stayed there. The biggest show was the one Cecil B. DeMille put on. For two days the workmen labored converting the park into a lawn and garden which was supposed to represent the grounds of an Australian hospital. The picture was *The Story of Dr. Wassell,* and the Writers' Building was used to represent the hospital. I don't know whether I got into it or not, but if you saw that picture and remember the hospital scene and a guy hanging three fourths of the way out of a fourth-floor window, that was my debut as a movie actor. Among other things they set up a big tree in the middle of the park and finally they were ready to shoot. Whenever DeMille is shooting even the case-hardened secretaries around the studio knock off work to watch it because The Master puts on a bigger show than the actors. They got everything all set for the hospital scene right after lunch. I was hanging out the window when I witnessed the arrival of The Master. He came around the corner by Paulette Goddard's dressing room. Walking with him, or, rather, a step or two behind him, were his personal aides—half a dozen of them. He arrived with dignity and a slow, deliberate step. He looked neither to right nor left, ignoring the mob of studio employees gathered on the side lines. He spoke not a word but came on into the sunlight and stopped finally alongside the big technicolor camera. His eyes were fixed on the scene before him and they stayed there. He took off his hat and tossed it over his shoulder without looking back. A hand came up and snatched it before it had traveled two feet. He took off his necktie and cast it into the air behind him. A necktie man grabbed it.

Slowly The Master unbuttoned his jacket, still staring fixedly at the scene. He let the jacket slip from his arms but it never came near the ground. A jacket man behind him swept it out of the air as it started to fall. I was surprised, then, to see Mr. DeMille roll up his own sleeves.

It was a fine experience to sit all afternoon and watch The Master make a scene, his voice roaring through the loud-speaker system. I remembered reading a story about DeMille, back in the days when he was making *The Ten Commandments*. Two of the principal actors, Theodore Roberts and James Neil, arrived at the DeMille office for a conference. They were in costume and they waited for more than an hour and finally a secretary came back to them and said, "Who was it you said was calling?" Mr. Roberts gave the reply.

"Just say," he told her, "that Moses and Aaron are waiting to see God."

A couple of secretaries came into my office and asked if they might watch the show outside my window. They had been around a long time and they said they never missed a chance to see DeMille in action. Otherwise they never paid a bit of attention to the business of movie-making.

"The other day," one of them said, "every secretary in this building ducked out because we heard that they were shooting Gary Cooper taking a bath and his knees would be showing. We all wanted to see *that*."

"Are you girls all crazy about Gary Cooper's knees?" I asked.

"Oh, no," she said. "Didn't you know about his contract? He has a clause in his contract that says his knees are never to be seen in a picture."

Going back to that first day, I got acquainted with Irene, the girl who ran the switchboard and presided over the central office, or loafing room, on the fourth floor. Irene was one of the most efficient and amiable gals on earth. When they came around and asked me if I wanted a secretary I said I didn't because I couldn't dictate my own name and I like to type my own stuff, so there would be nothing for a secretary to do. Irene, I said, could take care of all my secretarial needs. Nevertheless, they almost tried to force a secretary on me. Somebody told me that Ben Hecht and Charles Mac-Arthur did a writing turn at one of the studios some years back and that they argued that they didn't need a secretary. The studio insisted that they ought to have a secretary, so they hired a girl themselves. She occupied an outer office where she sat at a desk without any clothes on. Not a stitch. When visitors called, she got up from her desk, mother-naked, and escorted them in to Hecht and MacArthur. She behaved as if her nudity were normal, and so did her two employers. I didn't even want that kind of secretary. Well, I can say so.

They did send a girl around to my office and while I had nothing for her to do she started calling herself my secretary and dropping in whenever she felt like it and disturbing my sleep. Finally she began leaving poems of her own composition on my desk, so I went to Irene and told her I still didn't want a secretary and could something be done about it. Irene called the head of the secretaries and told her of my troubles and that precipitated a brawl that later became known as "The Revolt of the Angels."

It seems that the secretaries on the fourth floor were divided into two camps—the Irenes and the anti-Irenes. The anti-Irene girls claimed that their writers—the men they worked for—couldn't get any service out of Irene—that she spent all her time being nice to Dwight Wiley and Frank Partos and Frank Butler and me and a few others. They said Irene was a tyrant and a mean bitch. Thus it was that when Irene undertook at my request to drag an unwelcome secretary off my neck she got her own neck in a noose. The anti-Irene secretaries drew up a petition and signed it, demanding that Irene be banished from the fourth floor.

It turned into the God-damnedest, most wonderful mess you ever saw. It is a fact that for a solid week no work was accomplished in that building. Producers such as Charlie Brackett and Joe Sistrom got involved in it through long friendship with Irene. People talked about nothing else. There were meetings, both formal and informal, and whenever a group was seen in conversation somewhere on the lot, you could bet money that the topic was L'Affaire Irene. Delegations were formed among the pro-Irene writers, delegations composed of men and women earning up to $3,000 a week. These groups called on front-office executives and demanded status quo ante and cherchez la femme and quo vadis and everything else in the book. Meanwhile Irene went home after eighteen years of service at Paramount and sat there and cried. Roosevelt-haters never achieved the bitterness of those anti-Irenes. They stuck with their demands and grew meaner as time went on and I even heard talk that some of the girls were getting ready to scratch Irene's eyes out if she ever showed her face around the studio again. Eventually the pressure grew so strong that she was called back to work, but not on the fourth floor. She was assigned to duty in the secretarial department itself, headquarters for all the girls in the studio, but the going was too tough for her there and she went home again and stayed home.

I hope that by this time she's back in her chair on the fourth floor of the Writers' Building where she belongs. If she was tyrannical, it was a lovely tyranny. Some people got the idea that I was to blame for the whole explosion, but I deny it. I simply don't like to have poetry written at me. I like it even less than I like putting commas outside quotation marks.

CHAPTER XIII *How to Write for Movies Somewhat*

THERE is a distinct technique to writing a movie script just as there is a distinct technique to writing an opera. My experience with opera has been limited because of nature's shortsightedness in the construction of the horse. Horses are simply not powerful enough to drag me into the presence of all that hog calling. The cold fact of the matter is that I never sat through but one opera in my life.

Ten years ago I went to the first performace of Gertrude Stein's opera, *Four Saints in Three Acts*. I thought it was fine. They staged it on a bitterly cold night and many celebrities from the world of art, music, letters, and spread-the-legs dancing attended. I was there as a reporter and I still have the notes I made during the evening.

One of the most thrilling passages in the story came when

the Negro cast sang *andante bravura della fugue* and crazy-like a song that went:

"Did he did we did we and did he did he did did he did did did he did did he categorically and did he did he did he did he did he did he in interruption interruption interruptedly leave letting let it be all to me to me out and outer and this and this with in indeed deed and drawn and drawn work."

That is good stuff. Sing it over once. Or let somebody else sing it over for you. Or better than that walk up to a police officer and sing it to him.

Miss Stein's opera was concerned chiefly with Saint Theresa No. 1 and Saint Theresa No. 2 and Saint Ignatius and they performed with a variety of other saints, all portrayed by Negroes, and an assortment of angels. They did things about a telescope and a fish net, and the things they did with these things were quite interesting and set a new cultural high for that year he did he did he did. The plot began to reveal itself when members of the cast started scanning the horizon, searching for an unnamed object. They sang:

"How many doors are there in it how many doors are there in it how many doors are there in it how many doors are there in it . . ." and so on for a good, long paragraph until someone, a contralto, got to asking how many eggs there are in it, and one of the angels answered the question by singing: "If it were possible to kill five thousand Chinamen by pressing a button would it be done Saint Theresa not interested."

At this juncture Saint Ignatius brought forth his telescope and took a sight on the horizon which was made out of shiny, light blue oilcloth. Saint Theresa No. 1 then talked Saint Ignatius into letting her borrow the telescope but instead of examining the horizon to find out how many floors, doors, windows, and eggs were in it, she aimed it out at the audience, presumably to find out how many paying customers there were in it.

I concentrated hard on doors and eggs and five thousand Chinamen just as opera lovers down through the ages have concentrated, such being the method used to get at the core of the matter. I was concentrating, striving for the significance of this simple lilting thing, when I heard somebody on the stage who wanted to know how many *nails* there are in it. That threw me off a bit but right away came this:

"Four saints were not born at one time although they knew each other. One of them had a birthday before the mother of the other one the father.* Four saints later to be if to be if to be to be one to be. Might tingle."

Certainly, might tingle. Also might puke. I thought the whole thing most significant, particularly as related to the state of the world at that time, it being different then than now. I learned *so* much that evening that I can't understand for the life of me why the other operas, the ones they have down at the Metropolitan, confuse me.

The technique in writing movies is a trifle different from the technique employed so effectively in the Stein songs. One of the things I soon learned is that most screen plays are not written at all, but talked. Two or more screen writers get together in an office, clog up the atmosphere with smoke, chat a bit on international politics, then on domestic politics, then on studio politics, and finally on fourth-floor politics. They hash over the principal items they have read in the daily trade papers and they discuss the latest films they have seen, knocking them.

Then they go to work, *talking* out a situation, and then *talking* out the dialogue and action to fit that situation. A good many of them go through all the motions and facial contortions that later will be transmitted to the screen by the actors. Regulation equipment for a screen writer's office is a large mirror. This mirror is not hung there for use in powdering the nose or touching up the hair or pinching out blackheads. The writer stands before it and emotes and, having emoted, knows how to describe the effect he wants from hero or heroine.

Each writer, as a customary thing, works directly under an individual producer. These producers change from picture to picture. A writer gets word from the front office that he is assigned to the script of a picture being produced by, say, Seton I. Miller. Mr. Miller's office is on the third floor of

*Word seems to be missing here.

the Writers' Building. The writer and Mr. Miller spend hours on end talking over their story. Very likely they get into some lively quarrels and sometimes producers and writers quit speaking to each other for a few days. A writer wants a certain scene in the picture. The producer says it stinks. The writer says the producer stinks. The producer says the writer and all members of his immediate family stink. The writer says the entire studio stinks. And so on, until the writer stomps out of the place. They feud for a while until one or the other gets on the phone and makes an around-the-bush apology and then they start over.

When I had my first conference with Mr. DeSylva he asked me what I wanted to do. I said I didn't know and that I rather expected him to tell me.

"Go over to your office," he said, "and sit down at the typewriter and write me a movie."

"What about?" I asked.

"About anything," he said. "You've seen a lot of movies—now go write one."

"I don't know how to start. Have you got a book around here that tells you how to get started?"

"If," he said, "I catch you reading a book on how to write a movie, I'll take it away from you and pound you over the head with it."

I didn't have a producer to go fight with. He told me that *he* was my producer and that any time I wanted to talk things over, to come and see *him*. Later on I would phone his office and ask for an appointment and they'd say, "How about some time in November?" I'd see him on the studio street, and be damned if that guy wouldn't run from me. I'd trap him in the commissary, and no matter what I said to him, no matter how touching my appeal, he'd fling back his head and laugh, and then he'd say, "I'll get around to you one of these days." Once I got him cornered long enough to ask him for a collaborator. He said he didn't have any. He suggested that maybe I knew someone outside the studio who would make a collaborator for me and, if so, the studio would hire him. I asked for the Swedish Angel. He wouldn't let me have the Swedish Angel. In some respects Buddy DeSylva is a man of small horizons.

Anyway, I went back to my office after that first conference and started to write a movie. I got the first paragraph
on paper after four hours of deep thought. I did my deepest
thinking with a chair pulled up at the window so I could see
those messenger girls jiggle. I was starting to think about the
second paragraph when someone knocked on my door. A man
came in and asked me for a match. I gave him one, and he
sat down and asked me what I was writing. I said I wasn't
sure, and he told me he was writing a movie based on the
career of Frank Sinatra. Later on I found out my visitor had
been Marc Connelly and that he occupied an office across
the hall from me.

Dwight Mitchell Wiley came calling. Mr. Wiley and I
had become great friends and spent considerable of our time
in scientific observations out the window. We soon got wise
to one thing. Those girl messengers traversing The Campus
were constantly auditioning for movie jobs. We would watch
one of them come down the line past the dressing rooms of
Crosby, Lamour, Hope, Cooper, Barney Dean, and Goddard.
As she approached the administration building, where most
of the top producers have offices, a change would come over
her. She'd flick back her hair, toss her head like a horse that
has just broken wind, and, above all, throw those lovely
things into position. It's a wonder to me that some of those
mail girls and messengers didn't wear out a dozen sweaters
a day. They were always hoping, of course, that some producing genius would be gazing out his window in abstract
thought as they passed, would spot them, and cry out:
"Hold! Grab that lovely vision with the knockers before she
gets away! A perfect type for Prunella Van Cleve in my new
picture!"

The remarkable thing is that it happened sometimes.
While I was at Paramount the mail department lost three
employees that way. Two girls and one boy got parts in pictures. The boy was undeniably handsome. He wore himself
out auditioning across The Campus and then someone *did*
see him and pick him for a film role. He was cast as an aide
to Ernst Roehm in *The Hitler Gang*. He had auditioned
himself into the part of a fairy.

Mr. Wiley was working on a picture based on a series of

his own short stories. He couldn't see The Campus from his office, so he always came down to mine when he needed inspiration. He wouldn't let me raise the window because he had high place-phobia. He had it so bad that I sometimes marveled at his courage in climbing the three or four steps that led into the commissary.

Once he and his wife Rose went to New York and took a room at the Waldorf. Their room was on a corner of the building, high above the street, and when they got into it the first thing Dwight did was go to the window.

"Oh my God!" he cried out when he got a glimpse of the pavement far below. He quickly pulled the shade and issued orders that it stay drawn.

That night they went to bed, and Rose insisted on having the window open and the shade up. Dwight began to fret. He saw visions of himself getting out of bed in the night, going to that open window, and plunging to the street—a performance few people could survive. He worried and tossed and couldn't get to sleep. Finally he got up, carefully ignoring the open window. He dug into a bag and found his dog's leash. He tied the leash around his ankle and fastened the other end to the bedpost. Thus having defeated a horrible fate, he went to sleep. Sometime during the night he awoke feeling the need to go to the bathroom. He slipped out of bed and started across the room. Wham! He went face down on the floor and nearly tore off his nose.

That woke Rose up, to be sure, and she had a good long laugh, leading her husband to discuss matters calmly in terms generally employed by a mule skinner. When he returned to bed wearing adhesive tape over his wounds, he fastened himself in with the leash again. He was pretty sore about Rose's attitude. To his way of thinking there was nothing comical about the matter. So when her laughter subsided he began talking. He's a good talker. He told her that within every human being's mind lurks the dread germ of acrophobia.† In some cases, he went on, it is latent, but

† I had to search through the books for this word and it took me twenty minutes to find it. However, I came across another word I hadn't known about. It is "pho!" It is an exclamation signifying contempt or disparagement.

every human has it and it comes to life without warning.

"You've got it," he told Rose, "and you can't tell when it'll become activated. God forbid that it ever does, because it's a horrible affliction. It might very well come on you in the night and before you knew anything about it, you'd be over at that window, and out, and splattered all over the sidewalk down there."

Dwight continued in that vein for a while, and Rose began to get uneasy. Finally she got out of bed.

"I'll just be damned if *I'm* going out that window," she said. She found the belt to a bathrobe, tied it around her ankle and fastened the other end to the bedpost on her side. So they went to sleep like a pair of chain gangers, and bedogged if during the night Rose didn't get up and start for the bathroom, and down *she* went.

Dwight Wiley is a fiction writer and, like all fiction writers of my acquaintance, swears up and down that every story he tells is the truth. I can believe the first part of his story—the part in which Dwight himself hit the floor. But as for the latter part, involving Rose, all I have to say is: "Pho!"

Often during the "recreation hour" we gathered in Irene's office for long conversations of high intellectual content. Hundreds of writers had served time in that fourth-floor cell block and Irene knew them all. She was full of stories about them. Their eccentricities never bothered her, and she talked about them as though they were normal people. There was, for example, William Slavens McNutt, who found it impossible to work unless he had his shirt off and a bottle of beer in his hand. There was Russel Crouse, who was constantly beset by secretaries asking him to inscribe his latest book. He obliged them and in each case wrote something like this:

"To Mary Ellen—in memory of that beautiful moonlit night on the beach at Laguna when we tasted bliss and, as you so sweetly put it, went all the way. Passionately, Russy Wussy."

Once Dwight Wiley asked Irene what writer had been the previous occupant of his office. She thought awhile.

"Oh yes," she said, remembering. "The dope fiend."

"The dope fiend!" roared Dwight. "Whadda you mean dope fiend?"

"I mean he was a dope fiend," she said. "He's the one that committed suicide."

"In there?" cried Dwight.

"Right in that pretty little office of yours," Irene assured him.

"God's teeth!" howled Dwight. "Now I won't sleep for a month!"

The "dean" of the fourth floor was Frank Butler, who has been writing for movies something over twenty-five years. Mr. Butler usually works alone and dictates his stuff. He is a tall man who walks with a stoop, drinks gallons of coffee each day, calls everybody "Laddie" or "I say old boy," and wears clothes that would unnerve a hog. He has been in residence on the fourth floor for more than eight years. The floor is served by an automatic elevator with a heavy wooden door that snaps into place with the speed and force of a juke box dropped off the Washington Monument. For eight years Mr. Butler played a little game with that elevator. He used it perhaps a dozen times a day. He would step into the car and press the button. Then he would hold his index finger at the point where the sliding door slams into place. As the door shot toward his finger, Mr. Butler would withdraw his hand at high speed. Then he would smile with deep satisfaction and say something derogatory to the door, such as, "Aha! You vicious, bloody devil! Fooled you agayne!" Came the day, of course, when Mr. Butler's timing was off and the door got him. Broke his finger all to hell. He doesn't play the game any more.

Soon after I joined the geniuses of the fourth floor I was delighted to learn that Raymond Chandler occupied an office down the hall from me. For a couple of years I had been a Raymond Chandler fan, reading those superb detective novels he turns out. They are the hard-boiledest or hardest-boiled detective stories I've ever read and quite likely the best written. I wanted to meet Mr. Chandler right off. I expected to find a hulking guy with a flat nose and football-shaped biceps. He turned out to be the last man in the world I would have picked as the author of his books. He is a mild-mannered guy of medium size with black wavy hair, horn-rimmed glasses, and a sensitive face. He looks like a poet is supposed to look. He was born in Chicago and grew up in England where he got his schooling. Before World War I he contributed a few little things to London newspapers but never thought of himself as a man who might someday make writing his business. After the war he came to the United States and had his ups and downs. He got a job stringing tennis rackets at twelve dollars a week for a while, and later found himself mixed up in the oil business. He accumulated some money and in 1931 he and his wife were driving around California on a vacation. They stopped at a hotel in a small town, and that night before he went to bed Mr. Chandler picked up a pulp detective magazine at the news-stand. He read it all the way through and when he had finished it said, "Hell, I can write that kind of stuff." He started out, and he has never yet received a rejection slip. Moreover, he has seen a sort of Raymond Chandler cult develop, and now he is raking in that negotiable stuff from Paramount.

I was pretty well settled when Jack Wagner arrived on the scene. Mr. Wagner is one of John Steinbeck's close friends and has collaborated with Steinbeck on movies. Mr. Wagner, in fact, has collaborated with a lot of people in his time, for he dates back to the Mack Sennett era. He has a small superstition. Whenever he is inside a movie studio it is necessary for him to have a piece of wood in his hand. Usually he carries a splintered lath around with him. If he should ever leave home in the morning and forget to bring along this wood, he'll stop somewhere and break a limb off a tree before he'll go into the studio. He never lets that stick get out of his hand—even takes it to the men's room with him. I asked him several times about it but he shied away from a full explanation and said it was just a little habit he got into. Later on, when we got better acquainted, he told me the truth. Years ago he was a heavy drinker and kept himself adequately fortified from daybreak to dusk and beyond. He knew that studio executives sometimes regard drinking men as unreliable, so he began carrying a stick of wood. Each time he met a superior officer on a movie lot he would begin a forceful conversation, using the stick as some people use their index fingers, jabbing it at the chest of the listener. In this way Mr. Wagner was able to keep the executives three or four feet away from him and they couldn't smell his breath. He is now a teetotaler, but the stick-carrying habit stays with him.

Mr. Wagner was once invited to a highbrow Hollywood party, given at the home of one of the town's famous hostesses. Most of the celebrated guests were congregated in and around the swimming pool, but Mr. Wagner kept his clothes on because he doesn't care for swimming. He was minding his own business in a lawn chair when the hostess approached him. She said he should go in swimming, and he said he wouldn't think of going in swimming, and she pressed the issue, insisting that he join in the fun at the pool. He demurred.

"But I don't understand," said the hostess. "I can't understand why you don't want to go in. Really, *everybody* swims!"

"Listen, my dear Mrs. Lungwart," said Mr. Wagner. "The last thing I would do on this earth would be to take off my shirt in public. I'll tell you the reason if you'll promise to keep it a secret. Some years ago I was in Rio. I got stinking drunk with a couple of friends and passed out in a tattoo artist's parlor. They had me tattooed with dirty pictures from the waist up, terribly nasty things, and ever since then I've made it a practice never to take off my shirt in public."

Mrs. Lungwart said she understood perfectly and ceased her urgings. She did, however, devote much of her time thereafter to bringing drinks to Mr. Wagner. Her motive was apparent at once. She fed Mr. Wagner triple-strength highballs all afternoon, watching him closely, hoping he'd get barreled and rip off his shirt, so she'd get to see all those dirty pictures. He never did.

Mr. Wagner tells of the time years ago when he worked for a producer who decided to turn out a film about a nudist camp. This producer opened negotiations with an actual nudist colony and got permission to bring in a cameraman. It was stipulated that the half-dozen movie people should strip themselves naked and remain in that condition during the time they were in the camp. The cameraman was an obstinate, opinionated guy named Willie, and Willie objected to nudity on practical as well as moral grounds. He said the entire project was ridiculous but he agreed to cooperate up to a certain point.

"I'll take off my pants and shoes and socks and shirt and underwear," he said, "but by God I'm gonna wear my vest. I got to have a place to carry my screw driver and my pliers."

It was agreed that Willie could wear his vest and, thus attired, he went grudgingly about his duties. The camera was of primordial design and operated by a hand crank. It was perched on a tripod and the legs of the tripod could be folded together.

Willie was shooting a scene on a grassy hillside. He finished the job and prepared to move to another spot. He reached down and shoved the legs of the tripod together. Yipe! He had been standing too close. He let out a piercing scream and fell to the ground as though poleaxed, the camera on top of him. The legs of the tripod had locked on him and he was howling and clawing the air. The producer rushed to the rescue and pried the tripod open, releasing its wounded prey. They threw cold water on Willie and tried to comfort him with kind words. At last he got to his feet. He picked up a two-by-four and beat the tripod to splinters. Then he turned on the producer and would have slain him then and there except that the man was fast on his feet and got away. Willie put on his pants and the rest of his clothes and departed, announcing that he was finished. He never worked in pictures again, and disappeared from the scene. He probably figured people would laugh at him and point him out as the man who got his formal dances caught in a tripod.

A day or two after Jack Wagner reported for work at Paramount I had lunch with him in the commissary. We were leaving the place, walking along the studio street, when Jack suddenly seized my arm.

"Good God!" he said. "Look!"

Just ahead of us was a group of four men, standing talking. The man facing us was Adolf Hitler. Hitler was talking to the other three, talking earnestly, passionately. As we came up we heard him say:

". . . and so I says to this stinkin' heel, listen you son

of a bitch, no cheap rum-dumb agent is gonna get any 10 per cent outa me, and if you're not satisfied with that, how would you like a bust right in the snoot?"

It was Bobby Watson in make-up and uniform. We all had a lovely time while *The Hitler Gang* was being filmed.

The studio streets swarmed with Nazi storm troopers and usually they were marching in formation, goose-stepping to the commands shouted in German. Hitler and Goebbels and Goering and Hess wandered around the place. Watson, as Hitler, was so realistic that he often scared people. He had to give up eating in the commissary because pandemonium always followed his entrance. People heiled him and hooted him and threw buns at him and shouted dirty names at him.

Frank Waldman and I spent part of each afternoon roaming over the lot, sometimes confusing the people who were busy making pictures. Frank is a young writer from Scarsdale, New York, who went to Harvard but it doesn't show much at all. I recall one period when a costume picture was in production and the studio was overrun with women wearing hoop skirts that swept the ground. Every time Frank Waldman saw one of these ladies he'd step up to her with a frown on his face.

"Hey, sister," he'd say. "Your slip's showing."

To my knowledge he didn't get slapped once. Not for that, anyway.

CHAPTER XIV *The Tailing of Grantland Rice*

THIS will be a short chapter, and it has nothing whatever to do with the rest of the book. In this respect it is similar to all the other chapters. I have just taken an afternoon off for the purpose of watching the horses run at Belmont Park.

I go to the races not as an admirer of horseflesh; not as a person contributing to the breeding of fine horses (which is the reason all the other people are there). I read the dope sheets and study the tote board and determine for myself just which horse in each race is regarded as the finest and swiftest and stoutest. I find out which horse stands out above his fellows and then bet money that he's a bum. In other words, I follow the system that seems to have developed in our presidential elections: I don't bet *on* horses; I bet *against* them.

So here I was at Belmont Park with newspapers and charts and no precise plan of campaign for the day. Before the festivities began I was sitting on the clubhouse lawn getting some sun when I saw Grantland Rice. I promptly remembered something that happened a year ago at the same track.

Harold Matson, who is my literary tout, was with me that day, and we had gone through most of the afternoon with neither of us picking a winner. We were standing near the betting windows trying to make up our minds on a horse or horses for the seventh race. We were low in spirit and cash. Suddenly a man brushed past me. I looked up and recognized him and nudged Mr. Matson.

"Know who that is?" I said. "That's Grantland Rice."

"Well, get on his tail for God's sake!" said my agent, and I promptly got on Mr. Rice's tail. I scampered up behind him as he stepped into line before the five-dollar window. Soon he was laying down his money and I heard him say, "Number Three, three times." Then it was my turn. I didn't even know which horse Number Three was, but I shoved over a ten-dollar bill and said, "Number Three twice."

I still don't remember the name of the horse, but it won and paid something like thirty dollars to two, meaning a profit to us of about $150. That was the only winner we had all afternoon.

So it was that, seeing Grantland Rice again a year later, I decided to get on his tail and remain there through the afternoon.

There was a tremendous crowd of shovers and bumpers at the track. The customers were fighting to get in there and throw away their money and I was right with them. Somehow, though, the breaks were against me. I'd get behind that guy Grantland Rice, walking so close to him that I'd almost be climbing right up his back, and damned if he wouldn't get away from me. You understand, of course, that he doesn't know me and I don't think he ever suspected that I was trailing him around. I tried to be unobtrusive about it and maybe that's the reason I was always getting pocketed, or going wide in the stretch or getting bumped off the course. Never once did I get immediately behind him on the betting lines. One time I was two persons removed from him but I couldn't hear the number of the horse he bet on.

Each time I reached the window I had to bet on something, so I fell back on Frank Ortell's selections. I'd miss out on Grantland Rice and then I'd have to look down at my newspaper real quick, see what Ortell picked, and bet on that. Ortell had a bum day, a very bum day. By the time the seventh race was over I was sick of the whole institution of horse racing. I went back to a chair on the lawn saying the hell with Grantland Rice and the hell with Frank Ortell and the hell with everybody else including horses. I refused to bet at all on the last race. It was a long one starting from the gate directly in front of me. The horses came out and stalked around on the track for a while and pretty soon they were all congregated behind the starting gate. I was standing there looking at them, calling them names under my breath— names that reflected on their dams and sires. Several of them were acting frisky and one tried to run away. The horse standing nearest to me was behaving like a gentleman. He was barely fifteen feet away and it happened that I had my eye on him when he turned around. That horse looked straight at me. Looked me square in the eye. He just stood there and stared at me. I had the feeling that he wanted to say something to me, and I'm not one to ignore a horse that is trying to talk. I glanced at his number and like to broke a leg getting to the betting window before the race could start. I made it and slapped down all the money I had left. I didn't even take time to look up his name until I had my tickets and had started back.

That fiend out of hell was named Nebraska, and it is my hope that his owners sell him to Borden's. Or *give* him to Borden's. He deliberately deceived me. At least that's the way I felt about it on the train coming home. The way he performed in that race I personally could have outrun him with Grantland Rice riding me.

Now that I've had a chance to cool off I'm inclined to be more tolerant. Maybe Nebraska wasn't trying to tip me off to anything. Maybe he just happened to turn around like that to ease a crick in his neck, and saw me, and thought I looked funny, so he just took a good, long look. I know that if I were a horse and they brought me out on the track in front of forty thousand people, all jammed together, sweating and whooping and chattering and running into each other, I'd want to look at them. If I could figure any way to get out of it, I wouldn't waste my time running around that track as hard as I could go. I'd plant myself right there, sideways, and look at all those humans to my heart's content.

Nebraska's deception brought on another long period of speculation. What does a race horse think about? Does he know he's in a horse race when he's in one? Does he know that he's the favorite? When he turns around, as Nebraska did, and looks at the mob of people, does he know they are people? I don't suppose a horse gives much thought to people except when they come around bearing oats. Maybe a horse looks at all those people and considers them to be nothing more than a bunch of handles that sometimes have oats on the end of them and otherwise are of no use on earth.

I've asked any number of turf experts if a horse knows he's in a race and they all say he does. I don't believe it. Watch the horses when they come up to the gate with a minute to go before they start the contest. If they knew they were going to run a race they'd be looking each other over. They'd be peering around the gate for a gander at the track, deciding on strategical maneuvers. They'd snap their hooves to freshen circulation.

Philosophical speculation, as practiced by the professional philosophers, has never given much consideration to animals and their thoughts. What does a cow think about? Apparently that question didn't bother Spinoza. I can stand and look at a cow for hours, wondering what she has on her mind. What does she think is going on when she's being milked?

I'd like to know that, and I'd like to know about the race horses, and I'd like to know what a Canadian moose is thinking about when Roy Howard comes at him with a gun. I even wonder about birds and what goes on in their minds. Does a sparrow know what he's eating when he's eating something on the pavement? Does he know that it was left there by a horse, or does he think some bird-loving human tossed it out for him? If he knows it was left there by a horse, does eating it bother him at all, as it would me? It's an interesting speculation. Maybe he just pecks away at it and, being a philosopher like me, simply says to himself:

"Well, here I am eating so-and-so, but to *me* it tastes good."

CHAPTER XV *The Word Game*

EMILY KIMBROUGH, in her book about her adventures with Cornelia Otis Skinner in Hollywood, devoted a lot of space to a physical description of the Paramount plant. She told about the flowers and the architecture and the color scheme of the commissary.

She made some mention of Y. Frank Freeman but she seems to have missed his dogs. Y. Frank Freeman is the headman at the Paramount Studio. He's from Georgia, talks yall-talk, and drinks Coca-Cola for breakfast. I'm told that he is one of the shrewdest businessmen in the movie industry and that the "Y" in his name stands for "Young." There's a story about his bowsprit initial.

Some years ago Paramount was having one of those gaudy picture *premières* in Hollywood. As is the custom, bleachers were erected outside the theater, so several hundred assorted goons might witness the comings and goings of great and famous people. A newspaperman of my acquaintance decided to sit in these bleachers and write a story about the behavior and conversation of the idiot fringe.

During the dreary two hours in which the picture was being shown the bleacherites kept their places. Then the show was over and the flash guns started blinking as the celebrities emerged. A loud-speaker above the marquee was used to summon the individual automobiles. The voice, for example, would boom out, "RONALD COLMAN," and Mr. Colman's chauffeur would drive in and pick up his old marster. This, of course, was the high point of the proceedings for the yucks in the bleachers, for they could quickly identify the heroic personalities as they came out. The thing went along for a while and then the voice came through the loud-speaker:

"Y. FRANK FREEMAN!"

The echoes of the name were still bouncing about when somebody sitting behind my newspaper friend spoke up:

"Sounds like a legitimate question."

Mr. Freeman, I understand, is a trifle sensitive about his

"Y." During the first week or so of my encampment at Paramount I started signing interoffice memos with the name "Y. H. Allen Smith." In no time at all a producer dropped in to see me and caution me against this practice. He said Mr. Freeman would be offended if he found out about it and that if I were discreet I would desist. I'm not discreet, but I did desist. Who the hell am I to start kidding anybody about a front initial? Even if it is a "Y."

A movie studio is a newspaper office on a large scale, crowded with eccentric, capricious, temperamental screwballs. All you need do is shut your eyes and spit and you're bound to hit a genius. The geniuses come in three sizes: those who are geniuses and know they are geniuses and speak about it frequently; those who are actually not geniuses but somebody told them they were so they do everything but wear badges proclaiming it; and genuine geniuses who keep their mouths shut about their affliction and do their work.

The bootlicking that goes on is a sight to behold. In this connection Y. Frank Freeman's dogs serve an important function around Paramount. The dogs are German boxers and I personally consider them to be big, ugly mutts that I wouldn't want to have in a dark projection room with me. Mr. Freeman loves those dogs, however, and stables them right on the Paramount lot. Just inside the "DeMille gate" is a cage as big as a Fifth Avenue bus and in the cage are two dogs. Once I stopped and asked the gate policeman if the cage had been built especially for the Freeman pets.

"Nope," he said. "It was put up originally fer a wild line. Had a wild line in here fer some picture er other but he was too wild, so they took him away."

People come and go all day long at this gate and seldom even glance at the dogs. When Mr. Freeman is in the cage with them, however, it is a different story. The moment the big boss gets in there a crowd collects as if Dorothy Lamour were being auctioned off nekkid. This crowd generally consists of those producers, directors, writers, and department heads who are notorious for podex osculation. They fasten themselves up against the cage and go into spasms of baby talk. They oh and they ah and say isn't Judy cute and they bombard Mr. Freeman with questions about the age, ancestry, and eating habits of his dogs—matters that actually interest them as deeply as the philosophy of Bergson.

Once or twice a day Mr. Freeman releases his dogs from the cage and lets them gallop over to The Campus where they can chase each other around the grass, leap over the hedges, and frighten the goldfish in the pool. One moment The Campus is deserted. Then the Y. German boxers are in it, with their owner. Inside of a minute half the studio's minor executives are on the side lines, laughing fit to kill at the antics of the animals, risking their jugular veins trying to pet them, acting as though they would like to marry them. Mr. Freeman is an astute man and somehow I can't picture him sitting at his desk, checking over a list of names, and finally saying, "Well, I reckon we'll have Leander Dubbing handle this epic and give him a free hand with money. He likes my dogs."

Miss Kimbrough wrote about "a little sweetshop" across the street from Paramount. She described the place and commented that while there was a small bar, she had never seen anybody in the booths taking an alcoholic drink—that everybody ordered tea and Coca-Cola and chocolate sodas. I am pretty certain that Miss Kimbrough was not stiff when she visited "the little sweetshop," which is better known as Oblath's, but her powers of observation were off balance. I rarely missed an afternoon in "the little sweetshop," and I can remember once seeing Bill Dozier, head of the story department, drinking tea. At least he was drinking something out of a cup, and several persons stopped at his booth to watch the performance. Another time I witnessed the spectacle of a director ordering a Coca-Cola. He probably had an appointment with Mr. Freeman and wanted to have Coca-Cola on his breath.

Miss Kimbrough was still working at the studio when I got there. Back in New York Miss Skinner had suggested that I "look up Emily," correcting herself immediately by changing the phrase to "look Emily up." Soon after I arrived I wrote a note to Miss Kimbrough and asked if I might presume to call at her office and make her acquaintance. I got a note in response urging me to call soon. The note concluded: "I want you to come to dinner with me Saturday and hear some marvelous Russian music."

That scared me off. To my way of thinking the only marvelous thing about Russian music is that most of it is in Russia. Rather than listen to it I believe I'd try one of those Russian dances where you squat down, fold your arms, and start kicking to the front. Subsequently I was sorry I hadn't accepted the invitation because I learned that Miss Kimbrough planned on taking me to the home of somebody named Nina Koshetz, who weighs three hundred and four pounds and sits on a throne and has two noisy dogs, one of which eats nothing but caviar, beef stroganov, and other Volga vittles. This Nina Koshetz throws parties at which the guests sit around and talk about Life, and I would have enjoyed that. One time.

Miss Kimbrough also mentioned the Word Game, played each noontime by a group of writers and a scattering of producers and directors. The Paramount Word Game has been written about and talked about for years yet nobody, to my knowledge, has ever explained it. I was a regular participant and was known as a pigeon because I rarely won. Among the other regulars were Billy Wilder, Seton I. Miller, Mark Sandrich, Frank Partos, Dwight Wiley, Harry Tugend, Frank Waldman, Walter DeLeon, Charlie Brackett, and Jolly Joe Sistrom. No actors were ever allowed in the game, actors being considered subhuman. Betty Hutton forced herself in for five minutes one day, but she was expelled after she had spilled a pitcher of cream into Dwight Wiley's moribund lap and torn the pocket off Charlie Brackett's coat.

The writers' table is in a small anteroom off the main dining room and the Word Game is played at a long table seating about a dozen men. The game is played on a diagram containing twenty-five small squares. Years ago the players drew their own diagrams, but that wasted time, so they had a rubber stamp made and each day before lunch the table's waitress, Genevieve, cuts up a bunch of yesterday's menus and stamps them with the diagram. She puts a large stack of these stamped cards on the table and fills up a couple of tumblers with pencils. I brought away one of the stamped cards. It's good for two games. Here it is, just as Genevieve stamped it out, with a sample of a completed game.

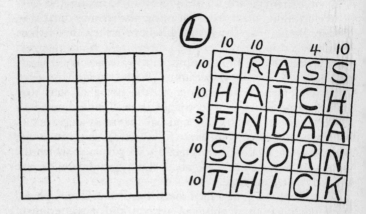

The purpose of the game is to fill out the card with words of three, four, or five letters, preferably five letters. The player chosen to start the game announces: "Play without L's" or "Play without E's." He may designate any letter in the alphabet and during that game that particular letter is not to be used. In the sample game, on the card above, the "L" is forbidden. Each of the players writes down the forbidden letter on the margin of his card, so he won't forget about it. Then the starter gives the first letter, putting it down in any square that he chooses. All the other players put that letter down in any square they choose. The next man gives a letter and everyone puts it down. Then the next, and so on around until all the squares are filled except one. The last letter is free, or wild. Each player may put down any letter he chooses to fill the last square.

The game is now finished, and each player counts his score. For each five-letter word he has been able to make, horizontally or vertically, he scores ten points. Each four-letter word gives him four points, and each three-letter word counts three. Two-letter words don't count. Proper names may not be used. Plural words are forbidden though an "S" may be used on the end of verbs and frequently is.

The players yell out their scores. Seventy is a wonderful

score and anything over fifty is excellent. The man with the top score doesn't necessarily win. He begins reading off, in a loud voice, the words he has succeeded in making. If any other player has one of his words, that player sings out. Suppose the top man has the word "light" and somebody else has it. The top man has to take off three points from his total score. Three points off for duplicated five-letter words and one point off for duplicated three- and four-letter words. Quite often the top man's score will be brought below the score of someone else, or someone else will have him tied. Then the player *now* having top score, or tie score, reads off his words, and he may be brought down. In case the thing winds up as a tie, the rule is one-tie-all-tie. If one man wins, he collects a quarter from each of the other players. If it's a tie game, the next game goes for fifty cents.

Maybe I haven't explained it well and maybe it sounds like a simple or stupid game. I can assure you, however, that some of the most brilliant men in the motion-picture business sweat blood over it. After you've played it for a while you'll learn that it is often best to follow certain patterns. You'll learn that it's a wise thing to have a vowel in the third square of the top line, in the second square of the second line, and the first square of the third line. Sometimes those will be all the vowels you'll get, and one of the three will be the free letter you give yourself at the end. You improve with practice and you also lose sleep. That little pattern of squares will haunt you, and you'll lie in bed at night with a montage of such patterns swirling in your head, and you'll find yourself talking in five-letter words, muttering such things as "Dwarf, light, ranch, porch, alert, night, skids, whorl, plank, bitch, chess, prods, skirt, claps, snarl, wrong, bench, brick, penny, yelps, shirt, musty."

I was told that some years back Harold Lloyd was producing a picture at the studio and got himself involved in the Word Game. He took the thing so seriously that he assigned a secretary to go through the dictionary and dig out all the five-letter words, which he then did his best to memorize.

Just recently Joseph Sistrom, producer of many fine pictures, left Paramount to undertake a special war assignment in London. He was gone for several months, and during his absence the Word Game players tried out a new method of scoring. They decided to count diagonal words. Somehow news of this radical innovation reached Mr. Sistrom in London. When he returned to the studio he promptly telephoned Charlie Brackett and Billy Wilder, who have offices together. They immediately began pounding questions at him about The Situation abroad. Mr. Sistrom interrupted them with:

"The hell with that! What's this I hear about changing the Word Game?"

The players often indulge in violent outbursts. They eat lunch, after a fashion, but the game continues right through the meal. They gulp down their food, yelling through the filet of sole, "I give a *G*" and "I give a *W*." It's not surprising that they have ulcers the size of fried eggs. When the game gets going nothing can distract them. Bing Crosby and Bob Hope usually eat at the next table and they are not exactly sedate in their deportment, yet the Word Game players ignore their ructions. Paulette Goddard might come in rigged in a costume that exposes her navel; it has no effect whatever on the players unless, perhaps, as inspiration for an attempt to make the word "belly." They bend over those cards, put sugar on their fried liver, pepper in their coffee, and try to eat their pencils. They have coined a simile: "As brief as a greeting at the writers' table." If Buddy DeSylva comes in to say hello, they say "Hi" and get back to clank and shirt and perch and dross and candy and whelp and milch and clock and anger. If a character actor comes over and asks a writer to please put some extra gag lines into a script for him, they roar at him to get the hell off the earth. If the air-raid sirens sound, they never raise their heads but try to make "alert" or "fight" or "blast" or "shell" or "wreck."

When a game is finished, words are sometimes challenged. This brings on horrific arguments. Once we all chipped in and bought a dictionary, but it proved unsatisfactory for two reasons—first, too much time was taken in looking up disputed words and, second, somebody stole the dictionary two days after we bought it. Billy Wilder, one of the most talented directors in the business, howls in anguish whenever a word of his is rejected. Mr. Wilder is an Austrian by birth. When the final verdict against one of his words is rendered, over his colorful protestations, he will stand up, fling his pencil to the floor, and announce ringingly:

"There will be no shooding on Stage Six dis afternoon. Furdermore, I am *leaving dis studio!*"

As a game progresses and the squares begin to fill up, frightening sounds come from the players. Each man has laid out a pattern of words, and now the bad letters are coming—*Y's* and *K's* and sometimes *J's*—letters that he cannot fit into his pattern anywhere, yet they must be put down. As, one by one, these final letters are called out there are vast groans that would seem to emanate from the very bed bolts of hell. Regardless of the presence in the little room of Dorothy Lamour or Barbara Stanwyck or Loretta Young, there are shrill, uninhibited curses. If you are trying to complete a word, say the word "wharf," and somebody gives a "C" or some other letter that shatters your whole plan of campaign, it is considered ethical for you to shriek at the dirty dog, calling him all the names you possess in your vocabulary, and you are not restricted to five-letter words in this contingency.

Charlie Brackett, the producer, is a soft-spoken man universally loved and respected. He makes an effort to keep an even temper during the Word Game, and when some wretched, unprincipled heel stabs him in the back with an unwanted letter, he tries to hold back the bad words, merely gazing at the offender with a wounded, sorrowing countenance. One day Mr. Brackett lost nine games in a row. Nine times he had dug down and brought up his quarter for the winner. Then he lost the tenth game. He sighed heavily and reached for his pocket.

"Can anybody," he asked, "change a St. Christopher's medal?"

When Mr. DeSylva hinted that I was a scarce commodity around the studio he exaggerated. I rarely missed the Word Game. My last official day at the studio was Christmas Eve. By noon the holiday parties were getting under full steam in the various departments and in the dressing rooms of the stars. The front-office executives had announced that *this year* there was to be no wassail around the place, no parties. The front-office executives had announced it, then smiled and quietly gone away. It was an afternoon in which people who spent three hundred and sixty-four days of the year in earnest work and solemn sobriety cut loose with a bang. It was an afternoon in which open season was declared on all secretaries. Joyous laughter sounded all over the lot, mingled with the shrieks of pretty stenographers being run ragged. Somewhere in all this happy family a stately brunette had grown even more stately under the spell of half a dozen highballs. She was talking to a little group, telling them that the studio was filled with phonies, that *she* knew the score, that nobody was pulling any wool over *her* eyes.

"Look at all them high-and-mighty bums," she said. "Look at Mister DeSylva and Mister DeMille. Who they think they're foolin'? Where they get that 'De' stuff? Well, brother, they ain't foolin' *me!* I don't fall for that 'De' stuff. To me, by God, they are Mister Sylva and Mister Mille!"

Elsewhere a writer was indulging himself in a tantrum. He had just overheard someone use the expression "cute as a bug's ear."

"Cute as a bug's ear!" he shrieked. "Jesus God! Did you ever see a bug's ear? I'm gonna get a picture taken of a bug's ear. I'm gonna have it blown up so it covers the whole side of this wall. *Then* let anybody come around and say somebody's as cute as a bug's ear. Uncutest damn thing on the face of the earth—that's what it is!"

Down in the all-but-deserted commissary five men sat at the writers' table. They were sober, and there was no mood of hilarity in them as they bent over their little cards. The silence was broken only by occasional remarks.

"I give an *L.*"

"Everybody ready? I give a *B.*"

"Oh, you filthy bastard! I give a *K.*"

And so on.

I was one of those five. Honest to God! I have witnesses.

CHAPTER XVI   *The Fame of Orph Gibberson*

HOLLYWOOD WRITERS are a peculiar breed. Another peculiar breed is the human race, and Hollywood writers are related to it. We have been discussing, during our examination of the Word Game, certain individuals named Harry Tugend, Billy Wilder, Charlie Brackett, Walter DeLeon, Frank Partos, and Jolly Joe Sistrom. Unless you are connected in some way with the motion-picture industry, you probably never heard of these people before. That statement will come as a distinct shock to the men themselves, or to most of them anyway. A screen writer has little realization of the fact that he is as anonymous, so far as the general public is concerned, as an assistant purchasing agent for a one-saw sawmill. The same is true of all but a few directors and producers.

Prior to my employment at Paramount I had done considerable prowling around the studio and while I had run up against an assortment of writers, producers, and directors, they meant nothing to me. As a yokel I was interested only in the stars. I wasn't able to understand how people I knew in the studio could walk past Gary Cooper or Claudette Colbert without giving them a glance. After I became an employee I soon found that I was able to pass Paulette Goddard on the studio streets without grinding my teeth. I am saying this for the purpose of developing a point. There is not a bit of truth in it.

The people who became interesting were the men who, unquestionably, are the real important cogs in the industry—the writers and producers and directors. Generally speaking, these men command bigger salaries than all but the top stars. They are famous, however, only among people who are in the business with them. A screen writer, unless he has already established himself in popular esteem through some other medium, as Steinbeck and Saroyan had established themselves, makes about as much impression on public consciousness as a split pea falling on a tombstone.

Just to reassure myself on this point I tried a little experiment a few nights ago. We had drop-in company at my house consisting of three couples. They were all, I knew, regular movie goers and they were above the national average in intelligence. Had they been average we would have played drop the handkerchief or spit on each other for amusement. As it was, we just sat around and talked. Then I made up a list of names, typing out carbon copies and leaving a blank after each name. I told my guests that the list contained names of people whose identities they should know. I included a few names of persons engaged in some business other than movies, such as Arthur Godfrey, Bill Corum, George Washington Hill, Abel Green, and Walter S. Gifford. The rest were screen writers, producers, and directors. Each guest was to identify the persons listed.

Five of them got Alfred Hitchcock right, though one woman put him down as a manufacturer of belt buckles. Three identified Leo McCarey correctly. Among the other answers turned in were:

DUDLEY NICHOLS, a *sports writer on the New York* Times.
PAUL JONES, a whisky distiller.
GREGORY LA CAVA, a violinist.
SAM WOOD, a golfer.
SETON I. MILLER, a shoe-store man.
BILLY WILDER, an eccentric dancer.
GENE TOWNE, a Kansas editor.
FRANK BUTLER, owner of Empire City race track.
LEWIS MILESTONE, an English author.
HOWARD ESTABROOK, a haberdasher.
DWIGHT MITCHELL WILEY, member of Lincoln's cabinet.

These same people could quickly tell you the name of Hedy LaMarr's current husband, the home town of Spencer Tracy, and Greer Garson's favorite depilatory.

One day a group of writers sat around in Irene's room, talking shop. One of them mentioned a name—let us say the name of Orph Gibberson.*

---

*I have always wanted to use the name Orph Gibberson somewhere. I like it because I think it's a wonderful name. Orph Gibberson was a man who lived down the block from us when I was a child in Illinois. He got drunk one night and somebody shot him and the bullet went clean through his body. It was common talk in our

"Got a note this morning from Orph Gibberson," said the speaker, proudly.

"The hell you say!" and similar expressions came from the others.

"Orph Gibberson?" I said. "Who's Orph Gibberson?"

They looked at me as though I had asked who's Franklin D. Roosevelt.

"Are you kidding?" asked the man who had got a note from Orph Gibberson.

"Never heard of him," I said.

"Good God!" spoke up another. "Orph Gibberson is only one of the top writers in this town. Where have you been all your life?"

Later I told Buddy DeSylva about that conversation. He admitted that it's true the public doesn't know who writes the movies and doesn't care. Yet, he said, he considers the writers to be the most important people involved in making movies. "After all," he said, "Shakespeare was right and the play's the thing." I knew that he was telling me that because I was a writer. He probably tells the directors that directors are the truly important factors, and the actors that they are the main cogs in the wheel. And all the time he is saying those nice things, he knows in his own heart that the executive producer is the guy who counts.

As a writer who has for years been an inveterate movie goer and who has had traffic with movie people, you might suppose that I would be attentive when the screen credits are listed at the opening of a picture. I never was, though. I fretted through those credits with my fellow balconyites, wishing to Jesus they'd get finished and the show would begin. No matter how those credits were tricked up, they still were dull stuff. They'd try presenting them by showing a book opening page by page. They'd do them with marquee lights; with leaves falling off trees and the individual credits printed on each leaf; with flowers bursting into bloom to reveal the names of the director and producer and so on. They did them with bombs bursting full in your face, and

neighborhood that Orph would have been killed instantly if he hadn't been full of whisky. As it was, he was up and around *and drunk again* in three weeks.

hands snatching away vaudeville posters. I heard once that someone had figured out a new gimmick for presenting the credits. The camera would come down on the butt end of a large ham. Then a large knife would appear and cut off a slice of the meat. As each slice of ham fell away it revealed

the title or the names of the stars, producer, associate producer, writers, director, make-up artist, water boy, utility second baseman, and the genius responsible for special plumbing effects.

The ham idea may have been used, for all I know, but there's another method of presenting credits that would be most effective and entertaining. Perhaps you have seen pictures in which the title and credits came riding into view on ocean waves. An idea, born in the mind of a certain screen writer, would be a variation of that technique. The camera is looking down on an ordinary toilet. A hand comes into view and jerks the flush lever. Water swirls in the bowl, and as it settles, wavering letters appear on the surface: "A Paramount Picture." The hand comes out again, another flush, another torrent of water, and then the words of the title, "Directed by John Farrow," and so forth. That's one I'd like to see.

Paul Jones, identified in my guessing game as a whisky

distiller, is a competent producer who has the Crosby-Hope *Road* pictures and a lot of other good movies to his credit. He became my producer during the last few weeks of my stay at Paramount. At last I had someone to talk to. Mr. Jones has been in pictures for centuries, and I soon found out that he is one of the great tangent-talkers of our time. He starts on a subject—let us say Bing Crosby. He has worked with Bing Crosby a long time, and since Bing Crosby is one of my favorite subjects, I am interested in what Mr. Jones has to say, so I settle back and listen. Mr. Jones proceeds something like this:

"Now, you take Bing and this picture. What we want to do along toward the end is . . . Here, look out the window. There goes Jack Hope. Bob's brother. There's a character you ought to investigate. Jack is the sort of guy who . . . What the hell is this letter doing here? Oh, it's from Bill Fields. Good old Bill Fields. Let's call him up. Damn this telephone. Can't understand how that wire manages to . . . Oh, come to think of it, I had a call from Buddy this morning about the reindeer. He said . . . Say, where'd you buy that suit? See this suit I've got on? Well, I'll tell you a story about how . . . It happened when I was working on . . . Speaking of suits, I worked out a routine once for a picture where a fellow tries to put on his coat and gets the sleeves all . . . Have a cigarette? I've smoked this brand since . . . Now, where were we? Oh yes. About Benchley. He's supposed to be over tomorrow, and I want to get you two together and talk over that business where . . . I almost forgot about Bing. If there's one thing I don't like it's jokes about Bing's horses. There was one occasion . . . By the way, what's the idea their feeding horse meat to dogs? Burns me up. I like horses better than I like dogs, so why the hell . . . Ought to be the other way around. Did you meet Hal Walker? He's the director on . . . See that picture there by the door? That's a picture with a little story . . . There goes Jack Hope again. Ought to get you together with him and if you want me to I'll . . . The way I look at it I think you and I are going to accomplish a lot, and if you'll just mark the pages where you . . . Oh, say, did you see the trade papers this morning? Where they said . . . Never mind . . . What were we talking about?"

There were a few occasions when I found Mr. Jones capable of listening briefly, and once I cornered him and tried to sell him an idea for the opening of a movie.

"Everybody," I said, "who goes to the movies hates those credits at the beginning. Nobody gives a damn about them except the people whose names are on the screen. Now, I've got an idea. Don't have the credits printed at all. Hire some ugly old guy, a bit player with dirty whiskers and all the symptoms of hookworm. Start right off by flashing his dopey puss on the screen. He's looking out at the audience. Then, in a doleful monotone, have him *talk* the credits. Have him recite the stuff in the dreariest manner possible, to correspond with the boring torture the audiences have had to undergo for years."

Mr. Jones was horrified.

"My God!" he cried. "Don't ever suggest a thing like that! The actors would cut you to ribbons!"

It has been suggested in these pages that screen writers are inclined to eccentricity. There's a writer in Hollywood who wears wrist watches on both wrists. He has watches on the inside of his wrists and on the outside, a total of four watches. When someone asks him the time he goes into a performance resembling the antics of a Javanese dancer, checking the time recorded on each of the four. There's another writer who was put away for a while. He was sitting at home alone one evening trying to read. He lived in a Hollywood apartment house. The radiator in the room had been knocking and clanking away all evening. The writer put up with it as long as his nerves would permit, then he got up, went into the kitchen, and returned with a heavy hammer. He walked up to the radiator and said:

"Okay, you son of a bitch. So you want to knock!"

Then he lit into it with that hammer. He broke the radiator all to pieces and hot water was squirting over him and steam pouring into the room and they had to come and get him. Nerves.

Taken as a class Hollywood writers are the dressiest people around the studios. They go in for peacock garb, turning up for work in horse-blanket coats, shirts with collar points a foot and a half long, and shoes that are two-toned except that each of the tones is two-toned, making them in effect four-toned. I have heard that William LeBaron, who once occupied Buddy DeSylva's chair at Paramount, couldn't stomach the sartorial eccentricity of his hired hands. He was himself a man who dressed with all the conservatism of Herbert Hoover. A writer would walk into his office for a consultation about a script. The writer would enter wearing kaleidoscopic sports clothes. Mr. LeBaron would look up from his work, contemplate the color scheme, then issue a grim order.

"Get out of my office! Go home and get into some decent clothes. When you're reasonably dressed, I'll talk business with you. Not until."

The last time I visited the cell block in the Writers' Building I stopped by to pick up my mail. Then I started down the corridor heading for the quarters occupied by Dwight Wiley. From somewhere came the voice of a man dictating a motion picture and, so help me, what I heard was this:

"I hate you! I hate you! I hate you!"

I was grinning when I stepped into Dwight Wiley's office. He was sitting at his desk and his secretary was off in a corner.

"You won't believe it," I said to him, "but just this minute, out in the hall, I heard one of your compatriots dictating and whoever it was said, 'I hate you! I hate you! I hate you!' "

Mr. Wiley didn't grin back.

"Why, you dirty heel," he said. "That was *me*."

The last I heard he was still there, and making good.

CHAPTER XVII   *Of Toothbrushes and Scalp Tonic*

SIXTEEN YEARS AGO John P. Medbury, then conducting a syndicated column of humor, stopped in to visit the offices of the Denver *Post* and stayed three or four weeks. Mr. Medbury had a large Lincoln automobile which he used in traveling aimlessly around the country. He usually wore a pullover sweater, linen knickers, sports shoes, and no hat. I was a runny-nosed reporter on the *Post* and I attached myself to this journalistic celebrity, trailing him around and fastening myself on him with the tenacity of a sheep tick.

One afternoon Mr. Medbury and I walked down Champa Street in Denver and I turned in at a drugstore to get some cigarettes. Mr. Medbury, bare of head and wearing his white pants, followed me into the store and stood off to one side while I transacted my business.

An inoffensive-appearing citizen walked up to Mr. Medbury, believing him to be an employee of the store.

"I want to get a toothbrush," said the customer.

Mr. Medbury just stood there and looked the man stonily in the eye. Slowly the expression on his face altered. He stared at the customer as a man might stare at a lifelong friend and business partner who has just confessed embezzling a million dollars.

Finally Mr. Medbury spoke.

"What did you say?"

"I said I want to get a toothbrush," replied the customer.

Again the long stare, and Mr. Medbury began shaking his head from side to side.

"Did you say *toothbrush?*" he demanded.

"Yes!" came back the customer, growing irritated. "I said toothbrush. I want to get a toothbrush. Anything wrong with that?"

"My friend," said Mr. Medbury, "you ask me if there is anything wrong with it. Good God, man! Have you taken leave of your senses?"

"What do you mean, sir?" demanded the citizen, hot anger struggling with complete confusion in his breast.

Mr. Medbury leaned forward, glaring into the customer's face.

"I mean," he said, "that you belong in a nut house. Coming in here and asking for a toothbrush! I suppose you're now going to tell me that you have hair growing on your teeth and that you've got to *brush* it. Right?"

The customer's eyes bulged. He stammered, fumbled for words, then came out with:

"I demand to see the manager!"

"Listen, you poor, deluded moron," Mr. Medbury said, "*I'm* the manager. Now, get the hell out of here before I call the loonywagon! Toothbrush, indeed!"

The customer seemed suddenly stricken with terror. He turned quickly and went out the door at top speed.

I caught a brief glimpse of Mr. Medbury a few years later at a World Series game in Philadelphia, and the next time I saw him was in Hollywood where he now lives, writing for the movies and radio. I began hearing stories about his unusual parties.

Once Mr. and Mrs. Medbury decided to have in a bevy of friends to celebrate John's birthday. They made up a list of thirty guests. Fifteen of these were people who love nothing better than formal dress. Given the opportunity to put on dinner clothes, they have achieved Nirvana. The Medburys sent invitations to them, specifying that the party was to be informal—that they should come in sports clothes. The remaining fifteen were people who loathe formal dress, wearing slacks and sweat shirts wherever possible. The invitations to these people stressed the point that the Medbury party would be rigidly formal—white tie.

Mrs. Medbury went to an employment agency for a one-day butler and got a pip, complete with proper habiliments and a British accent. Next came the food problem. Mrs. Medbury was at the moment lacking a regular cook. She remembered that the wife of her Italian gardener had a high reputation for making spaghetti. She engaged this lady and turned her loose in the kitchen.

The guests arrived, and from the beginning waves of bitterness coursed through the house. The guests in dinner clothes were furious and the guests in sports clothes were furiouser. The Medburys scurried around feigning sorrow, mumbling, "Really, there's been a mistake somewhere." The highbrow butler, bewildered at first, grew sullen and then outraged over this travesty on good breeding. The climax came when the sulking guests heard a mighty uproar from the kitchen. The unhappy butler, determined to retain his own sense of superiority, had made the error of telling the Italian lady how to make spaghetti. The Italian lady had told him to mind his own business. The butler *ordered* her to obey his dictates. Whereupon the Italian lady let go at him with forty miles of spaghetti, splattering him with it until she had emptied a heaping dishpan of the stuff. There was spaghetti on the ceiling and on the walls, from one end of the kitchen to the other. It was one of the loveliest parties the Medburys ever gave.

On another occasion a swanky affair was held in the Medbury home. The guests were mostly people of breeding and culture. As they entered the house the first thing they saw was the ladies' powder room directly in front of them, opening off the foyer. The door to this room was open and the light inside was turned on. In the little room was a toilet and sitting on the toilet was an elderly bum, unshaven and poorly dressed. His suspenders were down and he was sitting there, quietly reading a newspaper. As each group of well-bred guests came up to him, the women gasping at the rude picture he presented, he would raise his eyes, then make a gesture with his thumb.

"Medbury party to the right," he'd say. Then he'd return to his newspaper.

Mr. Medbury is but one of several thousand pranksters inhabiting Hollywood. Practical joking seems to be as much a part of studio life as is boss-licking. A man with a midget automobile (and there are many of them) had best anchor the thing firmly or put it in his locker, else he is likely to find it occupying the crosstree of a telephone pole when he goes to get it.

The japery on the sets is never-ending. Suppose there's a scene in which Ray Milland eats a cheese sandwich. He bites into it. The cheese is cold cream. Or suppose Bob Hope goes into an extended speech before the camera and during the shot he picks up a glass of water and takes a gulp. The water may contain alum, which puckers the mouth.

One of the town's most celebrated leading men has a small gag which he uses frequently. He comes up behind his victim. He dips his fingers in a glass of water. He flips the water onto the back of the victim's neck and, simultaneously, lets go with a big sneeze. He is still alive at this writing.

During my motion-picture career (whoops!) a certain screen writer was looking up a number in the Los Angeles telephone book when by accident he came upon a most unusual name—Gisela Werbezirk Piffl. That is the actual name. He was fascinated by it and concluded that something should be done about it. He grabbed the telephone and called the number. A lady answered.

"Is this Gisela Werbezirk Piffl?" he asked.

"Yes."

"Well, well, well," he said. "How are you, Gisela? This is Charlie Peabody. Remember me?"

"No," said the lady, "I don't believe I do."

"Ah, come on now, Gisela!" he went on. "You remember me! I went to high school with you in Omaha."

"I don't believe . . ." she protested.

"Back in Omaha, Nebraska," he insisted. "You remember me—Charlie Peabody!"

"I'm very sorry," she said, "but I have never been in Omaha in my life. I have never even been in Nebraska."

There was a long silence. Then he said:

"Oh. I see. I'm terribly sorry. It must have been another Gisela Werbezirk Piffl."

And he hung up.

If I seem to concern myself overmuch with stories of practical jokes it is because of the pure perversity of the people I know, and because I once had a newspaper assignment which required my spending a month collecting stories about famous pranks. Many of the practical jokers I know about should be given a high colonic with a Roman candle; yet there are others whose feats I almost admire. I recall the story of Waldo Peirce and the turtle. Mr. Peirce, celebrated in later years as a painter, once made his home in Paris. The wife of the concierge (French for orchestra leader) at his hotel grew fond of him and was constantly going out of her way to do him little kindnesses. As a gesture of appreciation Mr. Peirce brought home a present for her—a tiny turtle about the size of his thumbnail.

She was vociferously fond of that wonderful turtle and made all manner of French noises petting it and babying it and constructing a little house for it.

After a few days Mr. Peirce came home with another turtle, a size larger than the original, and secretly made a substitution. The lady was aglow with happiness. Her pet was thriving under her care, growing rapidly. A couple of days after that the turtle took on more size. Mr. Peirce continued to fetch in larger and larger turtles unknown to the lady, and before long she had a turtle as big as a flat hog. The beast was all but driving her out of her home, yet she was blissfully contented, overjoyed in the knowledge that her diligence had brought glowing health to the creature.

Then came the decline. The turtle started growing smaller. Day by day it continued to shrink until it was back to its original size, and the poor woman almost started wasting away herself worrying over what she supposed to be a sort of miraculous illness. I don't know whether Mr. Peirce ever told her the truth.

I can't resist putting down the story of Leon Kay's revenge. Leon is at this moment somewhere in the Middle East, serving the United Press as a war correspondent. He is an old friend of mine though I have not seen much of him since 1935 when he was sent to London. He could handle half a dozen languages and in the years just before the war he worked at a desk in the UP London bureau.

Soon after his arrival he sent a suit of clothes out to be cleaned. Something like two weeks elapsed before it came back, and when it did come, all the buttons were off the coat, trousers, and vest. It appears that the English cleaners remove all the buttons before cleaning a suit and, when they return it, they also return a small bag containing the buttons. This quaint custom struck Leon Kay as being uncivilized, impractical, and insane. In fact, it made him angry, and he swore that he'd get revenge on the English race if the opportunity ever came.

He worked the lobster trick on Saturday nights and amused himself through the dull hours by reading the letters-to-the-editor section of the *Sunday Times*. This London paper devoted acres of space to such letters. A reader would write in to report that he had sighted a water pipit, which is a form of bird, in a certain neighborhood. His letter would bring perhaps fifty others from people who reported that they, too, had seen water pipits, people who said they had *not* seen any water pipits, and people who said they hoped they would see some water pipits.

On one Saturday night Leon was reading a long series of letters to the *Times* discussing remedies for baldness. As he read he was eating a cottage pudding brought in by the office boy from a neighboring restaurant.

Suddenly Leon transferred his attention from the printed page to the pudding. It was a frightful blob of seal-brown stuff containing a scattering of raisins. Leon contemplated its unlovely texture for a bit, then a fine idea smote him.

That week end he searched through British cookbooks until he found the recipe for the pudding. Then he wrote a scholarly letter to the *Times*. He described himself as a person who had recently made the acquaintance of an old inhabitant of Kent, and this old inhabitant of Kent had given him a sovereign remedy for baldness. It worked wonders on the scalps of Kentish people, wherefore there was no reason to suppose it would not work wonders on the scalps of people elsewhere. After that Leon set down the recipe for the pudding.

"Please note," his letter concluded, "the presence of the raisins in this decoction. We know that raisins contain a plenitude of iron. Can it be that this iron is the essential element, the fertilizing ingredient, in the remarkable salve? I would greatly enjoy hearing from other *Times* readers who may have had experience with this Kentish elixir."

The *Sunday Times*, to be sure, printed it. There were responses. Several correspondents wrote in with long and learned disquisitions on raisins and their possible effect on follicles. One colossal liar said that he had heard tell of this splendid noggin lotion and was aware of its efficacy.

Leon Kay was satisfied. His revenge for the button incident was complete. Even now I imagine he sometimes chuckles when he thinks of the many elderly gentlemen throughout the British Isles who, at this very moment, may be solemnly kneading cottage pudding—raisins and all—into their glistening scalps.

CHAPTER XVIII   *Afternoon at Lucey's*

COME with me now for a rainy Saturday after-
noon at Lucey's. I hesitate to write about the place because
up to now the tourists have not found it. Movie people can
congregate in these cool precincts and nobody will bother
them. Saturday afternoons are soothing and restful after
a hard week of doing nothing. Especially if the rain is pouring outside and the flames are roaring in the two big fire-
places.

Much depends, of course, on the quality of the company,
or the lack of it. The little group in which I held membership was perfect. There would be Rufus Blair, a man of
placid temperament who only shatters one electric razor
against the floor of his bathroom each week. From a distance
of three thousand miles I can see him as the first glass of
bourbon is placed before him.

"Ah!" says Rufus. "Now for that tense, nervous feeling!
Who the hell wants to be relaxed?"

There would be Chuck Daggett of the Missouri Daggetts;
maybe Ted Bonnet from the DeMille menagerie; Fred Beck,
the city slicker from the Farmers Market; Gene Coughlin, of
the *News;* Fred Othman, who is likely the most popular
newspaper writer in Hollywood; Blake McVeigh, the historical novelist who has never written a historical novel;
Bill Morrow, formerly Jack Benny's writer and now of the
Army; and occasionally Mark Sandrich, Lou Smith, Jimmy
Starr, Barry Sullivan, Jimmy O'Toole, or Idwal Jones.
Women? Let a woman approach within ten feet of this con-
gress and she'll expose herself to a withering blast calculated
to shrivel the three and a half pounds of stuffing she wears in
her brassière.

Idwal Jones is the gourmet of the crowd, knows all about
fancy foods and how to prepare them. He looks upon most
restaurant cooks with Lucullan contempt, and I once heard
him observe of a certain chef: "That culinary scoundrel is
not fit to tote guts to a bear."

Many incidents and anecdotes come to mind from those

sessions at Lucey's. There was an afternoon when a new bartender took up his duties. Rufus Blair detached himself from our gathering and went to the bar and asked for a glass of brandy. The new bartender placed it before him and Rufus took a sip.

"Great God!" he exclaimed, choking and sputtering. "What kind of vile swamp juice is this?"

He characterized the brandy as swill, unfit for human consumption, pushed it back across the bar, and suggested that he be given bourbon in its place. The bartender gladly poured him the whisky, which Rufus tossed off. Then he started away.

"Just a minute," said the bartender. "You didn't pay for the whisky."

"Of course not," said Rufus, turning back. "I gave you the brandy in exchange for the whisky."

"But you didn't pay for the brandy."

"Certainly not," growled Rufus. "I didn't drink it. Why *should* I have paid for it?"

Then he walked back to the table and sat down, and we all watched the bartender, doing additions and subtractions in his head and all but counting on his fingers trying to puzzle it out.

If the mood is on him Chuck Daggett will narrate the epic of José Maniah and his death sentence. José Maniah was a cook in a Southwestern cow camp. To all appearances he was a lowly paisano yet beneath that rude exterior was the soul of a poet and the heart of a lion. A cowboy had the misfortune to cheat José Maniah in a game of cards whereupon José killed the man dead. A jury swiftly found him guilty and José was brought before a certain Judge Parker, a man who believed that Mexican blood was evil blood and the less of it in the world the better. Said Judge Parker:

José Maniah, stand up. You have been found guilty of a most heinous crime. Soon it will be springtime and down in the wild and beautiful valleys will be heard the bellowing of the frisky bull and the artless prattle of little children as they come home from school. But you won't hear any of it, José Maniah, because you will not be present. Nature will be putting on her gorgeous robes, and the birds will be singing their sweet carols to the sky, but you won't see any of these things because, José Maniah, you won't be here. As a usual thing it is a painful duty for me to pronounce upon a human being the sentence of death, and my mind sometimes revolts against the horror of such a duty. Happily, however, no such unpleasant sensations govern me this day, for I take positive pleasure in sentencing you to death.

The flowers will not bloom for you, José Maniah. The birds will not sing their carols for you. And after happy summer comes the dreary winter, but don't let that cause you any anxiety, José, for you won't be here. It is customary, at a time such as this, to invoke the tender mercies of a Higher Court. But if I thought God Almighty would have any compassion on a wretch like you I would never think or speak of Him again— you cold-blooded, saddle-colored, chili-eating, guilty, sheep-herding son of a bitch you.

José Maniah, I gladly and eagerly order that on the sixth day of the coming month you be hanged by the neck until you are dead, dead, dead. Take the son of a bitch away.

That might have been all had the sheriff yanked José out of the courtroom at once. But José Maniah had words to utter. He faced Judge Parker, and this is what he said:

That I have taken human life I do not deny, but it was under circumstances of the greatest provocation. So determined was this court to add another to its already long list of slaughtered victims that I early foresaw my doom was sealed. You have sat here through the proceedings of this hellish farce with a ghoulish glee portrayed on your every feature. You and your blood-thirsty jury remind me more of a lot of buzzards hovering over an expected victim, than of a body of men supposed to guard and honor the principles of human justice. Hear me, you half-starved hyena! You cannot break my spirit!

You speak of the pleasant odor of blossoms and the sweet singing of the birds, you grandson of a pock-marked whore. You announce to the world that I am to be hanged. As I gaze into your bloated, whisky-fogged face I find no surprise at your conduct. With mock solemnity and cruel sarcasm you have consigned me to an ignominious death. Very well, you disheveled barbarian, you wild-eyed, dirty-nosed, pot-gutted, carnivorous offspring of a cross-eyed maggot, I want you to understand that your words hold no terror for me.

You tell me that on the sixth day of the coming month I am to be taken out and hanged by the neck until I am dead, dead, dead. You hope in your filthy heart that my corpse is left dangling until the vultures come down and pick my bones clean. You do not even have the grace to call down the mercy of God on my soul.

And I, José Maniah, I say to you that on the sixth day of the coming month I will *not* be forever deprived of the sweet sounds and the pleasant odors of which you have spoken. As for hanging by the neck until I am dead, dead, dead—you can kiss my butt until it's red, red, red, and may God blast your dirty old soul!

That is the end of it, save for the legend that José Maniah broke jail a couple of days later, escaped into the hills, and was never recaptured.

A toast to José Maniah, and now someone recalls Dick Carlson. Dick was a young fellow working on a weekly newspaper in the Middle West when the Hollywood virus got him. He saved up his money and headed West. He made a quiet investigation of studio-publicity methods and then came up with an idea.

He approached the head of Paramount's publicity department and outlined his project. He knew how, he said, to get publicity for extra players—plenty of it. The publicity head was not interested; didn't care about getting publicity for the extras.

"But wait a minute," said Dick Carlson. "Every time you get a piece of publicity for an extra, you'll find that the name of the picture he's in and some of the details of that picture are mentioned. Here's what I'll do. I'll go on the set when a picture is being made. I'll take the extra players one at a time. I'll go to a man who's playing in a crowd scene. I'll interview him, and the first thing I'll ask him is the name of his home town. Suppose he says he's from Sapulpa, Oklahoma, or Logansport, Indiana, or Hattiesburg, Mississippi. I find out the name of a local paper in his home town and I write the interview with him for that paper. Local Boy in Movies—that's the idea. I tell what movie he's working in, the names of the stars he's working with, how he happened to get into the picture, the names of other pictures he's worked in, and so on. I can do three or four of those stories a day. Don't tell me that's not good publicity."

It was, indeed, a first-rate idea, and it worked. Dick Carlson was a young man of great energy and did his job thoroughly. He would descend upon a sound stage, drag an extra off into a corner, and start pumping questions at him. Finished with the one, he'd grab another. Before long he had become anathema to the assistant directors who, among many other things, have the unpleasant job of riding herd on extras. The cameras would be set, the lights blazing, the actors tensed, and then someone would discover that Mortimer Miller from Carmi, Illinois, who was supposed to be leaning against a lamppost and picking his teeth in the scene, was missing. They'd find him off in the shadows with Dick Carlson, and there would be much expressive language ricocheting around the premises over the delay. Soon Dick Carlson had become the most frequently God-damned individual in twenty square miles. He even became an issue. Directors and assistant directors stormed into the front office and demanded that this hellish half-wit be banished from the lot. The head of publicity would be called in. He would quietly spread out column after column after column of publicity on the desk—stories resounding to the glory of Paramount Pictures—all the work of Dick Carlson. So Dick stayed on, harassing the assistant directors, impervious to the curses poured upon him, delaying production more than overhead airplanes.

Then one day Dick Carlson up and died.

Two days after his death one of Paramount's top directors had a company at work on the back lot. This director had been among the most violent traducers of Dick Carlson. He was working now on a street scene. Members of the company were assembled in a short thoroughfare with store buildings on one side and brownstone fronts on the other. At the dead end of the street was a high wall. This was a part of the long wall marking the northern boundary of the studio. On the other side of the wall is Hollywood Cemetery.

Scenes of violent passion and sequences of side-splitting comedy are often played against sections of that wall, within six feet of the graves of the dead.

"Quiet, everybody!" came the assistant director's voice. That is another of his duties—yelling "Quiet!" eight or ten thousand times a day.

"Roll it," said the famous director.

The camera started. Along the sidewalk came two celebrated stars. The microphone followed them, dangling over their heads, picking up their whispered conversation as they hurried along. Then . . .

Bong, bong, bong, bong, bong, bong, bong, bong.

"Hold it!" cried the director. "What the hell is that?"

The assistant director hurried over.

"It's the bell in the chapel over in the cemetery," he said. Then he remembered something. "Hell," he said, "that's Dick Carlson. They're burying Dick Carlson over there this morning."

The director dropped into his chair and sat there, slowly shaking his head.

"Even dead," he muttered, "that guy screws up the works!"

☆ ☆ ☆

The story of Dick Carlson's parting gesture brings the talk around to cemeteries. A person engaged in even a casual examination of life in Hollywood cannot help but become graveyard-conscious. A great many residents of Los Angeles are elderly people who have gone there to spend their remaining days in the sun, and to die. It is altogether understandable. Anyone who wants to go out in a blaze of splendor would do well to choose southern California for a springboard. They believe in putting you away in style.

Feeling the urge one day to be among people who are unselfish, trustworthy, and incapable of back-stabbing, I spent a couple of hours wandering around Hollywood Cemetery. One thing I wanted to see was the Douglas Fairbanks sarcophagus, which is less elegant than the Taj Mahal but not much less.

As I went through the gates on Santa Monica Boulevard

a young woman was walking briskly ahead of me. She struck off down a winding drive and I decided to follow her simply because I didn't know my way to the interior of the premises. As I walked along about fifty feet behind her I wondered what her reason might be for visiting the cemetery. Maybe she would turn out to be the daughter of some forgotten picture star. Perhaps she was heading for the Rudolph Valentino crypt. No, that wouldn't be likely— she was too young. Anyway, I trailed along after her, and we were coming close to the Paramount wall when she arrived at her destination. She made a sharp turn and came up to a couple of men who were working a few feet from the roadway. They were gravediggers. One of them was an ancient citizen in overalls with a red nose and a tired look on his face. He was just standing there looking off into space. The other was a young man, a dark, Latin, good-looking guy. He was at work with a spade, standing in the grave. He raised his eyes as the girl approached.

"Hi, Joe," she said.

"Hi," said Joe. He wasn't very enthusiastic.

"Didja have your lunch yet?" she asked.

"Sure," he said. "Had it a hour ago."

"Oh," she said. "That's too bad. I just happen to be passing by and thought maybe we could go somewheres and have lunch."

Joe quietly put his spade down on the grass. He was still knee-deep in the grave.

"Lissen," he said, "how many times I got to tell you I don't want you comin' around here? For once and for all, will you kindly get the hell outa here and stay out?"

"But, Joe, I just happen to be passing by and . . ."

" 'Just happen to be passing by,' " mimicked Joe with fine sarcasm. "I know all about how you just happen to be passing by. Now, beat it, and don't let me catch you around here botherin' a man when he's workin' no more."

By this time I had moved on down the road, out of hearing, so I don't know how the discussion came out.

I looked around for the Valentino crypt but never did find it, though I've heard a lot about it. The cemetery once had a dynamic press agent whose job was to keep the institution fresh in the public consciousness and make the business of selling space easier. After Valentino was entombed this press agent had an idea. One August 23—the anniversary of the actor's death—he inveigled a reporter and photographer to stand watch with him near the crypt. Soon a big car drove up and out of it stepped a woman dressed all in black and wearing a heavy veil. She placed some red roses at the tomb, knelt briefly, and didn't seem to notice it when the photographer's camera clicked. When the reporter stepped out to question her, however, she high-tailed it into the car and escaped.

It was a master stroke for the press agent. Newspapers all over the country played up the story of "The Lady in Black." There was wide public speculation on her identity. So what happened? The next August 23 there were *two* ladies in black with garlands of red roses. The year after that there were more. And the thing finally reached the point where ladies in black were practically trampling one another underfoot to get to the tomb. All the cemetery press agent had done was hire the original lady in black. He didn't know he'd fetch out a rash of them in future years.

Expensive advertising campaigns and organized promotional stunts are as much a part of running a Los Angeles cemetery as keeping the grass cut. The cemeteries compete with the undertakers in attracting the public's attention. Among funeral directors in the classified phone book you may find:

ARMSTRONG FAMILY—"Where the Trust Is Sacred."

W. A. BROWN & SON—"The Only W. A. Brown Funeral Director in Los Angeles."

UTTER-MCKINLEY—Listing seven separate funeral homes providing "distinctive funeral services as low as sixty-eight dollars" and promising that "regardless of price, every Utter-McKinley funeral includes casket and forty-seven important items of service."

The ultimate, however, is achieved at Forest Lawn Memorial-Park. Here is man's most splendid achievement in the way of graveyards. From a scenic point of view it is a magnificent place, provided the viewer lacks the imagination that I have, an imagination that won't let me forget the ghastly things that are hidden away, underground and in the crypts. The lawns, the fountains, the flowers, the pools, the trees, the statuary, the edifices—these things are sufficient to overwhelm a lover of beauty. This "happy cemetery" with its "Resurrection Slope" is the same place that Bruce Barton, an advertising man, a Republican, and a Christian, called "a first step upward toward Heaven" in a signed and framed testimonial. Mr. Barton suggested also that tourists go back to their cities and towns and establish similar cemeteries, declaring that "not until that happens will we be able to call ourselves a truly Christian nation."

Forest Lawn is a big business enterprise founded by a banker who, back in 1917, acquired some property through foreclosure of a mortgage, went out to have a look at it, and while having that look also had "a vision." This vision led him to the conclusion that existing cemeteries "are wrong because they depict an end, not a beginning." Today the fruit of that vision is one of the first things tourists are urged to see in southern California, and it would take more than a full day to cover everything—the graves and crypts of the stars, the Wee Kirk o' the Heather, the $4,500,000 Mausoleum, the Tower of Legends, Babyland, and even the building which houses the Forest Lawn Life Insurance Company. Funerals and burials are not exclusively the business of Forest Lawn, for many weddings are performed there. Near the Wee Kirk o' the Heather is the Annie Laurie Wishing Chair, built of stones taken from the original Wee Kirk in Scotland. After people get married in the Wee Kirk they go out and sit in the Wishing Chair and maybe kiss each other. This is supposed to bring them luck, so that they won't be beating each other on the skulls with sash weights.

If you want to be buried in Forest Lawn you can make a deal for as low as forty-five dollars. That puts you on one of the lower slopes where, I suppose, you'll have a longer wait come Judgment Day. And if you don't have the forty-five dollars, arrangements can be made. One of the Forest Lawn advertising appeals sums it up pretty well in this fashion: "Everything in time of sorrow, in one sacred place, under one friendly management, with one convenient credit arrangement and a year to pay."

Chuck Daggett tells of the time a New York newspaperman arrived for his first visit in Hollywood as guest of a movie studio. The visitor was taken through the studio and then he said he'd enjoy seeing some of the other sights in Hollywood. He was escorted all over town, to the Hollywood Bowl, to that fantastic institution known as the Farmers Market, to assorted Brown Derbies, to the Sunset Strip, to Griffith Park, to UCLA, and to Grauman's Footprint. At last he arrived in Forest Lawn Memorial-Park. He drank in all the shining beauty, all the splendor of the place, and as he gazed upon its sheer loveliness he sighed and said:

"By God, these Hollywood people sure know how to live!"

Hey! What're we doing wandering around cemeteries? Back to Lucey's where somebody is telling a story . . .

A producer at one of the big studios was given an assignment to do a jungle picture. He was an all-around ball of fire; even his ulcers were dynamic. Right at the beginning he let it be known that he was not going to turn out any little old "B" picture. He called a preliminary conference of writers, half a dozen of them, men who had worked with him in the past. When he walked into the room only five of the six writers were present.

"Where's Ed?" he demanded. Somebody told him that Ed had reported he was sick.

"Sick!" roared the producer. "Sick, sick, sick! That's all I hear from that bum! Every time I want him for something he's sick! He's nothing but a God-damn nymphomaniac!"

The meeting started without Ed.

"Get this," said the producer. "I'm gonna do this jungle picture and it's gonna be the biggest, the greatest jungle picture in history. Everything about it is gonna be great. It's gonna have everything—the most tigers, the most lions, the most zebras, the most elephants. And a hippopotamus. Fellas, this picture is gonna have the biggest hippopotamus in the world in it."

"Where do you expect to get it?" a writer asked.

"I should worry my head about such things!" said the producer. "When I say I want the biggest hippopotamus

in the world, I want the biggest God-damn hippopotamus *in
history!* Now, *you* tell *me* where we get it."

They put the research department to work on the problem,
and in passing I'd like to say that the research departments
in the movie studios are superb. In no time at all the producer was notified that the biggest hippopotamus in the
world, at least the biggest hippopotamus in captivity, was
the property of the London Zoo.

"Buy the son of a bitch!" ordered the dynamic producer,
and negotiations were opened by cable. After a while a
price, something like $50,000, was agreed upon and the
question of transportation arose. The London Zoo people
urged that the buyer engage the services of the two regular
hippopotamus keepers—men who knew how to handle the
beast.

"How much salary?" came the cabled query. The two men
could be hired for fifty dollars a week each.

"No!" roared the producer. He was willing to spend $50,000
for the hippo, but he balked at fifty dollars a week for
keepers. "We got people in this studio," he said, "who can
handle any animal on earth. Why pay them guys?"

A couple of men from the prop department were shipped
off to London with instructions to bring back the hippo.
They got him on a ship and they got him off the ship and
into a special freight car. In due course the car arrived in
Los Angeles. The next problem was to get the hippopotamus
out of the freight car and into the movie jungle. But the
hippo wouldn't co-operate.

"He won't co-operate," they told the producer. This
phrase is a common one around the studios, whether applied
to a human or a hippopotamus.

"Drag him out of it," said the producer.

They ripped off the upper structure of the freight car,
leaving the hippo sprawled in full view. They built runways,
but the hippo spurned them. He was a sick hippopotamus.
He was out of his element. Those men from the prop department were capable when it came to handling period
furniture, but they really knew nothing about the mental
processes of a hippopotamus since prop men have little con-
tact with the front office.

After hours of wrestling with the problem they hired the biggest flat-bed truck they could find and backed it up to the flat car. They brought in a powerful crane. They fastened chains around the recumbent beast and they *drug* him off. There is no such word as drug, as used in the

foregoing sentence, but I like it and I'm writing this book, not you. They drug him onto the truck and drove him to the place where the jungle had been built. Now a new problem arose. The hippopotamus was prone to stay prone. They didn't want to drag him off the truck and onto the ground for fear they would break him. Then along came someone with a thought bordering on intelligence.

"That hippopotamus is sick as a dog," he said. "He has got to be up to his chin in water. An animal like that sops up water through his pores. He's been away from water so long he's a nervous wreck."

They agreed, then, that he should be put in water for a while. But where? Someone remembered a small lake out north of Hollywood.

"Lease the lake," ordered the producer, "and dump the bastard in."

They leased the lake. They drove the truckload of hippopotamus to the shore. He showed no interest in the water.

They didn't want to roll him off into shallow water for fear he'd founder in the mud and never get loose. So they summoned an army of studio carpenters and quickly built a heavy pier extending out to deep water. When the pier was finished and tested they backed the truck onto it. Next they brought up a hoisting engine. They blocked the rear wheels of the truck securely, attached a line to the front of the truck, and slowly tilted it upward. At an angle of around forty-five degrees the hulk of hippopotamus began to move. The great beast slid slowly off the tilted truck, then hit the water with a mighty splash. The job had been done neatly and without a hitch, and a great cheer went up among the workmen on shore.

The animal went under water at once and silence settled over the spectators as they waited for his reappearance. The seconds ticked off and nothing happened. More seconds, and still nothing.

The biggest God-damn hippopotamus in the world hasn't come up to this day.

CHAPTER XIX   *A Definitive History of Hollywood*

JOAQUIN MILLER, once the poet laureate of California, wore flannel shirts and high boots and let his hair grow wild until he looked like a bit player in a Republic Western. His real name was Cincinnatus Heine Miller but he took over the name Joaquin after writing a defense of Joaquin Murietta, a kindly, sweet-tempered, Robin Hoodish Mexican bandit who led an exemplary life except when he was going around robbing, shooting, stabbing, strangling, and bludgeoning people, which was most of the time.

Joaquin Miller was highly regarded by the people of England, who liked his hair. When he found out the English people considered him to be a great man, he hurried right over there in person because that view coincided with his own. He gave them many a laugh, and it is my private opinion that most of the Britishers who met him thought he was old Joe Miller, the man who didn't write *Joe Miller's Joke Book*.

This Joaquin Miller, as hinted, had a good opinion of himself. One day he was trimming his toenails, permitting the parings to fall on the floor. Suddenly a thought occurred to him. I am going to venture into pure speculation and attempt to reconstruct that thought.

"I," he told himself, "am Joaquin Miller. A great man. A man posterity will honor. No doubt about it. I am so great that everything about me is great. Even my toenails. Why should I throw these toenail clippings away? Are they not part of ME? Are they not a part of the great Joaquin Miller? You're damn right they are, and they ought to be preserved."

So he preserved them. Every time he trimmed his toenails after that he saved the cuttings. He put them in a big glass jar and by the time he died, in 1913, that jar was almost full of toenails—genuine Joaquin Miller toenails. He bequeathed his toenails to his daughter and I understand she kept them around the house, usually displayed in a prominent place, and when worshipful pilgrims came to call she would quite likely point to the jar and say, "My dear, dear papa's toenails."

That story of Joaquin's legacy calls to mind a little experience I had the first time I went to Hollywood. John Moynihan told me about a woman he knew, widow of an oldtime copyreader who had once worked on the same newspaper where I was employed. The widow enjoyed nothing more than to have newspapermen call on her, so she could hash over anecdotes about her late husband, and I was told that it would be an act of Christian charity for me to make such a call. I did.

The widow lived in an apartment in the heart of Hollywood. She welcomed me into her parlor and indicated a chair, and then she began chattering about "George." I hadn't known George, but I pretended that I knew him slightly and held him in high esteem—which was certainly Christian charity on my part because the bum was a copyreader. I asked about the circumstances of his death and had to listen to one of those clinical disquisitions that would wear out a cast-iron deer, and then she said:

"There's George. Right there."

I hadn't given much attention to the room and its contents but I did now. She had gestured toward a table next to my chair—a table on which my arm was resting. I glanced now at this table, a small feeling of alarm stirring around inside me.

"Right there," she repeated, "in that urn."

I got my arm off that table.

Sure enough, a small piece of pottery stood on the center-piece surrounded by an accumulation of other articles. Before I could focus real well she was enumerating those articles. George's things were all around him. His two pipes. A ragged pair of house slippers. A pair of shears a foot and a half long, such as copyreaders fancy, along with a crusted paste pot. Half a dozen pencils, gnawed nearly to shreds. And—believe me!—George's shot glass and the tumbler he used for chasers.

I remembered I had a date to bomb the Los Angeles *Times,* so I left rather hurriedly.

This chapter started off with the bit about Joaquin Miller just to demonstrate the amount of research I did while living in California. Almost all my reading was concentrated on the history of southern California with emphasis on the Cahuenga Valley. This is a failing of mine—the habit of studying the history of any locality I happen to be visiting. If I had a train stopover of thirty minutes in, say, Des Moines, I'd spend twenty minutes finding a book about the place and the remaining ten minutes trying to cram it all into my head.

The history of early Hollywood is comical, as is all history. I recall one book dealing with the town's early days which was, for the most part, just a recitation of names. The book might say, for example, something like this:

"On April 22, 1909, a meeting was held to organize a committee to handle the matter of hiring a new schoolteacher. Present were: . . ." There would follow a list of a hundred or so names. This technique is common among small-town historians. The more names they jam into their text, the more copies of the book they'll sell. Every person mentioned will likely buy a copy and so will his children and maybe his cousins-german. The technique is not limited to small-town authors, however. Some years ago in New

York a writer made a deal with a book publisher. If the publisher would issue his book, he said, he'd be responsible for a stated number of sales. The book was about theatrical and night life. It consisted of whole chapters containing little more than names. The guy would say, "At a first-night performance one is likely to see Hope Hampton Brulatour, Leo Lindy, Broadway Sam, Mark Hellinger (the former Gladys Glad), Cedric Crowell, Broadway Rose, Richard Mealand, Minerva Pious, Alfred E. Smith, Mrs. J. J. McCabe, Gene Austin, Milton Runyon . . ." and so on for half a dozen pages. Then the author would set down a list of people one might expect to see in the Hunting Room of the Astor, and at Sardi's, and at the Yankee Stadium. When the book was off the presses the author simply went to work on all the people mentioned and many of them, being hammy, bought extra copies to send to kinfolks just to show how important they were.

In studying the history of Hollywood and southern California I jotted down occasional notes. My own history of the place is inclined to be fragmentary because I don't have the space to include everything. However, I have tried to do a conscientious job, and I have no doubt my treatment will be recommended for use in schools and colleges throughout the land. Now, let us have done with frivolity. Knowledge, said the philosopher, consists chiefly of knowing things. Let us know things.

THE THUNDER OF DESTINY
or
WHICH WAY IS GOWER STREET?

The Santa Monica Mountains were not always there. The ground got restless a long time ago and started bulging around and up they came, providing pleasant hilltops for people such as Edgar Bergen, Greta Garbo, and Charles Boyer to have houses on.

In those ancient times there were no people in the valley, but imperial elephants, standing fifteen feet at the shoulder, the biggest elephants on record. Also there were swarms of saber-toothed tigers. These beasts have always had an evil reputation and may have been created to provide literary people with a useful simile, to wit: As ferocious as a saber-toothed tiger. The fact seems to be, however, that they would not bother trying to bite you. They had mean-looking upper canines that curved downward, lapping over their lower jar even when they had their mouths open as wide as they could get them open. Those teeth were so long that their owners couldn't bite *anything*. Given a juicy piece of meat, they were unable to get their mouth to it unless, like Jim Moran, they were equipped with the peculiar ability to eat a tomato through a tennis racket. Perhaps the tiger could lie down, flatten the side of his mouth against the piece of meat and drag it in back of the saber teeth. Otherwise he was in a bad fix, and those long teeth were of no use to him except perhaps for loosening the earth around tomato plants.

Came the Indians. These were of the Cahuenga tribe and their language was called Kokomcar. Most of my information about the Indians comes from a translation of their own histories. I didn't translate it myself. Dr. Rockwell, the only person east of the Rockies conversant with Kokomcar, did the job for me.

The Indians never wore any clothes. The girls went naked except for lovely earrings made out of abalone shells. They might as well not have worn them. They shampooed their hair with clay to make it look nice.

These original citizens of Hollywood lived in thatched huts something on the order of wigwams. They were lousy housekeepers. When the house got overrun by vermin and began to smell like a twenty-hole privy, they didn't bother about cleaning it out. They simply burned it down and built another.

They ate badgers, skunks, gophers, rats, and crows, and had roasted locusts for dessert. They were a peace-loving people and didn't believe in killing anybody, except one another. Thievery was unknown among them if we are to believe the Rockwell translation, which I don't.

If a wife were caught in the act of infidelity, her husband could do one of two things. He could take a club and beat her brains out, or he could go have a look at the wife of the guy who wronged him. If he liked the interloper's wife he could have her, while the other fellow could keep the unfaithful woman and welcome to her.

Immediately after the birth of a child, mother and baby were taken to the tribal hospital, called the sweat house. This was a sod-lined hut where water was poured over hot rocks. The mother and child were required to take up residence in the sweat house. When they had perspired themselves dry as a corncob, they were wrapped in heavy furs so they could *really* sweat. The treatment had to be taken twice daily for three days. This is probably where birth control originated.

The mother was not allowed to share her husband's bed until the child was able to run. Dr. Rockwell informs me that a tribal literary classic, *Tzordinn Guggle Ze Bell Tolls*, is concerned with the dilemma of a husband under this taboo. This husband became the parent of a ggukk (a tribal word meaning moron, or average person) and while the ggukk appeared to be physically normal, he was incapable of running even at the age of eighteen. His father waited eighteen years and then crept up to the ggukk and started beating him on the head with a sockful of lemon seeds. The sock split at the seams and the seeds were scattered over the ground. Hence the lemon industry. I do not consider this tale to be adequate from a literary point of view because it never does get around to telling whether that ggukk ever ran a step. That, to me, is more important than lemons. Think of his old man.

The first Hollywood residents, these Cahuenga Indians, had all manner of cures for their afflictions and they had all manner of afflictions. They would take charcoal made from wild cucumbers and rub it on the head to cure baldness. For a pain in the side they applied a wet poultice of live red ants. If they were just generally sick, they were given a rattle to shake.

They had a Jimson-weed ceremony that was quite nice. It was for boys stricken with puberty. These boys would be herded together in the place of assembly. The priest would mix up a large bowl of Jimson-weed soup, which is said to be stronger than vodka. Each of the boys was required to drink some of the stuff. When they had all been given their share, the men would finish it off. Everybody then got up and began dancing around and making bird noises until they fell down and passed out. The rite is no longer practiced in the Cahuenga Valley—for little boys.

Now come the Spaniards. They went up and down the land establishing missions. They were having wars all the time and some of the wars were fought right where Hollywood stands today. The battles were heroic. A typical engagement, the battle of Cahuenga Pass, was fought in 1845. The Mexican governor, Micheltorena, heard that a revolt was brewing in the Southland. He came marching down the coast with his army. The rebels moved up from San Diego and were joined by the total population of El Pueblo de Nuestra Senora la Reina de Los Angeles de Porciuncula (now L. A.). The rebel horde went out to meet the Governor's troops and did so at Cahuenga Pass. The historic site is now marked by an establishment serving ice-cream sodas made out of carrots, or spinach, or the juice of water cress. The artillery duel lasted for two long days and nights. Wives and children of the rebels stood on the hilltops and wept and wrung their hands as the guns boomed.

At the start of the third day of carnage Governor Micheltorena checked his casualties. They were:

Horses killed—1.
Mules wounded—1.

Micheltorena decided against further wanton sacrifice and capitulated. Thus ended Mexican rule in California. I think.

The missions converted the Indians—the ones they could catch with lassos. The Indians didn't want to be converted. They had a sneaking suspicion that the coming of the Mexicans had done them no great good. For one thing, they had to wear clothes and they didn't like that. For another, they began taking down with diseases which they didn't understand. The men got these diseases from the women, who got them from the soldiers and then tried to tell their husbands that they got them off toilets. The husbands didn't fall for the explanation because there *were* no toilets. It was the custom of the soldiers to ride around on their horses until they spotted an Indian lady they fancied. They would lasso her and practice the Rhythm system with her right there in public. The mission priests objected to such conduct and were always feuding with the military about it.

The technique of these soldiers calls for a digression because it reminds me of a story told by my friend Ben Serkowich. He said that out West when the earliest rodeos were organized the cowboys had an extra event known as corset-dogging. It was similar to bull-dogging or calf roping except that the cowboys didn't use horses. A young woman would be turned loose from a chute and she'd light out down the field. Then the cowboy contestant would be released from another chute. He'd tear out, on foot, in pursuit of the running woman, and he'd be carrying a corset. His job was to catch the woman, throw her to the turf, get the corset around her, and lace it. The cowboy who finished his corset-dogging in the best time won the contest. I'm skeptical about the whole thing. Ben Serkowich is an authority on Western lore by virtue of having said hello once to Buffalo Bill in an Omaha hotel. Buffalo Bill didn't answer him.

One history of Los Angeles takes up the conversion of the Indians in great detail. These Indians, as I've said, didn't want it because it meant going to work in the mission fields; also it meant being baptized, which was pretty close to taking a bath, and *that* was ignominious and degrading. The soldiers were given the job of going out and capturing converts, but the mission fathers sometimes joined in this pious work. The book tells about one priest who was a skilled horseman and expert with the lasso. He would come charging into the village, pick out an Indian with big muscles, lasso him, drag him back to the mission, "tie him and whip him into subjection, Christianize him and set him to work within an hour, then away for another without rest, such being his zeal for the conversion of infidels." It was also a custom to fetch in the little Indian children and baptize them and then hide them away in the mission. When the mothers arrived, pleading to get their kids back, they were

told that they could not see their children until they themselves submitted to baptism.

So, what with venereal diseases and one thing and another, the Indians died out.

Back in 1937 a mechanic named Jesse Zelda filed suit
against William Randolph Hearst asking $40,000 damages.
He complained that while he was repairing a truck on San
Simeon ranch an ostrich crept up to him, knocked him down,
and then stomped on him, rendering him unconscious. I
have never been to San Simeon but they say life there is
full of little surprises. I know a Hollywood writer who was
invited to spend a week end at the Hearst ranch. He drove
up the coast alone and was passed through the outer gates.
He had to drive quite a distance to reach the big house,
traveling over winding roads.

"It was wonderful," he said. "I went sailing along with the
top down and the scenery on every side was absolutely out
of this world. Then I turned a sharp corner and hit a camel."

This little accident would not have been so surprising to
him if he had known anything about the history of California. One of the first settlers in Hollywood was a man
named Greek George who arrived with a drove of camels
which he brought over from Smyrna. The United States
Government was then experimenting with camels for desert
transportation, but the scheme never worked out, and Greek
George found himself owner of a couple of dozen of the
animals. He was not a wastrel, this Greek George, and he
wasn't going to throw away some old camels just because
he couldn't figure out anything to do with them at the
moment, so he held onto them.

The scheme for camel caravans was launched by Jefferson
Davis when he was Secretary of War. A Lieutenant Beale
sold Davis on the idea, Beale being as gone on the subject
of camels as Woody Hockaday is gone on the subject of
feathers. Right up to his death this Lieutenant Beale drove
a team of camels around the California countryside, hitched
to a buckboard. He is said to have been, unwittingly, a great
force in the California temperance movement.

The project for camel caravans in the Western deserts might have been successful had it not been for the opposition of the mule men. It is ever thus. The mule breeders set up a tremendous fuss and launched whispering campaigns against the camels, saying among other things that the female camels did too much senseless traveling. So the camel people had to give up the battle and the camels were sold at auction. A man named McLeneghan bought a lot of them, took them to Los Angeles, and looked around for something to do with them. Along came old Greek George from Hollywood with his camels, offering to race the McLeneghan camels. Thus for a while camel races were a part of life in Los Angeles, and around the Spring Street hotels there were little gatherings of men called "camel players" who were dedicated to improving the breed of the dromedary and whose unchallenged leader was known as "Harry the Camel." There was much wagering at the camel track, particularly on "the daily hump" which involved picking the winners of the first and second races. The foundation of one of the greatest fortunes in southern California had its origin in a lowly saloonkeeper's shrewd selection of his "daily hump."

When interest in the sport abated, something had to be done with the camels, so they were shipped to Nevada for work around the mines. Somehow they didn't fit into this industry, so the miners got rid of them by simply shooing them off into the Mojave and Colorado deserts. They wandered around the desert wastes for many years and were responsible for occasional tall tales brought in by prospectors. Some of their descendants are quite likely still roaming the cactus land, destined someday to scare the britches off a geologist or a *Life* photographer. As late as the 1920s a camel appeared on the outskirts of Banning, California. The beast did so much damage and brought on so much nervous prostration among domestic livestock that the citizens finally got up a posse, went out after him, and shot him.

☆　　　☆　　　☆

We come now to The Curse of Lost Felix. This is a bit of history dealing with a part of Hollywood where I lived and did a lot of visiting. The region is accurately called the Los Feliz section after the Feliz family which gave its name to Los Feliz Boulevard. The Negro girls who work as servants in the district have corrupted the name, however, and say, "I'm goin' down to catch the bus on Lost Felix." Hence, to many residents of the neighborhood it has become Lost Felix.

It is a land with a dandy curse on it.

Don Antonio Feliz was the last of the line and died in 1863. His final illness was of a nature that made it impossible for him to speak. He had neglected to write a will and he was dying, so something had to be done about it. A lawyer was called in to supervise the job. He was a smart lawyer and he knew, among other things, that Don Antonio owned a tremendous chunk of property.

The dying man could not speak the phrases that he wanted in his will, but the lawyer figured out a device that would have the appearance of legality. The old man was propped up in bed. The lawyer had a neighbor in the room for the purpose of witnessing the procedure and taking down notes. The lawyer would address the dying man something like this: "You bequeath all the land to William Tecumseh Biggerstaff?" Don Antonio would nod his head, and the witness would write it down. Then the lawyer would ask if he bequeathed the house to William Tecumseh Biggerstaff. (I made up this name to represent the name of the lawyer himself.) Another nod of the head. The lawyer was sitting next to the bed, almost on top of the old man. He had a stick of wood fastened to Don Antonio's neck and each time he asked one of the questions he would waggle the stick and the head would nod and the bequest would be written down. When the business was finished, the old man died and the lawyer had become a man of property.

Now, Don Antonio had a niece named Petranella, which was considered a pretty name in those times but now sounds like something to squirt on mosquitoes. Petranella had been raised in his home and was all but a daughter to him, and it had always been understood that he was going to leave his entire estate to her. At the time of the stick-waggling fummadiddles she was away from home, but when she got

back and found out about the will she blew a gasket. She
marched out to the front porch and let go with The Curse
of Lost Felix. It was a dramatic thing, the way the history
books have it. She called down a curse on every person who
should ever come into possession of that property, or have
anything whatever to do with it. She decreed that the
crooked lawyer would soon come to rack and ruin, and he
did. She said that the cattle would all die, and they did.
She said that the crops would fail, and they did; that there
would be woe and death on the land for all time to come,
and there has been. She called down famines and murders
and suicides and conflagrations and floods and disease and
deformities and miscarriages and all manner of similiar
disasters. Down through the years Petranella's curse has been
upon that land, and just a few years ago, when fire swept
through a canyon there and burned up a lot of workmen,
the newspapers suggested that The Curse was functioning
again.

A charming character called Colonel Griffith J. Griffith
was the last man to own the blighted land all in one hunk.
Colonel Griffith was a cocky, fat little Welshman with curled
mustaches adorning a loud mouth. He arrived in Los Angeles
around 1882, and his eye fell on a young woman whose
family had a lot of money. He made little progress toward
winning her hand until he decided to try poetry. He engaged a hack writer who turned out a poem extolling Miss
Mary Mesmer, and he mesmerized Miss Mesmer by having
it printed in a local paper as a paid ad.

Before long Colonel Griffith had acquired the land of
Lost Felix and had become a power in the community. The
Curse didn't bother him for a long time, but when it got
him it got him good. One day in a Santa Monica hotel room
he handed his wife a prayer book and told her to get down
on her knees and get right with God. He told her he was
going to kill her because she and the Pope were plotting
against him, conspiring to catch him out on the street and
assassinate him. Then he shot out her left eye. His trial was
one of the great courtroom shows of the time and his chief
lawyer was the brilliant Earl Rogers. The prosecutor, in his
summation, made an acid remark to the jury that no rich

man was ever convicted for such behavior in southern California. That crack angered the jurors. They'd show him! For an act that was worse even than killing his wife, Colonel Griffith was sent to the penitentiary—for two years.

The Curse of Lost Felix gets them one way or another and its manifestations take on mysterious forms. There's the case of a man who was once a brilliant writer and public speaker. He took up residence in the Land of Lost Felix and, forthwith, a sort of palsy seized his tongue and nowadays he babbles nonsense. I refer of course to Mr. Rupert Hughes.

CHAPTER XX   *The Yuck from Yucca Street*

FRANK LLOYD WRIGHT once decided that Hollywood was an ideal spot for a home. The celebrated architect built himself a house on top of a bargain-basement mountain at the north edge of the town. In order to get to this house, unless you are a fool and prefer climbing, it is necessary to enter the side of the mountain, get into an elevator, and have yourself boosted to the top of the peak.

Mr. Wright moved into his home and examined his surroundings, giving particular attention to the caliber of his fellow citizens. At length he reached a conclusion and put it into words. I've not been able to find it anywhere in print but it was recited to me as follows:

"It is as though God had taken hold of the United States at the tip of Maine, just as a person might take hold of a handkerchief. He lifted that one corner and began shaking it, and all the unstable elements in the country were shaken loose and deposited down in the opposite corner. That is southern California."

Having reached this opinion, Mr. Wright forsook his home and moved away. The house is now among the goods and chattels of Fred Othman, who is able to find vast entertainment in the doings of his Hollywood neighbors.

☆   ☆   ☆

Southern California's regional literature is fascinating, and near the top of the required reading list is the Los Angeles Telephone Directory. It holds the interest. It is one of those books you can't put down, although at times there is a strong temptation to put it down with force on the head of some Chamber of Commerce executive. An American custom, common in large cities, requires certain business enterprises to make an effort to get their names listed at the very beginning of the phone book. The champion in Manhattan, for example, is the AAAAAA Ace Paper Box Corp. Six *A*'s and a word beginning with *A*. Los Angeles doesn't go in for such half measures. The first name in the L. A. book is: AAAAAAAAAAAA Alteration & Repair Co. Twelve *A*'s and a word beginning with *A*. In the Los Angeles directory the AAAAA Termite Control Co. barely managed to squeeze into fifth place.

One blustery afternoon I amused myself by leafing through the Los Angeles Classified Directory. Here are a few items I found:

Trixy of Los Angeles—abdominal supports.
Smith's Domino Parlor.
B-Glad Manor—an apartment house.
Fred Allen Body & Paint Shop.
Wise Men's Civic League.
Mission Village Motel—"most unique motel in California—$1.50 to $3.00—where you can meet movie stars—Erected by Robert E. Callahan, Noted Author."
Bakery Without a Name, on E. Florence Ave.
Cut 'n Curl Beauty Salon.
Pat's Powder Puff (evenings).
The Primp Shop.
Squirt Company, beverages.
Absolutely Reliable Bicycle Shop.
Be Married in the Wedding Manor—Appts on short notice by telephone with pipe organ, music, candles, flowers, and palms. The entire expense is $5.00 to a Bridal Pair alone or with 10 persons. With 11 to 30 persons, $10. With 31 to 100 persons, $15.
Borderline Cocktail Bar, on Tweedy Boulevard.
The Hangover—a Vine Street night club.
J. J. Roberts, Jr.—manufacturer of dog houses and dog beds; "Dude Ranch for Dogs" in Pasadena.
Paramount Pest Control Service—"Call Dr. Kilzum—His Patients All Die."
Zig-Zag Liquor Store, on Whittier Boulevard.

That's enough to give you an idea. Somewhere else I heard about an institution in Hollywood specializing in "custom-made uplift form-fitting brassières." I already knew that stuffing bubby socks is more common in Hollywood today than stuffing turkeys. I suspect that most girls there are militantly modest about where gents shall put their hands solely because the gents would quickly determine that mountains had been made out of molehills. A studio still photographer told me about a session with a glamorous actress. He wanted to get her in a series of sexy poses. She arrived for the sitting in a form-fitting gown, but the way he wanted to pose her, the bust was altogether inadequate. She was in a hurry to get away and had no time to go back for the reinforcements usually employed in such cases. The cameraman poked around his studio and found an old pair of nylon stockings. These were crammed in the proper vacancies and patted around until the required effect had been achieved. The photograph that resulted became extremely popular with the armed forces and was pinned up by the boys in far-off jungles and on shell-torn beachheads, causing many a lonely warrior to sit down and quietly bite tent stakes in half.

Here was a field I wanted to investigate, but I'm handicapped. I couldn't very well go to that brassière store and ask for a fitting, and I was inclined to be timid about barging in as a reporter. So I sent my wife—told her to go down to the place, get herself stylishly busted, and report back to me.

She said they really go about the thing scientifically and that the process is more complicated than filling a tooth, although they don't drill. In the first place, she figured they'd take some measurements and let it go at that. Not at all. She was told to strip to the waist. The lady engineer who handled her case then stood off and took sights on the issues involved.

"Petite," she finally said. "Yes, you are the petite type."

(I have spent two solid days in forceful argument getting the patient's permission to use the above-quoted diagnosis. I call it a major triumph.)

There were all sorts of posturings, such as bending over to let things hang, leaning backward to put muscle strain on the things, and so on, with much taking of notes, and then the blueprints were handed over to the construction department. My wife asked a good many questions in this haberdashery-for-knockers. She learned that padding is practiced

today almost as widely as shoe-wearing. At one point she took up the matter of her own classification as the "petite type" and said that this designation was not exactly flattering to her.

"Oh, my dear," said the lady, "you should never worry about that. You should see the parade of breasts that come through here. My dear, I have *two* customers who have *four* breasts each!"

My representative gasped in astonishment, but the lady declared her statement to be God's truth. In each case, she said, the four-mammaed customers were equipped with breasts occupying the time-honored positions. The spares grew out six inches below the normal pair. One of these fortunate women (or unfortunate, if you choose) was around thirty years old. All four of her breasts were of approximately the same size and they were not petite. She didn't give a damn beyond the fact that whenever she bought a brassière she had to have a special job. She couldn't very well go into a department store and say, "I'll take a Mabs Pliant-ease and while you're at it, sew a Hickory Perma-lift on the bottom of it."

"When she comes in for a fitting," said the expert, "we have to build her a bra that extends from the hips to the shoulders. It runs into money."

The other girl upon whom Nature bestowed bountiful gifts and then some is around eighteen years old. She is undergoing a series of treatments aimed at causing her lowers to recede without affecting her uppers. The treatment involves taking hormones, and the lady in the brassière plant says it is beginning to show results. If I were the doctor in such a case I believe I would hesitate before giving such a treatment. Nature can sometimes be unpredictable. The girl is given hormones and the duty of those hormones is to eliminate two of those four breasts. Hormones have no intelligence. You can't point to the two breasts you want done away with and expect a hormone to understand. I'd be afraid the hormones would go to work and wipe out the wrong udders—maybe take away the upper left and the lower right and leave the girl built on a bias.

But enough of such scientific matters.

During the early stages of my employment at Paramount I lived at the Hollywood Knickerbocker Hotel. Visitors to Hollywood who wish to put on a large front usually take up residence in one of the classy hotels in Beverly Hills, but the Knickerbocker has always suited me. My admiration for the establishment is shared by Dr. Rockwell, translator of the Kokomcar papers. Doc always stops at the Knickerbocker when he is in Hollywood, contributing to the establishment's daffy charm.

He is the world's champion faddist. If you remember the great days of vaudeville you remember Doc Rockwell. If your memory doesn't go back that far, I'll describe him. I'd like to pay him a compliment on his looks, but in the interests of unalloyed truth I am compelled to say that, with a little more meat on his bones and some fur growing out of his shoulders, he could make a living posing at the American Museum of Natural History in an exhibit called "Neanderthal Man at Bay."

Doc is the kind of man who always carries a large pocket knife with eighty or so attachments. He is forever fixing things. He makes his home in Maine now, being retired from show business. Once a year in New York we have what Fred Allen calls "man hog day." This is the day that Fred succeeds in luring Doc out of his hideaway in Maine, getting him down to Manhattan, and putting him on the Allen radio show as a guest performer.

In his time Doc has tried every religion known to man, and he has undertaken every diet he has ever heard about, plus a few he invented himself.

Once he kept himself for months on a diet consisting of raw vegetables and a beverage of his own devising called Vitafizz. This was a mixture of milk, lemon juice, and bicarbonate of soda. Alton Cook, who is one of Doc's close friends, went on an expedition with him to the end of Long Island during his Vitafizz phase. Alton and the others, when mealtime came, would repair to a restaurant. Doc would head for the A & P for his vegetables, milk, and lemon juice, return to the car, sit down on the running board, get out his knife, and go to work. Later on he decided that a diet of beer and green salads was the very thing a man needed, and he stayed with that one a long time. For several years waiters in the restaurants he frequented knew what was needed whenever Doc Rockwell sat down and called for "my chemicals." They'd bring him hot water, hot milk, and a saucer of after-dinner mints. He'd mix the milk and water, then stir in the mints and drink the thing off.

He is looked upon as a great man in the Maine community where he lives, for he is an authority on all fields of knowledge. He once tried to run a resort hotel. After buying the building he found out that the plumbing was in bad shape. He approached a local plumber and got an estimate on the job. The price suited him, so Doc told the plumber to go to work and install a completely new system. He didn't know that the plumber he picked had been drunk for twenty years, and he didn't go around to supervise the work. When he finally inspected the finished job he found that the drunken plumber had achieved effects that could have been exhibited at Coney Island for profit.

"He put in an international hookup," said Doc, "with pipes running across the middles of rooms and some of them sticking through the walls so that the building, from a distance, looked like a square porcupine."

Never daunted, Doc went to work himself, tore out all the plumbing and reinstalled it himself. Thus he learned about plumbing.

During this period he began experimenting with popcorn. He had a room filled with large glass jars containing popped corn, and he kept his experiments a secret. Finally he revealed that he had been trying to invent a popcorn laxative. It was not satisfactory. Caused constipation.

His resort hotel had barely started operations when it caught fire. Doc stood and watched the flames eating away his building.

"I don't care," he said. "The salt cellars were always getting plugged up."

He became an authority on fire insurance.

He has a big house now and there are always a series of experiments in progress. Doc may be taking up knitting, or geology, or color photography, or tea-leaf reading, or meteorology. Back in the days when he lived in New York he thought he might become a professional writer. He concluded that the best place to write was in the reading room of the New York Public Library. He'd go to the library every day, get a book, take it to one of the long tables, sit down, ignore the book, and try to write. One day, lacking a breath of inspiration for literary work, he picked up the book which he had chosen at random. He glanced at the first page and got interested and didn't leave until he had read it. It was a law book. He went back and ordered more law books. Now he knows law.

He is a sucker for a printing salesman. He can't resist having letterheads and calling cards printed. One letter head describes him as "Dr. Rockwell: Maker of Fine Cigar Ashes since 1889." Another identifies him as "Dr. Rockwell. The Happiest Man in the World." And one of his cards says, "Dr. Rockwell: Explorer. Discoveries Made at Reasonable Rates. I Furnish Own Bicycle."

He is proprietor of a small fishing boat, a rude, clumsy-looking craft in which he cruises rivers and channels along the Maine coast. The arrival in summertime of the gentry, with their expensive cruisers, has always been a source of irritation to Doc. He'd be chugging along through the channels when one of these shining vessels would come up behind him and swish past him, the haughty people on board giving him a glance of contempt. Doc fixed that. He installed an engine of tremendous power in his decrepit little boat. Nowadays in the summertime he finds great pleasure in his river cruises. The snobs in their swift cruisers come up behind him as he dawdles along. They approach him intending to pass him by. Quietly he puts on speed. He lets the lordly boat draw abreast of him. The dashing yachtsman, perplexed, believes for the moment that his own engine is misbehaving. Doc, at the throttle of his shabby tub, casts mild, condescending glances at the people on the cruiser. Then the pilot of the cruiser, deeply chagrined, puts on full speed. His boat begins to leap ahead, and Doc casually shoves over his own throttle. The little fishing boat all but takes off, shooting past the cruiser as though it had been fired out of a rifle. Doc derives much pleasure from this sport. He is unquestionably a great man. If you ever get an opportunity to meet him, don't miss it. He'll talk until your ears begin to flap like the wings of a wild duck, and he'll never utter a dull word.

One evening I was sitting in my room at the Knicker-bocker when I developed an urge to drink a couple gallons of beer. I telephoned downstairs for it, and in five or ten minutes one of the Filipino boys arrived. Unlike the other bellhops, he didn't knock. He simply walked in, confronted me, and said:

"My name iss Junior."

He was a handsome, cheerful little guy. A woman might be inclined to call him "cute," for which I would gladly slug her. He had some bottled beer on a tray but he didn't take it to the kitchenette where I had a refrigerator. He put the tray down and hopped over to the radio, switched it on, and when the music of a dance band burst from the speaker, he began leaping around the room like a Comanche Indian with snapping turtles in his loincloth.

"Junior iss jitterbug," he announced.

He was still smiling when he left, saying:

"When you call down, say Junior. I come quick."

From then on I did specify Junior when I called downstairs and he always came quick. I tipped him well, but I was repaid many times over by the service he gave me. And each time he came into my room he repeated that original performance, tuning in jazz music and executing his unique version of jitterbug dancing.

Whenever it came time for him to knock off work it was his custom to call at my room and find out if I needed anything. If I wanted a moose-meat sandwich on pumpernickel with scalloped edges, Junior would get it.

One day I asked him casually about the Philippines. Did he have relatives there? The smile faded from his face.

"Junior got one sister, one brother, one mother," he said. Tears came into his eyes and began flowing down his brown cheeks. He tried to smile, but it wouldn't work. "Jops got Pilippines now," he said. "Jops got Pilippines only little time. Junior go get Jops."

I didn't quite get what he meant.

"Junior in duck," he explained. "Monday I go take pizzical."

I realized then that Junior's elaborate cheerfulness had been a pose. He jitterbugged no more. He came as usual, even when he was not called, but he wasn't the happy Junior of the past. He knew that I knew what was going on inside him, and there was no use keeping up the pretense any longer.

One Sunday afternoon a soldier friend of mine named Ted Perkins came up from Wilmington and we were sitting in my room when Junior arrived. By now he seemed to take a proprietary interest in me, and the moment he saw Private Perkins he demanded: "Who iss this?"

I introduced Ted and Junior appeared to regain some of his old zip.

"Right dress!" he cried out. "Left face! At ease!"

Soon Private Perkins was putting the little guy through the paces of military drill. Junior knew it all and, by the testimony of my soldier friend, executed every movement perfectly. He then revealed that he had studied the drill and other military matters under a Filipino friend already in the Army.

He took his "pizzical" and passed it.

Then one morning I awoke to find Junior standing beside my bed. He was no longer in his green bellhopping uniform. He was in civilian clothes and he was smiling. When he saw that I was awake, he went to the radio and turned it on.

"Junior jitterbug!" he said, and he jitterbugged.

He came over and stuck out his hand.

"Well, Mr. Smiss, I go. In duck."

"You're inducted today?"

"Yess. Today I in duck. Good-by. Junior go get some Jops now."

Then he was gone, and I knew that I had lost a good friend. I never heard from him after that. I do know that a lot of boys got some Jops, and I'd almost bet money that some of them were got by Junior.

Castle Argyle doesn't stand within the territory of the old Rancho Los Feliz but it's right next door to the accursed acres. It is a white building seven stories high with a patio, a goldfish pool, and Donald MacBride.

The building is on a hill two blocks north of Hollywood Boulevard and one block over from Vine. This was my home during eight months of 1943. The apartment I occupied was on the top floor facing south with a little terrace. From this porch I could look down on the whole of Hollywood. Off to the left I could see Paramount, as well as RKO and Columbia. Given a little more fire-power than I possess I could have spit on the corner of Hollywood and Vine. Directly below me was Yucca Street, named after a screwball tree, and off to the right I could see the Goldwyn Studio, Grauman's Hoofprint, and the beginning of Beverly Hills. Sloping upward to the right of Castle Argyle is a hill covered with a profusion of foliage. This mass of greenery with occasional splashes of color made a pleasant prospect. There were trees and bushes of diversified sizes and shades. I could follow the practice of other authors and go into extensive detail about this flora, making out that I was observant and erudite, remarking, for example, that among the lovely items were hickory-nut trees and cinnamon and slippery ellum and cetera. I won't do it for two reasons. I don't care for that sort of padding, and if I did, I'd have had to go downstairs to find somebody who could tell me what kind of trees they actually were.

In its time Castle Argyle has been the home of many movie people before they got into the swimming-pool brackets. Gary Cooper and his parents lived there, and other tenants ranged from Fatty Arbuckle down to Clark Gable and William Bendix. Several actresses are now in residence at Castle Argyle, but I made the acquaintance of only one movie personality there—Donald MacBride. He is a character and a character actor who usually plays hard-boiled cops, judges, district attorneys, and the like. As is the case with most actors Mr. MacBride is a fine conversationalist and uses his face to advantage when telling a story. He and I had a regular date on Monday nights to attend the wrestling matches because the finest acting in all Hollywood may be seen there.

One night we witnessed a particularly fine demonstration of skillful wrestling. The two gentlemen of the main event were large and powerful athletes and the customers knew they just downright despised each other. One was a ferocious, clean-cut individual called Wild Red Barry, who wrestles largely with his fists and has a knack of seizing his opponents

and hurling them at Row F, Section 5, Upper Tier, Kindly
Refrain From Throwing Bottles at Performers. The other
was a dark-haired citizen named Tony Ross. Mr. Ross, when
he is not busy wrestling, leans on the ropes, faces the audience, and calls its members bad names, sometimes inviting
them up to have their spines cracked, sometimes spitting at
them, but always addressing them with remarks reflecting on
their ancestry and sex habits. It is his further pleasure when
he is at work to get his opponent on the floor and stamp
vigorously in said opponent's face.

Mr. MacBride and I usually got ringside seats so we could
be near an old gentleman who always had the same seat up
against the apron of the ring and who was always accompanied by a woman considerably younger than himself.
These two were the most enthusiastic of all the spectators.
The old man always had a heavy cane with him while the
woman carried a bulky handbag and usually had a pop bottle
in her hand. Whenever the wrestlers got themselves tied in a
sheepshank-with-granny knot near the edge of the ring where
these two citizens sat, they made haste to get themselves un-
tangled and away from there. The old man and the lady
always had their favorite among the performers, and they
were not above lending him a hand when they could reach
his opponent. I have seen the old guy leap to his feet and
whack a wrestler on the noggin with his cane until the
blows rang out like the dull bonging of Big Ben. If the
wrestler she despised got near the lady, even though he might
be bleeding in eight places, she would crawl halfway onto
the apron of the ring, pour Coca-Cola in his eyes, and then
whack him with the bottle.

The tête-à-tête involving Wild Red Barry and Tony Ross
was a lively affair full of pretty little surprises. The old man
and his lady favored Mr. Barry, diligently pounding Mr. Ross
on the head, face, and hands whenever opportunity afforded,
and Mr. Ross paid his customary tribute to them by quoting
from the works of D. H. Lawrence, James Joyce, myself,
and other great authors. At one point Mr. Ross demonstrated
his fine science by seizing Mr. Barry's ears and pounding Mr.
Barry's head against the ring post. Mr. Barry retaliated by
taking hold of Mr. Ross's fine head of hair with both hands

and swinging him around in a circle, accidentally letting go and sending Mr. Ross flying into Row D, Ringside, Kindly Don't Strike the Wrestlers as They Come Up the Aisles. Mr. Ross got to his feet, shook the cobwebs from his keen mind, spoke feelingly to the customers on whom he had landed, took a poke at one man who got in on a pass, went back into the ring, knocked the referee down, kicked him in the stomach to make sure he'd stay down, seized the long wooden box containing the championship belt, and began pounding Mr. Barry on the head with it. Mr. Barry retreated through an inch and a half of gore, pausing in his delaying action long enough to kick Mr. Ross in the groin. Mr. Ross howled as though someone had just given him a prophylactic with a brace and bit. He bent over double in his fine agony, whereupon Mr. Barry got a running start, jumped high in the air, and came down on Mr. Ross, mashing him to the floor, and to all appearances breaking his neck, pelvis, shoulder blades, and skull. This was the end of Mr. Ross, and as the half-crippled referee was counting him out the ringside lady gave him a farewell wallop with the Coca-Cola bottle. It said in the paper next day that Mr. Barry won the match with a four-figure scissors.

Mr. MacBride and I were quite pleased with this scientific demonstration put on by two superb, clean, sporting young athletes and made our way to the Brown Derby for some supper. Afterward we took a walk before climbing the hill to The Castle. We passed a little hotel and out of the entrance came Mr. Wild Red Barry and Mr. Tony Ross, chatting affably and leading a Pekinese dog on a leash. Darned if they hadn't made up!

Back in 1937 Mr. MacBride was one of the principal actors in the stage hit *Room Service*. This was his first major break in the acting business and led to his employment in Hollywood. *Room Service* had a long run, and Mr. Mac-Bride became a lively prospect for "the bite." He has explained at some length the technique of "the bite" as practiced on Broadway and he told me the story of a typical "bite" in the lush days of his *Room Service* run. I have a transcript of that narrative. Donald MacBride talking:

I had finished the matinee and was heading down Broadway, bound for the Lambs Club. The sidewalk was jammed with people and I had reached a point between 44th and 45th when this baby trapped me.

"Donnie!" That's what he yelled out. My own mother never called me Donnie. "Hello there, Donnie!" he sang out. He had closed in directly in front of me, so I couldn't get away. I said "Hello," though I had never seen the lug before in my life.

"Donnie, old boy!" he went on, grabbing me by the hand. "Imagine running into *you* just like this! I never expected to meet you like this, not now, Donnie, not now that you're *up* there. But let me tell you this, baby. It's grand. It's grand to tell you how we all feel about you. I've been intending to stop in at the theater and tell you, but it just seems that something always comes up.

"Donnie, it's a beautiful thing—a *beautiful* thing, to see something happen that you've always *wanted* to see happen. You know something? It's always the *stinkers* that get ahead. Always! You seldom see a *real* guy make it. God knows, Donnie, *you're* no stinker. We all know that! And another thing. Gettin' up there, that don't make a stinker a real guy. That only makes a bigger stinker out of him. Right? You're modest, Donnie. Modest like a God-damn flower! Yes sir, like a God-damn flower! I want to tell you, fella, your modesty is *refreshing!*"

I just stood there and took it. I nodded now and then, or mumbled something that didn't mean a thing. The crowds were flowing by on either side of us, but this baby went right on.

"Of course, Donnie, I wanted to come up to your dressing room and tell you. You musta thought I was a heel, now didn't you? You musta thought that if the piece had been a flop I'd have been around soon enough, to crow over you. But you know *me* better than that, baby. You know I haven't been around because of a good reason.

"You know of my loss, of course."

I shook my head. I didn't know of his loss. He bowed his head, but not long enough for me to get away. His eyes were wet. Then he says:

"I lost Flo. I thought you'd heard."

"Flo?" I said.

"Yes, of course. Don't tell me you didn't know. Don't tell me you didn't hear of that crushing blow. (A deep sigh.) Yep, Donnie, they musta needed Flo up there (a gesture toward Heaven) more than I needed her down here.

"All that suffering is over now, Donnie. You—you above all know what I went through. Night after night after night. No sleep. I was a nervous wreck. I'm not over it yet. It's been tough—tougher than even you could realize."

By this time I had my hand in the pocket where I kept the two dollars. That's the stabilized sum—two bucks, no war tax—and a man with any sense keeps it in a "bite pocket" ready for use.

"About Flo, Donnie. You know, I don't regret it one bit. When the time comes for me to go, when I take *my* curtain, and when I get up there (again the gesture) and meet the Guy with the Whiskers—listen, Donnie, I'm in the *red* with him! I'm *IN!*"

I was getting weary of it now. I'd been yelling my head off all afternoon on that stage and I was tired, and I wanted to get to the Lambs and a double martini. By this time I had the two bucks out of the bite pocket, hidden in my hand.

"From now on," the guy continued, "I'm coastin'. All I gotta do down here is keep my nose clean. The Guy with the Whiskers knows I've led a good life. He has Flo there with him, just waitin' for me. And Donnie—I've got my ticket in my pocket. The Old Guy knows that. Lemmy-take-two-bucks."

Voof! Just like that.

My hand came out and he took the money. He stood there, casually folding the two bills. I started to push by him. But he had one thing more to say. His entire attitude, now that he had the dough, had changed.

"Say, Don," he said. No more "Donnie" now. He was hard, authoritative, talking from the corner of his mouth. "Say, Don, I happened to catch your show the other night. Mind if I hand you a little piece of advice?"

"Not at all," I said.

"That part, baby. *Give it a little more guts!*"

CHAPTER XXI   *How to Play Stud Poker All Night*

I DON'T feel good today. The hell with writing anything.

CHAPTER XXII   *The Magnificent Splinter*

WHEN Paramount and I parted company as of Christmas Eve, Buddy DeSylva presented me with a special pass permitting me to wander at will through the studio, confuse producers and directors, demoralize the publicity department, and play the Word Game. I decided to stay in Hollywood for a couple of months longer.

For one thing I had become acquainted with a fine fellow named Edgar Bergen.

One day Margaret Ettinger took me up to her office above the Brown Derby, unlocked a drawer in her desk, and brought out a yellowing booklet. She let me examine it after warning that it was to be handled with extreme care. It was a paper-bound thing called *Herman's Wizard's Manual: Secrets of Magic, Black Art, Mind Reading and Ventriloquism, as Performed by All the Celebrated Professors of the World.* The first article in it is titled "How to Cut Your Arm Off Without Hurt or Danger." Others included: "To Make a Watch Stop, or Go at the Word of Command," "How to Turn Water into Wine," and "How to Cut a Man's Head Off and Put It into a Platter a Yard from His Body."

Miss Ettinger guards that little book as though it were the Kohinoor diamond, because it is the birth certificate of the most famous boy in the world. About thirty years ago a Michigan farm boy named Eddie Bergren saw an advertisement for this *Wizard's Manual,* sent in his two bits, and in due course received this very copy.

He applied himself to such paragraphs as this:

As a beginning the student should strain a little from the chest as if in pain, making a prolonged grunting sound in a high key.

Let the air escape slowly, keep the lips and teeth but slightly apart. Having tried this a few minutes, attempt to say such words as "Oh-oh, dear," "I say!" "Halloo!" et cetera, straining a little all the time.

That two-bit investment paid off on a grand scale. Today Edgar Bergen is one of the most popular and highest-paid entertainers in the world. The mocking, impertinent dunderhead he created—that devastating critic of our life and times denominated Charlie McCarthy—is celebrated from Hollywood Boulevard to the Burma Road.

I spent several afternoons and evenings at Bergen's home and hung around the guy while he was doing his radio work, and came away from it all with a vast admiration for him.

Because he has appeared in half a dozen movies Bergen, as an individual, is now known by sight to the public. In the early days of his success, however, he was no more than a name and a voice. I remember back five or six years ago when he arrived in New York on a train which also carried Dorothy Lamour and Don Ameche. I was down to meet the train as a reporter and several hundred yucks were jammed into the station concourse, where the cops strung ropes to keep them in check. The train pulled in, the fans broke through the ropes, and there was a beautiful bit of confusion on the platform alongside the train. Miss Lamour and Ameche were posing for press photographers and a publicity man shoved Bergen alongside the film stars. One of the cameramen let out a yell: "Git that lug outa there fer cry sake!" Bergen picked up a large black suitcase and started toward the station concourse just as the wave of hysterical fans burst upon the platform, screaming for Charlie McCarthy. They almost knocked Bergen down as he pushed his way into the concourse and quietly sought a taxi. His suitcase contained the arrangement of wood and gadgetry which constitutes McCarthy. Nobody recognized him.

Because he has always subordinated his personality in favor of Charlie, few people understand Bergen. His intimate friends know him for an amiable, entertaining, sweet-tempered man, a fine host, and a one-man hobby lobby. He is genuinely shy and generally self-conscious among strangers, and when he is without Charlie McCarthy he is not especially funny. It is not uncommon for him to arrive at a party and find himself all but ignored because he hasn't brought along his dummy. Almost everybody regards him simply as a straight man for Charlie.

Rehearsing his radio program in private, one might assume that he would leave the dummy in the bag, reading his own lines and Charlie's lines and letting it go at that. It is altogether necessary, however, that he have McCarthy perched at his side; otherwise, his producers say, his delivery is flat and uninspired. The moment Charlie is alongside him the lines seem to take on sparkle and zip.

Nothing irritates Bergen more than a ventriloquist who talks about the innards of his dummy—who permits photographers to take pictures of nude dummies, revealing their mechanical workings. His own attitude toward Charlie is distinctly that of a fond parent toward a boy of twelve.

On stage Bergen usually works with two dummies, McCarthy and that grotesque goon, Mortimer Snerd, whose human counterpart may be found in large number around the stage doors of broadcasting studios with autograph books in their hands. Most ventriloquists of the past have worked with two or more dummies. Finishing with one, they would customarily drop it to the floor and pick up another. Bergen realizes that an animated jaw-wagging dummy in hand can be made to appear alive, but if that same dummy is tossed on the floor it becomes a lifeless pile of junk. Whenever McCarthy and Snerd are in view, they are talking or gawking around. A few feet to his right on the stage Bergen always has a low, curtained cabinet. Comes time for the appearance of McCarthy. Bergen walks behind the screen, his head in view, his manner eager and expectant. Charlie begins talking before he is even seen. He might yell, "Berr-r-r-rgen! Git me outa this foul rattrap!" Charlie is carried to a tall stool before the microphone. Bergen doesn't rest the dummy on his knee. The stool brings Charlie's head to the same level as Bergen's and they talk, so to speak, as man to man. Even cynics in the audience have difficulty, after a minute or so, remembering that McCarthy's voice is the voice of Bergen.

The illusion that Charlie is an actual flesh-and-blood being has been demonstrated many times but never more tellingly than on the day Bergen was given his first chance in radio. Back in 1936 he was auditioned as a possible guest performer on the Rudy Vallee show. One advertising-agency executive scoffed and snorted at the idea of putting a ventriloquist on the air. This man was in a position to scuttle the deal but someone talked him into attending the audition. He sat in the studio control room passing sarcasms and making things generally tough for the nervous Bergen. The ventriloquist had prepared a script for the audition but he wasn't using it, having memorized the lines. He started off, exchanging quips with Charlie, and the executive in the control room grew more derisive. Suddenly Bergen fumbled. He had forgotten the next line. The scoffer, of course, haw-hawed and I-told-you-soed. A young man hurried over to Bergen with the script in hand. He held it in front of Bergen's eyes and Bergen quickly scanned the forgotten line. "Okay," he said, "I've got it now." The young man started to move away when Charlie McCarthy stopped him. "Hey!" piped Charlie. "Let *me* have a gander at that." The young man turned and unwittingly thrust the script in front of the dummy's face. The sneer disappeared from the puss of the man in the control room and he simply muttered, "Well I'll be damned!" Bergen and McCarthy were on their way.

Where Bergen is inclined toward bashfulness in the presence of strangers, his wooden alter ego serves him well as a release from his shyness. Bergen is the very acme of gentle, polite deportment, but Charlie seldom pulls a punch. He has ridiculed and insulted most of the great names in show business, privately as well as on the radio. During the production of a Bergen movie, for example, Charlie talks almost incessantly between scenes. Bergen, as Bergen, never criticizes directors or other members of the company. Charlie takes care of all such complaints. The dummy tells them off in devastating language employing gutter terminology that would shock a racker in a poolroom. A mild complaint from Charlie might be: "How long does this lard-head expect us to keep working? It's time to go home and by God I'm a-goin'!" He violates studio ethics right and left while Bergen stares blandly off scene.

Once they were rehearsing a shot in which Bergen and

McCarthy were perched on stools at a soda fountain. Next to Charlie sat a beautiful young woman wearing a gown cut so low that, had she bent over, her shins would have been showing. Bergen glanced at this startling vista and, like the gentleman he is, modestly averted his eyes. Not Charlie. That young man glanced, too, then leaned forward, almost crawling onto the counter, took a good long look, straightened up, flopped back on the stool, opened his mouth, and said: "Yeeeeeeeeeeeeeow! I'm hungry!" The young lady couldn't very well slap a chunk of wood.

Bergen's home is a beautiful nine-room house on top of a Beverly Hills mountain. The house is built around a large patio complete with barbecue pit, flourishing magnolia tree, and a wooden horse for Charlie when he is in a mood to

punch cows. Most of the rooms open on the patio including Charlie's own suite. The patio door leading to Master Mc-Carthy's quarters is decorated with a knocker in the shape of a woodpecker—a gift from Greer Garson. Charlie has a large bedroom, an oversize closet, and a bathroom. The latter serves as powder room for the ladies whenever Bergen has a party at his home. Charlie has been known to utter bitter, resentful remarks about this feminine intrusion on his privacy. He is usually sitting up in bed and he'll watch the girls entering and leaving his bathroom. Then, on occasion, he'll shock them by coming suddenly to life and screaming at them to get the hell out of his can, and if they can't find any place else to go, to use the back yard.

In the closet and the large dresser are the McCarthy habiliments. He has a bigger wardrobe than Bergen. There's a complete fire-chief outfit, a cowboy suit, Foreign Legion uniform, baseball suit, jockey silks, Mexican fiesta costume, an Eskimo ensemble, and various uniforms reflecting his honorary membership in the military. There are Stetson hats of all types, sweaters and sweat shirts, snazzy sports clothes, and full-dress rig. Charlie is equipped for every occasion.

On a table among many gifts sent to him from all over the world stands the special Oscar awarded Charlie in 1937 —a wooden duplicate of the statuettes handed out each year by the Academy. Charlie's is the only talking Oscar ever awarded. Bergen picks up the figure, holding it by the base, and its tiny lower jaw moves as it cries in a thin, high voice: "Put me down, you big ungainly jerk! I belong to Charlie McCarthy!" Also on the table is Charlie's first invention—a pea shooter with telescopic sight.

McCarthy's personal library stands on his desk and includes the *Boy Scout Handbook, Letters to Strongheart, How to Fly,* Emily Post's *Etiquette, A Modern Handbook for Boys,* and a thin volume called *How to Be a Ventriloquist,* by Edgar Bergen. Lying on the desk is a sheet of paper covered with a childish scrawl in pencil. It says:

Dear Techur:
    Please excuse Charlie McCarthy for being absent from school yesterday because he had a bad attact of ~~larin lorayng~~ larengytis.

                                    Yours truley
                                    Mister Bergen

Bergen's home is a five-minute drive from Sunset Boulevard yet the house occupies a lonely eminence commanding a panoramic view which stretches from Los Angeles City Hall to the Pacific Ocean. The first time Bergen drove me up Benedict Canyon he put himself into the character of a rubberneck bus driver in order to identify his neighbors. His routine went something like this:

"On the right we have the new home of lovely Kay Francis. Now, look off to the left and you see the magnificent estate of Charles Boyer, Great Lover, French style. Beyond that is the lonely abode of Katharine Hepburn. Ahead in the distance may be seen the old John Gilbert place—another Great Lover. It is now the home of Miriam Hopkins. On the left, way ahead there, is Falcon's Lair—home of Valentino, still another Great Lover. Yonder is the King Vidor residence, and the house with the blue tile roof was the honeymoon home of Lana Turner and Artie Shaw. Off to the right here is the home of Mister Nash of Nash automobiles. And here before our eyes is the John Barrymore place—Great Lover on the screen, Great Lover in real life. Now we negotiate this turn past the Barrymore garage and . . . Watch carefully! Here! You are now gazing upon Bellevista—home of the Greatest of the Great Lovers—Edgar Bergen!"

Since his mother's death in 1943 Bergen lives alone with a housekeeper and a versatile fellow named Bill who drives his car, takes care of the grounds, raises chickens, beats off coyotes who come to get the chickens, supervises the barbecues, and keeps the swimming pool in shape. Most frequent visitors are Bergen's writers, and most of the weekly broadcasts are put together in his den.

He did his own writing in the first years of his radio success, then the pressure of increased activity became too much for him and he began hiring gag men. One of his first writers was Ukie Sherin, better known these days as stooge to Bing Crosby. Ukie, according to Bergen, had a unique theory about writing comedy for radio. He'd show up on schedule at Bergen's home without a line on paper. He thought his job was to make Bergen laugh; he didn't seem to be concerned about the radio audience. If he could get a howl out of Bergen, he figured he had earned his pay. Thus each time he came to the house he'd tell a few moss-backed jokes, then suddenly hurl himself into the swimming pool with all his clothes on. This performance always got a laugh from Bergen but contributed nothing whatever to the radio show.

Bergen's chief hobby is flying. Deprived of that recreation by the war he rides, swims, plays tennis and golf, and goes for long walks in the hills around his home. He tinkers in his workshop, cooks Mexican dishes, and attends regular meetings of Los Magicos Society, where he and other amateur magicians show off before one another. At Indio, California, he has a fifty-acre ranch devoted mainly to date palms and alfalfa. He is a member of the Society of Cinematographers and has made a color film of Hollywood sights—a picture he has shown to thousands of homesick servicemen in Alaska, the Aleutians, and Newfoundland. His reading is mainly in scientific fields. He studied medicine briefly at Northwestern University and he has investigated chiropractic. His interest in this subject is responsible for a disconcerting habit. Where other people crack their knuckles, Bergen cracks his neck.

Once he hired a new writer who came to his house for the first conference. Bergen, sitting opposite him, suddenly took hold of his own head with both hands, gave it a sideways jerk, and a loud, bony crack sounded in the room.

The writer gazed at his new employer for a moment, stood up, and said: "Well, so long, Mr. Bergen. I quit."

Recalling the incident, Bergen comments: "I was merely giving myself a simple adjustment. The guy should have known that every Swede is a masseur at heart."

Bergen is one of the neatest, most orderly men alive—a perfectionist in everything he undertakes. In his workshop adjoining the house there's a place for everything and everything in its place. The jars of bolts and nuts and nails look as though they had been packed by Fanny Farmer. He loves to tinker in this little shop where he keeps spare bodies for Charlie and where in the last few years he has continued to improve the mechanics of the dummy. Charlie can now walk quite realistically when led by the hand. He can stand alone, hold a spoon or pen, and before long he should be able to kick girls who trespass in his bathroom. Among other gadgets to be found in the workroom is an electric ant trap which Bergen invented. He has been inventing things since boyhood and can remember, back on the Michigan farm, trying to devise a mechanical strawberry picker.

He doesn't have to be coaxed into adopting new hobbies. One week his radio script called for a comedy sequence in which Charlie became a beekeeper, using Bergen's top hat for a hive. Bergen, the perfectionist, undertook some research on bees to insure scientific accuracy in the script. He sat up all night reading bee books and the following day ordered a colony for himself. He still has them.

Bergen is a first-rate host. Dull moments don't exist when he's having guests. Everyone, of course, wants to inspect Charlie's quarters. Bergen also enjoys showing off the rest of his house and grounds. His theater is a soundproof room containing comfortable chairs and sofas, a projection room at one end and a small stage at the other. Back of the stage is a bar. The films he shows include some of his own making and a collection of old silent pictures. He acquired most of John Barrymore's silent films from the actor's own collection.

He indulges his ventriloquial talent often without a dummy. One evening we were in his little theater looking at Lon Chaney in *The Phantom of the Opera*. Around midnight I suggested it was time to go home.

"Just a minute," said Bergen. He went to a wall phone, took down the receiver, and a far-off telephonic voice was heard saying:

"Yes, Mr. Bergen."

"Get my car out," ordered Bergen.

"Why?" came the voice.

"Listen, you numskull, I'm driving downtown."

"Is that guy Smith still around?" asked the voice.

"Yes, he's here."

"Well, tell the son of a bitch to go home!"

On another occasion we were standing in the wide driveway before the house. Bergen's Doberman pinscher was at his side. I looked at the dog and asked its age. Bergen said he wasn't sure. He reached down and took the dog's upper jaw in his hand.

"Pupchkin," he said, "tell the man how old you are."

Then he wagged the dog's jaw and the dog said gruffly, "I'm . . . four . . . years . . . old."

A hundred yards down the hill from Bergen's house is the garage belonging to the Tower Road estate of the late John Barrymore. The walled-in estate itself is directly across the road from Bergen. Barrymore's fondness for animals and birds and the strong affection these creatures always had for him has been adequately described by Gene Fowler. Pupchkin loved the actor and made a practice of hanging around the garage, waiting for his friend to come home. The garage is still there, surmounted by a weather vane representing Ahab coming to grips with Moby Dick, and though Barrymore has been dead for two years now, Pupchkin keeps her vigil. She trots down the road late each afternoon and stands by the garage doors, waiting.

The neighborhood was a bit livelier in the time of Barrymore.

"He was a lonely man in his last years," says Bergen. "He'd come to visit me now and then. He'd come up this little stretch of road and I'd know it was Jack because my dog would be out yelping for joy. Usually he'd come to visit me because someone at his house wouldn't give him any more to drink. He'd never ask me for a drink, but I think he did some of his greatest acting just glancing significantly at my bar. I'd accommodate him, but I never would give him much, and we'd sit here by the hour and talk. You've heard about the peculiar tricks his memory played him. He could talk brilliantly about things that happened thirty years ago, but he didn't know what day it was."

Having always admired John Barrymore, I was interested in his last and favorite home. When I found out that Bergen had the keys to the place I asked him if I might look it over. We crossed the road, unlocked the gate, and entered. It was like going to a funeral. The entire establishment occupies just a few acres, yet there are sixteen different structures containing more than fifty rooms, several pools, a bowling green, fountains, and a skeet range among other things. At the top of the property near the swimming pool is the biggest totem pole I ever saw. Down below Bergen pointed out a tall, grotesque-looking tree with a single skimpy branch sticking out near the top. Barrymore was accustomed to sit in one of the courts and shoot the limbs off this tree with an elephant gun. We went up the iron stairs into the tower which served him as hideaway—a circular room he could enter by way of a trapdoor. There was no way of getting him out short of dynamiting.

The two or three hours we spent roaming through the empty buildings, most of them falling to pieces for want of attention, were among the most pleasantly depressing I spent in Hollywood. When we got back to Bergen's house he excused himself, went to another room, and when he came back handed me a book.

"You liked Barrymore," he said. "Here's a book out of his library and you can have it if you want it. He liked it."

At first I didn't notice the name of the book, being so pleased at getting a volume that belonged to The Monster. Then I turned it over and saw it was *Low Man on a Totem Pole*. Inside the front cover was his bookplate and on the opposite page he had written his name and address. He had read it with a pencil at hand and had marked passages here and there, underlining, or placing exclamation points in the margins. All of the passages he had marked were irreverent.

CHAPTER XXIII *Notes on a Swan-Hater*

THEY GAVE A DINNER not so long ago to honor W. C. Fields for having finished out forty years in show business. The speakers started speaking in the middle of the green beans and the gooey sentiment was passed around in washtubs. Orators such as Eddie Cantor and George Jessel stood up and talked and let the tears flow down their cheeks until it was almost necessary to club them to the floor in order to stop them. Why they call those weepers comedians is one of the larger mysteries of life. There were other recitations, long and dull, and it was coming along toward two or three o'clock in the morning. The newspapermen were fidgeting and squirming and yawning and now and then gulping water to avoid heaving up their leg of lamb with mint sauce.

At last the toastmaster struggled to his feet. Everyone

uttered a quiet prayer, hopeful that this time he would dismiss the class. He didn't.

"And now," he said, "just one more speaker and we'll call it a night. It is my pleasure, gentlemen, to present you with Dr. Leo C. Rosten, who has a few remarks."

The newspapermen groaned. A doctor yet! Probably a professor ready to give a paper on "The Anatomy of the Belly Laugh." Dr. Rosten was not known to them at that time as the genius who, among other brilliant achievements, had given the world the incomparable H*Y*M*A*N K*A*P*L*A*N.

He stood up and said:

"It is my opinion that any man who hates dogs and little children can't be *all* bad."

Then he sat down, and the newspapermen emerged from their torpor and cheered him as if he had just announced the death of Hitler.

I believe it to be true that W. C. Fields actually hates dogs and little children. In one of his pictures where he played the part of a pitchman, a little child was pestering him, interfering with his spiel. Mr. Fields was supposed to keep trying to push the child away with his hand. Instead of that he kicked the brat in the face.

The first time the Quiz Kids were taken to Hollywood they were asked to enumerate the three things they most wanted to see. They listed the La Brea pits, Griffith Park, and W. C. Fields. It required some powerful argument to get Mr. Fields to agree. He said he would permit the kids to visit his home briefly provided they were "all encased in tiny strait jackets." This stipulation was beaten down by the publicity men and the day came for the visit.

Mr. Fields sulked in his office while the kids were shown over his grounds. Then Gerard Darrow crept into the room.

"Mr. Fields," he said timidly.

"Yaaaasssss," said Mr. Fields. "What is it, my little touch of bubonic plague?"

"Could I have a glass of water, please?"

Mr. Fields looked at Gerard for a long time. He rubbed his hand over his face and stared at the ceiling.

"Water?" he said. "Let me see, now. Water. Water. Oh,

yass. Bleeeeve I have heard of the stuff. They told me some of it fell on the property here one night. 'Bout a glass full. Ran right off. No, my boy, I regret to say I cannot satisfy your desires. Haven't got any. Now, I could fix you up with a nice scotch and soda . . .'"

Gene Fowler is one of Mr. Fields's close friends and tells about the time the comedian was in the hospital with a broken neck, a bothersome thing at best. Mr. Fields refused to obey most of the regulations governing the conduct of patients with broken necks. He insisted on having a pitcher of martinis at his side all the time, declaring that while his neck might be broken, his gullet wasn't. One afternoon the nurse left him alone for a while and during her absence he got out of bed, martini in hand, and strolled over to a window, exercising caution in holding his head so it wouldn't fall off. Outside the window he saw a big tree and in the tree were some little men busily engaged in screwing light bulbs into the branches. Mr. Fields quickly turned and went back to his bed. He poured his martini back into the pitcher, got into bed, and began buzzing furiously for the nurse. When she came in he was lying there with his eyes tightly closed.

"Nurse," he said weakly, "please go over and look out that window."

The nurse obeyed.

"Are you at the window now?" asked Mr. Fields, his eyes still closed. "Look out and tell me what you see."

"Well," she said, "there's a big tree out there and in it are some little men screwing light bulbs into the branches."

"Allah akbar!" said Mr. Fields. "Pour me a drink, quick."

He had forgotten that it was coming up Christmas.

There's another Fields Christmas story I picked up at Paramount. The studio has a locksmith on the grounds and one Christmas Eve this gentleman's phone rang. It was Mr. Fields, screaming hysterically for help. The locksmith hurried over to the Fields dressing room and found the comedian pacing the floor and wringing his hands.

"I have murdered my best friend!" he cried. He pointed to the door of a closet. "He's in there—smothering to death! In God's name, varlet, do something about it!"

The locksmith found a key broken off in the lock.

"I swear before God it was an accident!" cried Mr. Fields. "Oh, my good dear friend! Hurry, hurry, hurry! If he dies I'll kill myself!"

He wept and groaned and held his head in his hands and the locksmith was genuinely alarmed. He went to work quickly and in short order swung open the closet door. Mr. Fields's manner changed at once.

"Thank you, my good man," he said, and stepping into the closet, began carrying out bottles. "You have saved my life. I have my entire stock of Christmas booze in here. A small snort for you?"

When Paul Jones telephoned Mr. Fields at my request and told him I'd like to call, I was in Paul's office and could hear the comedian's voice over the phone.

"You know him," said Mr. Jones. "The fellow who wrote *Low Man on a Totem Pole* and *Life in a Putty Knife Factory.*"

"Never heard of the son of a bitch," came the Fields reply. "Tell him to come over anyway. I'm lonesome. Tell him I read one of his books and I'm halfway through the other one. Tell him I'm one of his greatest admirers."

When the phone conversation was finished Mr. Jones said:

"Bill's dying to see you. He's read one of your books and he's halfway through the other one. Says he's one of your greatest admirers. Go on over there tomorrow."

Mr. Fields lives in the accursed land of Lost Felix. He rents a huge, beautiful house across the way from Cecil B. DeMille's home. From the road I walked through a long colonnade and pressed a button at the front door.

I jumped like a goosed archimandrite when the door spoke to me.

"Whadda you want!" it said. I located a small screen, covering a loud-speaker, and told it who I was. The door clicked open and I walked into a large foyer. Off to the left was the living room. This was a room of baronial proportions —beautiful walls and drapes, a room almost big enough for skeet-shooting. The furnishings in this splendid drawing room were quietly simple. In the center stood a pool table and around the walls were tall stools with chromium legs. The "string" for keeping score was stretched across the recessed part of the huge fireplace. Mr. Fields favors pool and billiards, he says, because the table breaks his fall.

No guide was needed to locate the Master, for his voice was turned on. I got on the beam of it, went up a flight of stairs, and walked into his office. He was sitting behind a desk, which he uses to hold up highball glasses. He stood up and held out his hand as I approached and said without punctuation:

"Glad to see ya have a snort."

A young woman came into the room and Mr. Fields introduced her as his pick-up girl. Said she picks him up when he falls. She went across the room to the bar and fixed him a fresh drink and got me a bottle of beer.

What followed was a lovely afternoon. I took no notes and asked few questions. It is difficult to put Mr. Fields's discourses into print, retaining their full, pristine flavor. The thing can be done with Jimmy Durante, but the alphabet we use is feeble and altogether inadequate when it comes to recording the ebb and flow of Fieldsian accents.

"All tired out," he drawled. "Been over wrasslin' a bear. Fella over at United Artists called me in. Got these two bears, with a trainer. Says I've got to wrassle one of the uncivilized beasts for the still pictures. Not me. I says to him, 'George, I'm a physical coward. Tremble even in the presence of small birds and angleworms. Don't mind admitting it. If it ever becomes necessary for me to wrassle a bear, I retire from the cinema. I leave the damned picture business to rot in its own evil pollution.' But George was a persuasive man. He told me how tame the bears were. Wouldn't harm anybody. No danger at all. I'm about to become convinced. Then one of these nasty beasts raises up, hauls back his right arm, and takes a swipe at his trainer. Had long fingernails, too, that bear. So I say, 'That will be all, boys. Muh coat and hat, if you please.' They grabbed me and said I couldn't walk out on them, said they had to get the still pictures. So they dressed up a human in a bear suit. A powerful-built fella. I took one look at him and I said, 'Why, I'm more frightened of you than I am of the bears.' He promised not to fracture any parts or portions of me, and we got the pictures. A very trying experience. Very."

The telephone rang and Mr. Fields told someone to come right over.

"Greg La Cava," he said. "Old drinking companion of mine. Says he's thirsty."

Soon Mr. La Cava, a producer-director who could be called a genius except for the fact that Orson Welles has debased the term, was with us. He and Mr. Fields began reminiscing. The young lady got up from the desk at the side of the room and fixed fresh drinks.

"They hate the two of us over at Dave Chasen's," said Mr. Fields. "Everyone shudders when we enter. Strong men quake when La Cava and Fields walk in. Others mutter soft prayers to their Maker and there are occasional faintings. Important men in our community lurch to their feet and stagger out, taking their wives to shelter."

For years these two men have played golf together. Mr. Fields dearly loves to rattle and distract Mr. La Cava on the tee. As Mr. La Cava addresses the ball, Mr. Fields will take up a position immediately behind him, making just enough noise to let his presence there be known. Mr. La Cava will say:

"Listen, you son of a dog, get the hell out from behind me."

Mr. Fields moves a few feet. He waits until Mr. La Cava has started the backward swing preceding his drive. Then he speaks up timidly:

"Is this all right?"

Invariably the remark spoils the shot and Mr. La Cava fouls up the welkin with improper wordage. Once they were playing for $100 a hole and Mr. La Cava got so furious that he played fourteen holes without using a club—simply *kicked* the ball around the course. When it was over he was still fuming and Mr. Fields, thinking perhaps that he *had* been in the wrong and noting that Mr. La Cava owed him $1,700, suggested:

"Listen, Greg, as far as the money is concerned, we won't count this one. I don't want your money."

This attempt at placation brought a horrendous scream from Mr. La Cava.

"God damn you!" he roared. "You cheap, petty, two-bit crook! You'll take my money and like it! I've got more money than you ever heard of, you filthy heel!" He whipped out a checkbook and began writing furiously, never once halting his bitter flow of invective.

"That check is now a museum piece," said Mr. Fields. "I still have it. The greatest handwriting experts in the country have been unable to figure it out."

One day they were on the green, cursing each other with customary vividness, and they failed to notice the arrival of two other golfers—both priests. Mr. Fields saw them first.

"Father," he said to one of them, "I beg your pardon."

"I know just how you feel," said the priest.

They played the rest of the way around with the padres, who proved to be fine company, and when the match was over invited their new friends to dine with them.

"We took them to Chasen's," said Mr. La Cava. "There was greater consternation than usual when we walked in with two priests. We made our way to a booth. Nobody believed they were real priests. A well-known Hollywood Irishman came around to the booth and started cursing us. He said they had put up with a lot in the past, that they had been tolerant of our behavior up to now, but that this was the last straw. He said, 'For you two bums to go out and dress up a couple of extras as priests of the Church and bring them in here is too much for me to swallow. You are a pair of —— ——' The Irishman gave it to us with all the stops out. And Bill kept turning to the priest at his side and saying, 'Father, I don't understand this. The man is psychopathic, I presume.' When it finally dawned on the Irishman that the priests were genuine, he damn near got to his knees apologizing."

Mr. Fields showed me the rest of the wing where he spends most of his time. The office is a large room and among other things has a blackboard on the wall where Mr. Fields chalks down appointments. The day I was there the notation was: "Stay home and meditate on the follies of humankind. P.S. Get stiff."

Next to this office is a large chamber containing a steam cabinet, a rubbing table, a barber chair, and a huge refrigerator stocked with beer. The barber chair has an interesting history.

"Went on the wagon once," said Mr. Fields. "Only time I ever have the d.t.'s is when I go on the wagon. Go two days without liquor and I begin to see things. Really see snakes. Only difference between my snakes and other people's snakes is that my snakes come at me with revolvers and baseball bats. Time I was on the wagon I couldn't sleep.

Tossed all night. Took pills, but it didn't do any good. Then I remembered something. Remembered that every time in my life I ever got into a barber chair I fell asleep like a little baby. Bought me this barber chair. Slept in it every night."

Back in the office Mr. La Cava told about the time Mr. Fields lived in the vicinity of Toluca Lake. He wandered off one afternoon and they finally found him on the shore of the lake. In one hand he had a bottle and in the other a black-snake whip. He was quietly lashing at a swan.

"The bastard hisses at me," he explained. "Hisses at me every time I come down here seeking solitude. Can't stand to be hissed at."

I interrupted the pleasant crackling informality of the

talk to ask one question. Would Mr. Fields describe his daily
routine?

"Muh daily routine," he began. "Days when I'm not working, get up between eight-thirty and nine, or nine and nine-
thirty, or nine-thirty and ten, somewhere around there. Have
breakfast. Always breakfast on fruit."

Mr. La Cava interrupted.

"You bulbous-nosed liar!" he said. "Tell the truth. You
know you breakfast on martinis."

Mr. Fields had been talking to and looking at me. He
paused, and his face froze into an expression of painful
distaste. Slowly he turned his head and looked at Mr. La
Cava.

"SHUT UP!" he roared. "The son of a bitch is from the
prasssss!"

He turned back and continued the story.

"Have muh breakfast, just as I said. Then I have six or
eight double martinis, depending on how I'm feeling. Seems
to be an idea knocking around that I'm a drinking man. A
misconception and a gross canard. Why, I'll take oath that
sometimes I go till twelve o'clock noon before I have a drink."

"That," Mr. La Cava interrupted again, "is on the days
when you don't wake up till a quarter to twelve."

Mr. Fields didn't deign to turn his head this time. He
wrinkled his nose as though he smelled something rotten,
and spoke without looking at his friend.

"I ignore you," he said. "I keep my face turned away from
you, so I will not forget that I am a gentleman and spit all
over you. Now, where was I? Oh yassssss. After breakfast I
come upstairs and look at muh desk. Want to see if it's still
here. It always is. Then it's time for lunch. Always drink
muh lunch. Immediately after lunch I have a martini. Back
to the office then, back to the drudgery."

He stopped talking for half a minute, reached around to
a ledge behind him and came up with a revolver. He laid it
down on the desk before him, then turned slowly and gave
Mr. La Cava a significant look.

"Do muh serious drinking in the afternoon," he resumed.
"Never kept a record of it. Always believe in conserving
paper. When dinner's ready, they come and pry muh head up

off the desk. Always eat dinner. That is to say, eat a little dinner, and then have a brandy."

"Just the one brandy?" I asked.

"Good God!" he exclaimed. "Are you mad? Have bottles and bottles of it. Please don't get the idea I'm overfond of liquor. I only drink the stuff when I have the desire to drink it. Nobody has ever seen me stagger. After all, I have my canes."

Again he reached behind him and this time came up with a pair of canes. He stood up, a cane in each hand, and leaned on them, and then started walking, bent forward, supporting himself with the canes.

"This," he said, "is the method I use in going to bed. If someone is kind and thoughtful, considerate of muh health and well-being, they hang these canes within reach wherever I happen to be sitting in the evening. Pegs all over the house for them. With these two canes, walking like this, I am sometimes able to get into the bedroom and into bed without falling down. If I cannot find the canes, if I don't have the strength to grasp them, or if I can't see them, I am lost, and I sometimes drop like a stunned ox and remain there until this young lady arrives in the morning and unfastens me from the floor."

Thus his description of the daily routine on days when he is not working. What about work days?

"Please don't speak of those days," he said. "Have to get up at seven o'clock. See yonder red barrel on the bar? Go examine it."

I walked over to the bar and picked up a cask about a foot high, constructed of red rubber with a hard rubber cap that fits over the top. I noticed that the little barrel was looking a bit soiled and ragged around the edges.

"Before departing for the studio," he said, "I whip up a quart of martinis, tasting the mixture now and then to make certain that the ingredients are correct. I fill the little barrel with ice, in case I should stumble on a highball or so during the day. When I leave for the studio I have the little barrel under one arm and a quart of martinis under the other. That's all I drink when I'm working. A man should be temperate during working hours. The little red barrel is one of muh fondest possessions. As you see, it is getting a bit worn. Made a great effort to obtain others like it, but alas! They are not available. Rubber shortage, you know. I tell you, the war has hit me hard!"

Somehow Mr. Fields got onto the subject of Mack Sennett, who was once his employer. Mr. Sennett's days of glory are long past and he lives now in a small Hollywood apartment, complaining over the way the world has passed him by.

"Hard man to get along with, Mack Sennett," said Mr. Fields. "Always had a bad habit. Chewed tobacco. Sit around by the hour and chew tobacco even when it interfered with his taking in alcohol. Wouldn't bother me so much except that he's always *talking* about chewing tobacco. Says it's the greatest thing in the world. Says it kills germs. Says he's got the cleanest mouth in the world. Sits around talking about his cleanest mouth in the world and spits all over the carpet. Remember the time I was having a big party on a Sunday afternoon. Lived in Beverly Hills then. Seems that a couple of high society girls came out from New York. Rich girls. Had the movie bug. Wanted to be actresses. Had beautiful clothes. Drove around in a limousine that had its inside lined with pink silk—cushions and walls and all. Prettiest thing you ever saw, the inside of that car, all pink silk.

"Somehow these girls met Mack Sennett. Knew his name and thought he was still a big power in the movies. Mack thought he saw a chance to get back into the business, introducing these girls to pictures. He called me up. Told me all about it. Asked if he couldn't bring these girls to my party. Knew a lot of stars would be there. Wanted to make a big impression on the girls. I said okay.

"So here they came—Mack and the two girls—riding in that pink silk limousine. Everything was fine. Mack sat over in a corner and chewed tobacco awhile, then he'd drink awhile, then he'd sit and chew some more and deliver his lecture on how clean his mouth was and how the germs couldn't live in it.

"Girls finally said it was time for them to be going. I went to get Mack. He was a little wobbly, but still chewing tobacco. Straightened himself up and walked with me out to the beautiful car. Got in the back seat. Sat down between the two girls. Guess he forgot to spit before he got in the car. Leaned over one of the girls and spit out the window. Only trouble was, the window hadn't been wheeled down. Splashed and splattered all over that beautiful silk upholstery, all over the expensive clothes those girls had on. Girls went away mad and left him behind. Had to have somebody else drive him home. Good old Mack! Poor fellow always got bad breaks."

A maid came into the room, finger to her lips.

"Shhhhhhh!" she said. "Everybody keep quiet."

Mr. Fields looked at her.

"God-damn landlord here again?" he demanded.

"Shhhhh!" she said. "Don't say a word, Mr. Fields."

"God-damn landlord," he insisted. "Throw him out!"

"No," whispered the maid. "Quiet, now. It's two girls down at the front door. They want autographs. I told them you weren't in."

Mr. La Cava got up and so did I. We decided it was time to leave. Mr. La Cava drove me back to Castle Argyle. He said the landlord crack was just a gag on Mr. Fields's part. The comedian is a wealthy man, doesn't need to work.

"Bill's just like the rest of them," he said. "Can't stay out of the picture for any length of time. He could go back in the hills and build himself a beautiful home and just sit there and drink with his friends. But he won't do it. He has no illusions about fame, but he gets restless unless he's in there performing occasionally. He's not after the adulation of the mob. He knows the I.Q. of the mob.

"We went to Jack Barrymore's funeral. They were great friends, as you may well imagine. The procession went through a section where the sidewalks were crowded with women and children. A lot of big stars were in the automobiles. As each car went by and the crowd recognized a star, a tremendous yelling and cheering went up. They yelled for Bill, too, ignoring the fact that Jack was taking his last ride up ahead. Bill just looked at them and shook his head and said, 'God-damn morons!'"

Edgar Bergen has worked frequently with Mr. Fields both in pictures and radio. Mr. Fields likes to compose his own gags and insert them in his scripts. Quite often these gags are considered to be unsuited to radio. There was one script in which Mr. Fields had occasion to refer several times to a mythical concert singer. He insisted upon calling her "Madame Pussy de Pussy." The radio people tried to explain to him that the name was hardly proper fare for radio. Mr. Fields argued stubbornly for it and they finally told him that he couldn't use it.

"God help us!" cried Mr. Fields. "This place has been taken over by the forces of evil! What, I demand, what in all this world could be more innocent than a little kitten!"

CHAPTER XXIV   *Best of Breed*

WE WERE ABOARD the Sante Fe's Super Chief running between Chicago and Los Angeles and I was sulking. We were having domestic difficulties. In the first place, we were riding in a drawing room, and I was spending my time looking for cowboys. Every time I cross the continent I spend the Western portions of the journey looking for cowboys. I've seen many a mesa devoid of its wild horse; I've looked upon whole counties of purple sage without spotting a rider of it. Yet I'm almost always at the window, hopeful of seeing a man on a horse.

We were going through a dry and dusty part of the country and the simple act of looking at it made me thirsty, so I ordered a drink. I pushed a button and the porter came. He had to go forward several cars and notify the bar steward, then the bar steward made the delivery. This procedure struck me as a waste of valuable time.

"The thing that's wrong with this train," I said to my wife, "is the absence of telephones. They ought to have telephones, so a man could call the club car and tell the guy to bring a drink."

My wife looked at me with an expression which suggested she considered me daft.

"Well," she said, "if that isn't a hot one! They should make you get off this train and ride a freight. Here you are—sitting in luxury, lolling in a drawing room on the finest train in the country. You don't even have to move your lazy carcass to press the button. Think of the pioneers. (She went to college and knows about pioneers.) Less than a hundred years ago they were traveling across this same country in their covered wagons. Most of the time they were hungry and had nothing to eat. They were thirsty and couldn't find water. They were sick and had no doctors. Sometimes they managed to cover as much as ten miles a day if they were lucky and the Indians didn't get them. They were real men. And you . . . Here you sit! Bellyaching because they haven't got telephones on the Super Chief, so you can get your scotch thirty seconds faster than you get it otherwise. Sometimes!"

That didn't set well with me. After the inefficient delivery system had completed the cycle and I had my drink, I finished it and stomped off to the club car where I met a man who said he made a fortune as a fire-engine salesman. I spent a couple of hours in the club car and then went back to the drawing room. The sight that met my eyes when I opened the door was staggering.

Here we were, occupying this elegant drawing room on this most excellent of trains, and my wife had been doing the washing. She had strung lines from corner to corner and from these lines were hanging wet socks, underwear, a dripping brassière, and sundry other articles of clothing.

"Good God!" I said. "Have you no sense of refinement? Why didn't you call the porter and have him gather up all the Pullman towels and wash *them* while you were at it? This is a fine thing! Suppose I had run into Charles Boyer up there in the club car, and asked him back to my drawing room for a drink?"

"Charles Boyer," she said, "probably washes his *own* socks."

So, what with one thing and another and the fact that we would be in Kansas before nightfall, I was sulking. I sat beneath the clotheslines and stared out the window. The Super Chief pulled into a siding to wait for a military train to pass. I was just staring at the bleak scenery when I saw a bird.

This bird was suspended in mid-air about ten feet above the ground. It was headed in an easterly direction and it was flying, yet it wasn't going anywhere. I watched it for ten minutes and it didn't move forward or backward as much as six inches. I could tell that the wind wasn't strong, which might have explained the bird's lack of progress. Somehow the thing fascinated me. I didn't know what kind of bird it was and I couldn't figure out its motive in flying at a standstill.

"Furthermore," I said suddenly to my wife, "when I get back to New York I think I'll take up bird-watching." I don't know why I figured that would be a way of getting back at her.

I might have done it, too, just to get even with her. I gave some serious consideration to the matter. I saw a book advertised and I think it was called *How to Watch Birds*. It seems incredible to me that an entire book could be written on the subject. I tried to get it but the store didn't have a copy and I let it go for a while. By the time it was in stock again, I had lost interest in bird-watching. If I had the book now I know what kind of binding I'd want on it. I already have a book bound in half-calf. I'd want *How to Watch Birds* bound in half-ass.

I don't mind glancing at a bird now and then, but after careful consideration I don't think I'd care to go out deliberately, creep up on a bird, and just sit there and watch it. I think maybe birds get more amusement out of bird-watchers than bird-watchers out of birds.

It might be fun, in fact, to become a bird-watcher watcher. Brooklyn could be a good field for that sport. The bird-watchers of Brooklyn have an organization called the Brooklyn Bird Club and during the first years of the war their hobby became quite precarious.

Whenever these Brooklyn people went out bird-watching, other people didn't know they were watching birds but suspected them of watching something else, such as war plants or harbor installations, and the next thing they knew the F.B.I. was around watching *them*.

The game became doubly hazardous because it is the custom of bird-watchers to use field glasses. These glasses are considered essential to Class A bird-watching in Brooklyn because a Brooklyn bird is inclined to be suspicious of human motives and a watcher seldom gets close enough to observe him with the naked eye.

One day a Brooklyn bird-watcher turned up near the shore of Jamaica Bay, blithefully pursuing his hobby. He was whipping his field glasses around, watching for birds to watch, when the law closed in on him. He was carted off to a near-by Army post and cross-examined. I remember reading about the case in the papers. They asked him what he was doing on the water front with field glasses. He said he was watching birds. You can imagine what he went through before he was released, before he was able to convince his captors that he was simply looking for a linnet.

So the Brooklyn bird-watchers had to curtail their activities. For the time being they confined their activities to wandering in the Brooklyn parks, glancing casually at birds, and letting it go at that. There was one small group that refused to be intimidated. These people set up a sort of bird-watching black market. They made a practice of assembling deep inside a large cemetery where they spent hours just watching the hell out of birds. They reasoned that even if they were caught at it, nobody would likely accuse them of hanging around military objectives in a graveyard.

The balance of this chapter will be about dogs.

A man signing himself G. L. Wyndham published an article knocking dogs in the American *Mercury* last winter. Mr. Wyndham developed an eloquent argument in an effort to demonstrate that dogs are dumb, dirty, and depraved. The magazine is still catching hell from its readers, most of whom wrote letters urging that Mr. Wyndham be taken out and whittled with a knife until deader than Kelcey's knuckles. Attacking dogs is more dangerous than attacking the efficacy of prayer.

A Mrs. Walter Ferguson, who writes a syndicated column, got sore in print one day about the fact that dog owners were pestering war-ration boards in behalf of their pooches. An amazing number of citizens applied for ration books to be made out in the name of Fido McGonigle or Sport Ten Eyck or Laddie Lastfogel. When these requests were turned down the applicants (the human ones) generally exploded with wrath and said what the hell kind of a democracy is this anyhow? Mrs. Ferguson got tons of mail as a consequence of writing that column. She was called such a variety of names that even Eleanor Roosevelt's personal collection couldn't come up to them. One correspondent concluded her letter to Mrs. Ferguson with the wise observation: "God must have loved dogs because He gave them His name spelled backward."

A writer so ill-advised as to speak of a dog in anything but glowing phrases is quickly denounced as a human viper, a drooling lunatic, a succubus, and a honey-dipper in the bottomless pit. He becomes, in popular disesteem, a fiend more depraved than Hitler. At the time Reinhard Heydrich was happily killed a New York newspaper discussing the matter referred to him as a dog. Forthwith came a letter from a lady, writing in behalf of her dog, protesting against use of the word "dog" in reference to such a man.

I want it understood that I am not speaking disparagingly of dogs. I have been gnawed twice by dogs whose owners assured me they wouldn't hurt a fly. But it was my fault both times for going around like an idiot with legs on me.

When I was a boy I had a dog named Dud. He was my companion for a long time until the day when several of us fashioned a rope elevator and hauled him into a barn loft where we had a hideout. We no more than got Dud into the loft when a bat flew out from behind a rafter and the dog went after him. The bat shot out an open window and Dud didn't hesitate, even though he knew nothing about the science of aerodynamics. He went sailing through the window and died on the ground below. He was given a funeral that would compare favorably with the last rites for a Tammany sachem, more than a hundred boys and girls attending. Since then I have never owned another dog though I have known and enjoyed the company of many and I have come to hate a few and yearn for the privilege of doing bodily harm to them. As I have said, though, I am not writing against dogs. I'm only setting down a few stories about *people* who have dogs.

For a number of years I have collected stories about dog owners and their peculiar deportment. My clippings and notes filled a large envelope but now that I examine its contents I find that much of the material is missing. I have a suspicion that a dog came in and found the envelope and chewed up part of the material. Pardon me. I mean a dog lover came in and chewed it up. I remember distinctly that the clipping which started the collection was a brief, unbiased story about a dog-catering service set up in London. In addition to the usual services, such as shampooing and hair-cutting and toenail-burnishing, this company delivered regular meals for dogs. The thing that struck me as unique was a paragraph stating that the caterer provided fish dinners on Fridays for dogs belonging to Roman Catholic families. That clipping is missing, and so are the ones dealing with the hot controversy over whether dogs should be given the Purple Heart, Silver Star, Distinguished Service Cross, and other decorations designed for humans.

Hollywood is a fine town for the collection of stories about people with dogs because almost everybody has one or more. The dog population of New York is tremendous. An air warden in the Central Park area was assigned the job of taking a census of a large apartment house. His report showed that occupants of the building included seventy-two dogs and one baby. The people in my own neighborhood are partial to dogs. I'm glad that I was girlish in my childhood and learned to skip rope, for this ability stands me in good stead nowadays when I make a progress along the streets of Jackson Heights. I consider myself one of the most adroit leash-hoppers in the Borough of Queens. It seems to be proper technique, when walking a dog, for the owner to take one edge of the sidewalk, the dog the other edge, and a leash in between. I have a friend who, just a few evenings ago, came along the street and encountered a woman whose leash was blocking his way. He stopped, she stopped, the dog stopped, and the leash stopped. He stood there, expecting her to reel in her dog and make a passage for him but, as is the custom among dog-walkers, she looked upon my friend as a mere human and did nothing of the kind. It dawned upon him that he was expected to get off the sidewalk. Rather than make a scene he did just that, but on arriving at the other side he turned around and said to the dog owner:

"Lady, you are a God-damn *woman*." This remark was irrelevant and unfair. The lady might easily have been a man.

A city editor of my acquaintance, a man who would swiftly throw out a story reporting the end of the war if it were necessary to get a story about a dog on Page One, was talking to me one day about the intelligence of dogs.

"A dog," he said, "is just naturally smart. Knows how to figure things out. I remember one day when I was at the dog races in Florida. You know how the mechanical rabbit runs around the edge of the track and the dogs race after it. Well, there was one dog that finally figured the thing out. He had been coming out of the box time after time, maybe hundreds of times, and chasing after that rabbit and never catching it. Then he got smart. He reasoned the thing out in his head. The day I was there he came out of the box with the rest of the pack. All the others lit off down the track after the rabbit. Not this dog. He slowed down, hopped over the fence, raced across the infield, jumped the other fence, and got into the back stretch. That dog had it figured out that the way to nab the rabbit was to take the short cut and head it off. He was in the back stretch before the rabbit ever came around the bend. I tell you, a dog is a smart animal."

"Did he get the rabbit?" I asked.

"Well," he said, "that's the sad part. The rabbit is mounted on an iron hoot nanny that sticks out from the rail. There stood the dog, waiting. The rabbit came charging down the line. The dog watched it, standing tense. When the rabbit was about fifteen feet from him, that dog lunged through the air to meet it. Broke his neck."

A sad story, all right. That city editor has always been a man capable of recognizing smartness at a glance, whether in man or beast.

Sidney Whipple came back from a Christmas shopping expedition one day to tell of a small adventure he had in Saks Fifth Avenue. He was waiting at the jewelry counter while a girl was wrapping his package. Up came a richly dressed woman with a tiny dog on a leash. Sidney, always amiable, bent a little way down and started to pat the dog on the head. The dog snarled and tried to take off Mr. Whipple's finger. This was most embarrassing to the lady. She spoke a few scolding words to her pet, employing the customary baby talk, then turned apologetically to Sidney.

"Don't you pay a *bit* of attention to him," she said. "He's just angry because I won't take him to the toy department."

A friend of mine, let us call her Mrs. Parks, was visiting my apartment in Hollywood one afternoon when she made a telephone call to an elderly woman who was her friend, the widow of a rich industrialist. The elderly woman appeared to have half the money in the world and she also had a dog. She asked Mrs. Parks to do her a favor.

Her dog was sick, she said, and confined to a dog hospital. Would Mrs. Parks go to the hospital and "take him his toy?"

"I would go over myself," she said, "but if I did it would just upset him. The doctor recommended that I stay away for a while. He's a *very sick child* but I'm confident he'll pull through. I know he misses his toy and I want him to have it. If you'll take it over to him I know he'll realize I've been thinking of him night and day."

Mrs. Parks agreed. The "toy" proved to be a thick Turkish towel with a knot tied in the middle. It had been freshly laundered and knotted. The wealthy lady caressed it and kissed it before handing it over for delivery.

"You know," she told Mrs. Parks, "I've always understood dogs better than most people. Once I accompanied my dear husband on a business visit to the White House. He had to see President Harding on a business matter. We had never cared much for Mr. Harding, but when we got to the White House we were introduced to Laddie. Laddie took to us both, immediately, and the President said that ordinarily he did not like strangers. The President said, 'It proves Laddie is very discriminating.' Well, we were converted to Mr. Harding right then and there."

For a final dog story I give you Butch Blair in "The Great Impersonation." Butch is a German shepherd, patriarch of the assorted animals inhabiting the Rufus Blair home. Butch weighs more than I do and knows it. He has grown old and developed new eccentricities with age. For example, he eats Pocket Books. The Blairs can't keep Pocket Books in the house. No matter where they hide them, Butch will find them and eat them. I think it's a form of exhibitionism on his part. He thinks it is clever because he does most of his Pocket Book eating in front of company. Every time I ever arrived at the Blair home, Butch promptly set up a clamor and raced around the house until he found a Pocket Book. Then he'd fetch it to the center of the living-room floor, lie down with it, and quietly eat it, whether it be *The Pocket Book of Etiquette, The Case of the Howling Dog, Mrs. Miniver,* or *See Here, Private Hargrove.* Mr. Blair tells me that Butch once tried to eat a copy of *Life in a Putty Knife Factory* but it made him violently ill, causing him to throw up an earlier meal consisting of *Jeeves, Green Light,* and *Mission to Moscow,* and since then he never touches my stuff.

Whenever possible the Blairs take Butch with them on out-of-town trips. Once they went to San Francisco, engaging a bedroom on The Lark, a train which is customarily greeted in the Los Angeles station by shouts from railroad workers who cry, "Hark! Hark! The Lark!"

The Blairs got Butch into the bedroom without difficulty but from then on there were unpleasant developments. Butch has a habit of exposing his fangs and snarling, presenting a prospect that would frighten the late Albert Payson Terhune. Moreover, Butch is suspicious of anybody in a uniform. The conductor who came for the tickets was the first victim of this suspicion, and the transaction finally had to be consummated under the door. White-jacketed waiters all but got their heads torn off whenever they tried to bring Mr. Blair's bourbon, and they ended up by refusing to serve him. During the night Butch spent all his time trying to climb into the upper berth where his master was losing sleep. The dog barked and howled and screamed, and the other passengers pounded on the walls, yelled their protests, and complained bitterly to the train officials.

At last they reached San Francisco. Mr. Blair got Butch off the train and started down the platform. He encountered the conductor and, with the intention of placating that gentleman, said:

"Butch didn't behave himself very well on the trip, did he? I hope he doesn't act up like that on the return trip."

"Are you taking him back to L. A.?" asked the conductor.

"My wife is," said Mr. Blair. "Going back next week—on The Lark."

"Oh no, he's not," said the conductor. "That dog is never going *anywhere* again on The Lark. That dog made this run a hell on earth and I intend to say as much in my report. You'll not get *him* on The Lark, or on any other trains belonging to this company."

"We'll see," said Mr. Blair abruptly. He is a man who loves nothing more than to find an obstacle that needs surmounting.

Yet the conductor's mandate gave him some worry. He planned to remain in San Francisco awhile and Mrs. Blair was to return with Butch. Mr. Blair was determined that Butch should ride The Lark back to Hollywood.

He went out and bought a pair of dark glasses. Then he bought a Seeing Eye dog harness.

He took Mrs. Blair and Butch to the station. Mrs. Blair had on the dark glasses and Butch, wearing the harness, was supposed to be impersonating a Seeing Eye dog. He did all right until they got through the ticket gate. The moment he reached the platform and saw the train he went into rebellion. He wanted nothing whatever to do with that iron monster. He started growling, flopped down on his belly, and refused to move another inch.

By good fortune another conductor was in charge of the train, else the plot would have died right then. In any event, passengers and trainmen were treated to a unique spectacle.

Down the platform came a blind woman, *dragging* her Seeing Eye dog along the concrete. Over the stubborn dog stood a man, cursing the animal fluently. The blind woman dragged that dog all the way down the platform and then the man spent ten minutes wrestling with the animal, boosting him into the vestibule of the car.

In spite of Butch's rebellious performance, they got away with it.

If, by chance, this chapter has ruffled your composure, I have a way of getting you back into a pleasant mood.

Mother memory cellophane bellboy melancholy belladonna flamingo wilderness tambourine lavender.

Those are the ten most beautiful-sounding words in the English language as chosen in a nationwide poll. Read them over again if you want to. Feel better?

CHAPTER XXV   *Dinah's Fan*

THIS IS BY WAY of apology to Señor Jack Pfefer, the wrestling impresario. Señor Pfefer, whose views on the sweet mystery were set down in *Life in a Putty Knife Factory,* has been described by Fred Allen as a man with six toes on each foot. "Jack got his start in life," says Fred, "stamping out forest fires for a living."

One afternoon I encountered Señor Pfefer on Vine Street in Hollywood. Immediately I went to work on him with a business proposition. I wanted to hire his prize possession, the Swedish Angel, to serve as my secretary and collaborator at Paramount.

"Anyting in the vorld I do for you, my frand," said Señor Pfefer, "vith the sole exsaption of not that. Does Paramount vant to hire the Svedish Angel, let Paramount hire the Svedish Angel as movie star. Already has been offered the Svedish Angel to Paramount, but they are dumbbals. Everybody knows the Svedish Angel is a great ector, should be starred up in pictures. But no. Vith me is strickly a business metter. For you, my frand, I lat you have him but not for Paramount, them bums. Now, if you . . ."

With rude disregard for a great man, I suddenly left him in the middle of a sentence and hurried across the street. I had spotted Miss Fanny Rose Shore and I didn't want to miss her. I didn't want to miss her because of all the dames in Hollywood I consider her to be the most admirable, the most sensible, and the most fun.

Miss Fanny Rose Shore sings superbly under the more familiar name of Dinah, and I had to tell her something. We have been friends for a number of years. When we first got acquainted I was a newspaper reporter and she was struggling upward from a small start as a singer at a radio station in Manhattan.

The thing I wanted to see Dinah about was a telephone number. During our friendship she had become the No. 1 gal singer of the nation, a top radio star, a movie celebrity, and a favorite of the servicemen. And trudging along in her wake I had become a book author. She was always inclined to rib me about how fast she was going forward and how I should hurry up or she'd be forced to quit speaking to me in public. One day I met her on the street and she whooped in triumph.

"You don't rate any more," she said. "I'm really up there now! Guess what has happened! *I've got an unlisted telephone!*"

H. L. Mencken has said that the final test of fame is to have a crazy person imagine he is you. The next to final test of fame is to have an unlisted telephone number. Even H. L. Mencken is in the book. So the reason I left Señor Pfefer so abruptly and descended upon Fanny Rose Shore was to inform her that *I* now have an unlisted number. She took it well. Wasn't a bit jealous about my triumph. Even asked me for my autograph and then traded phone numbers with me.

That little meeting there on Vine Street brought back a couple of memories. Once when I was in Baltimore Dinah was playing a local theater and I made a date to take her to lunch. I called for her at her theater dressing room and we sat around and talked awhile. She told me I had to quit calling her Fanny Rose. She said that when she was a schoolgirl the other kids were always making jokes about her name. One kid would say, "Fanny sat on a tack." Another kid would say, "When Fanny sat on a tack, did Fanny rise?" And the other would reply, "Fanny rose, shore!"

Dinah had to change from stage clothes to street dress. She began taking things off there in the little dressing room. Upon reaching an interesting stage in these operations, she said:

"Now, turn around. Face the wall."

"Can't I just put one hand over my eyes?" I said. "I got a sore neck."

She made me turn clear around and stay turned around until she said she was ready. Women are so distrustful.

We had lunch and went back to the theater and sat around some more and were just gabbing when someone knocked on the door. It was a messenger with a package. The package had been forwarded from New York. Dinah opened it and found a small phonograph record.

"What the Sam Hill is this?" she said. Then she saw a piece of paper with some writing on it. "Oh, sure," she said. "It's from that boy. He writes to me all the time. Let's play it."

She put the record on her portable machine and we sat down to listen. I took notes on it because it represented a great stride in the march of civilization. It went approximately like this:

"Hello, uh, hello, Dinah. This is Arthur Pomeroy Verplanck of Binghamton, New York, your fan forever. I have my own recording machine now. Uh, oh yes, thank me, I mean thank you for your lovely Christmas card. It was lovely, Dinah. Holy smoke! That's Dad playing the radio in the other room. Don't mind that. There goes Mother, telling him to turn it down, turn it down. Now, lemmy see, what can I say to you? I have, uh, maybe you notice, I have a terrible cold. Yes. I have a terrible cold. Lemmy see, now. Here's my mother now, Dinah. C'mere, Ma. I don't know what to say to her, Ma. She's such a wonderful girl, such a wonderful girl, I don't know what to say. You say something, Ma. You got a cold too. We all got colds up here, Dinah. Here's Ma. Say something, Ma. (Tired female voice comes in.) I don't know what to say. I just don't know what to say. She has a lovely voice when she sings. (Back to Arthur Pomeroy Verplanck.) Yes, that's it. That's what I wanna say. Dinah, we love your singing. I have this terrible cold. Gee, Ma, I don't know what to say. A lovely girl like that. Like Dinah. Here, Ma, you say something. Go on now. (Tired female voice again.) I don't know what to say. (Arthur Pomeroy Verplanck comes back.) Well, anyway, she's got a beautiful voice. I'm your fan forever, Dinah. When you get through playing this, Part One and Part Two, sit right down and write me a nice letter and tell me how you liked it. Now, uh, don't you fail me now, Dinah. When this side is finished, turn it over. It's a sorta surprise for you on the other side. But just remember I got this awful cold. Uh, this is Arthur Pomeroy Verplanck of Binghamton, New York, signing off. Turn over."

Part One was finished.

"Well, I'll be darned," said Dinah, shutting off the machine. "I think that's the sweetest thing. Wonder what on earth is on the other side."

"Yes," I put in. "Hurry up and play it. He said there's a surprise on the other side. I can't wait."

She turned the platter over and Arthur Pomeroy Verplanck's voice came through again. He spoke of having this awful, terrible cold and apologized for it, and then raised his voice in song. He sang "I Don't Wanna Set the World on Fy-yerr." Sang it all the way through.

When Part Two was finished we sat and looked at each other a bit, and I started to say something. Dinah cut me off.

"Maybe it *is* corny," she said, "but I think it's downright sweet."

CHAPTER XXVI *Arkansas Medley*

THE SUBJECT MATTER of these state papers might have been Arkansas if Buddy DeSylva had subjugated his emotions, used his head, and withdrawn his offer of employment at Paramount. For a long time I had hankered to visit the Wonder State, live there awhile, and try to absorb some of the atmosphere.

There was a chance that I would be turned back at the state line because the people and the government of Arkansas are sensitive about their commonwealth. If a furriner comes in and writes about their backwoods citizenry, they will hold him up before the world as a snake-in-the-weeds, a deformed second cousin to a razorback hawg, and a liar to who-laid-the-chunk. Let one of their own boys carry the folksy drama of Arkansas life to the rest of the world and that is okay; they make a hero out of him.

Bob Burns, for example. Bob can tell stories about Arkansas that reasonably should wither the toes of Chamber of Commerce executives; yet he is one of the state's primary exhibits in the pride-and-joy department. There is one story Bob hasn't told on the radio or elsewhere in public. A few years ago he and Mrs. Burns were on an automobile tour of Arkansas and were scheduled to arrive at a certain small town at the lunch hour. Word reached this town that the great Bob Burns was coming, and the proprietor of the local restaurant, where the visitors would have to eat unless they were packing their own lunch, got busy stirring up interest.

When Mr. and Mrs. Burns arrived they found the town's total population, including cats, jammed into the restaurant. The proprietor was doing the biggest business of his career but he thoughtfully held a table for the distinguished visitors.

It was not a quiet, leisurely meal for them because Bob was kept busy shaking hands, patting babies on the head, and listening to home-talent talkers.

At last the restaurant proprietor approached Bob.

"Mr. Burns," he said, "I have got a supply of five hunnerd pitcher post cards advertisin' are beautiful little city. I can git five cents apiece for these cards, but if you was to sign your name onto them, I could git twenny-five cents apiece for them. I would be mighty proud for you to do this."

It was a wearisome job but Mr. Burns set to work and signed every one of those cards. Then it was time to go. He pushed his way through the crowd to the counter where the proprietor stood at the cash drawer.

"Well," said Bob, "we got to git a move on. How much do I owe you?"

"That'll be sixty-five cents," said the proprietor, beaming.

Bob considered the thing for a moment. Sixty-five cents?

"How does that figger out?" he asked out of curiosity.

"Well," said the smiling host, "I'm only chargin' you for Mrs. Burns's dinner. *Yourn* is on the house!"

Bob gave me another story that I can't resist setting down here:

I remember the time we had the big blizzard down home. Snow piled up to the second-story windows. Everybody was marooned in their homes. My uncle was lookin' out the second-story window of his store. There wasn't nothin' but a sea of snow as fur as the eye could reach. Not a sign of life. Suddenly on top of the hill, where Main Street dips down to Lick Skillet, he saw snow a-flyin' up in the air. It kept gettin' closer and closer. On down the middle of Main Street came this flurry of snow flyin' every which way.

Finally it was right under my uncle's window and he could lean out and see what it was. It was a little old man with long whiskers that had been shovelin' a trench through that deep snow. My uncle says, "Where in the world did *you* come from?" The little old man says, "I dug my way here from forty miles back in the mountains." So my uncle says, "You musta been desperate to dig your way forty mile through this blizzard." And the little old man says, "I'll say I was desperate. We bin out of nutmeg for two weeks."

The Wonder State is equally proud of Chet Lauck and Norris Goff. These two boys are from Mena, Arkansas, a town that was named for the tail end of Queen Wilhelmina's name and then misspelled. Chet Lauck and Norris Goff have been broadcasting dialect dialogues for fifteen years under the names of Lum Edwards and Abner Peabody. A stranger to Arkansas might suspect that their names would be stricken from the vital statistics of the state and that the governor would law-sue 'em. To the contrary, the main United States Highway traversing Arkansas has been named, by legislative act, the Lum & Abner Highway. And whereas the town of Pine Ridge was pure invention at the beginning, it now exists in fact. The only character in the Lum and Abner broadcasts bearing the actual name of his living counterpart is Dick Huddleston, the storekeeper. The town where he lives and keeps store was called Waters until Lum and Abner began using Dick's name on the air. Waters is now officially Pine Ridge.

Chet Lauck and Tuffy Goff are youthful, good-looking, college-bred men who live in Hollywood and broadcast from there. They write their own scripts, and it is my opinion that those scripts contain some of the best regional humor produced in America.

Being a devout follower of Pine Ridge doings, I succeeded in making the acquaintance of Lum and Abner and now I no longer need to visit Arkansas. I know all about it. Lauck and Goff Arkansawed me dizzy. They told stories that are true and stories that are pure folklore, and they know how to tell them.

They have a shrewd grasp of the small-town character, and I got vast enjoyment out of their analysis of the Arkansas attitude. In every little town there is usually a group of men who loaf together on the main street, passing judgment on the world about them. These men appear to look upon mules as being more important than humans. They'll be sitting in front of a store when a team of mules comes in view, pulling a wagon. There'll be a man on the wagon, but they don't care about him. They're interested in those mules.

"That off mule yonder," one of them will say, "that's the same mule that Old Man Wivvett got from the Widder Binks when she moved to Oklahoma, and then give to Ortho Hackenstaff when Ortho married up with Sairy Wivvett."

"Yer dead wrong," says another. "That ain't the one. That off mule come from the county seat two and a half year ago, bought at auction by Caleb Bogle and the first week kicked his hard man and broke his laig in two places."

They'll argue the matter heatedly until the team draws closer and the mule in question is definitely identified as the one Old Man Wivvett "give" to Ortho Hackenstaff. Whereupon the man who had been correct in his identification would slap his thigh and say:

"I knowed I knowed 'er!"

The small-town man of Arkansas places great stock in his knowledge of animals and their ways. Norris Goff tells of the time Ezra Seestrunk got lost in the woods, far from town. Ezra had his dog with him and after hours of wandering hit upon a scheme for finding his way back to town. He cut himself a switch from a tree and began to whip the dog. The dog lit out through the woods, running about half a mile, then stopping to wait for Ezra. When Ezra would catch up, he'd beat the dog some more with the switch and the animal would run another half mile. Before long Ezra and dog were home. "A beat dog," said Ezra, "will head fer home ever' time."

There's the story of the Gasper family and the first automobile. The Gaspers lived in a small house alongside a dirt road. The road consisted of two deep ruts, dug out by the wheels of countless farm wagons—two wriggling, wavering lines stretched across the countryside.

It was a hot summer day when the first automobile came down that road, and Willie Gasper was at work in a field half a mile from the house when he first sighted the monster. Willie lit a shuck for the house, shouting a warning to his paw and maw. Paw took one look at the thing coming down the road, traveling a wild zigzag course with its wheels in the wagon ruts. Paw ordered Maw and Willie to take cover, then threw the sofa across the doorway for a barricade, grabbed up his shotgun and crouched behind it. Just as the clattering devil came abreast of the house Paw drew a careful bead on it and pulled the trigger. The charge struck the side of the car and the man at the wheel gave up his post in terror, leaping to the ground and running like a jack rabbit for the woods. The car went jiggling on down the road, following the ruts. From behind the stove Maw spoke:

"Did ye kill it, Paw?"

"Nawp," said Paw. "Didn't kill it, but 'y God I made it leave go of that man it had."

CHAPTER XXVII   *A Preface*

Deep within the wellspring* of my secret nature is just a smidgeon of sentiment. It rends my spirit to see a thing deprived of its natural companion—a scarecrow without a crow to scare; a Tommy Manville without a helpmeet; an Old Gold bereft of its apple honey; a lovely dell without a farmer in it; a ballplayer without balls.

Because of this weakness, then, I have taken in a poor, homeless preface. It is a good preface, well disposed toward the world, yet it has been knocking around for months and months, lonely and forlorn and anguished.

Fred Allen is the father of this preface. A long time ago

---

*"Wellspring" is a word I made up out of my own head, on the spur of the moment. Darned if it isn't in the dictionary! Means the same thing *my* word means!

a man came to him and said that he was getting up a book on horses. He said his book would be a sort of anthology and that he needed a beguiling preface and would Fred Allen provide it?

Mr. Allen set to work at once and turned out a fine preface for a book about horses. On the day he finished it he telephoned the man for whom it was written, and the man said he had run into difficulties and his horse book wasn't to be published after all.

Mr. Allen wearily chucked his composition into the waste basket. Then a notion occurred to him. Someday, he said to himself, somebody might sit down and write a book about horses and, having written it, ask Mr. Allen to turn out a preface for it. He salvaged the sheets and tucked them away in his files. From then on he answered phone calls eagerly, and fairly snatched letters away from the mailman, but no request for a preface about the horse ever came.

During one of his dispirited moments Mr. Allen happened to tell me about his lone and lorn preface.

"The poor thing," he said, "is languishing up there in my apartment, wasting away for lack of a book to go on the front of."

I'll confess it: I was touched. I offered to provide a haven for that preface. I said I could even find a place for it in a book which, while not a treatise on horses, has the word "horse" in its title. I'm glad I adopted that preface. I think it will become the standard authority on the horse. Up to now scholars have had to lean on such works as *The Horse; Its Treatment in Health and Disease* (1906) J. Wortley Axe; *The Horse and Its Relatives* (1912) R. Lyddekker; *Lehrbuch der Pferdezucht* (*Berlin,* 1926) Schwarznecker, and *Today's Best Bet* (1944) Fred Keats.

These are overshadowed by the Allen opus. Mr. Allen, long famous as an authority on the behavior of horses' behinds, now takes his place as the Nestor of Nags, the Plutarch of the Percheron.

It has been impossible for me to put the horse preface in the place where prefaces customarily are found. It appears here at the end of my book because that seems to be the next-best place for it. Here it is:

Preface

THIS BOOK is dedicated to the horse. Most books are sold in cities. Since the automobile has driven the horse from metropolitan streets there are millions of people living in cities, potential book purchasers, who have never seen a horse. To them the horse is a spavined relic of the past, a denizen of yesteryear, who has trotted down the bridle path of time in the wake of the dinosaur and William Jennings Bryan. If the compiler of this horse anthology hopes to interest city readers in his equine treatise he must first acquaint them with the horse. He has passed his problem on to me. I have rounded up a set of dehydrated statistics and some random, unauthenticated facts that I hope will tend to clarify the horse. The city reader who consummates this miscellany will know what the horse is, where the horse came from, and what the future holds in store for the horse. This digest prospectus I call . . .

THE HORSE
(Reading time 5 minutes—for the first furlong)

The first horse was foaled from space approximately forty-five million years ago. This was millions of years before man first appeared on earth. The horse stalled around the Western Hemisphere several million years hoping that man would come to pass. The horse finally tired of waiting and became extinct.

This first horse was not the quadruped of noble dimensions the world knew later. Eohippus, the dawn horse, was about the size of a thyroid cat. The first stallions thought nothing of returning home and finding their mares neighing over a litter of tiny horses. History tells us that Eohippus was very neat. When the first horse became extinct no litter remained.

After the ice age the earth was defrosted and man, a little chapped and blowing on his hands, appeared. The horse returned. Man became attached to the horse. They roamed the earth together. Man noticed that the horse could travel much faster than he. When they set out for distant places together, the horse would jog along and arrive hours ahead of man. The urge for speed was born in man. He realized that if he could get on the horse and keep his seat, he and the horse would arrive together. Man would have company on his journey. Time would be saved.

Man started riding the horse. At first complications ensued. Man had no way of telling the horse how far he was going. When man arrived at his destination the horse galloped on. When the horse was exhausted, he stopped. Man had to dismount and walk back to where he was going. This was confusing. It was taking man longer to go from where he had been to where he was going than it formerly took him to go from where he was to where he wanted to go. Man had no way to stop the horse.

After many centuries man started bemoaning his fate. As the horse sped past his destination man would shout "Woe is me!" A century or so later the horse got the idea. When man cried "Woe is me!" the horse would stop. "Woe is me!" was shortened to "Woe!" The first man in England to own a horse added an "h." Ever since that time a horse has stopped whenever its rider has shouted "Whoa!"

When man found he could control the horse, he longed for greater speed. The horsewhip was invented. Man went to war on horseback. Alexander the Great tried to put his army on a horse. Alexander had more soldiers than he had horses. The wagon was invented. This proves that originally the horse came before the wagon.

Down through the ages the horse has been oppressed by man. The ancient Scythian rode his horse all day, killed him at night, ate his flesh, drank his blood, and used his bones and hoofs to make armor for the next day's mount.

The horse helped the white man to liquidate the Indian. The horse helped till the soil. The horse hauled the covered wagon, making possible the development of the West. The horse has dragged fire engines, ice and brewery wagons through city streets. The horse gave his all until early in the twentieth century (circa Henry Ford), when he saw the handwriting on the garage. With the coming of the machine age the horse gave way to the automobile, the tractor, and the truck. The horse was only to be found at race tracks, at polo matches, on bridle paths, and in Republic movies. The day of the horse was done.

It may be said, however, that without the horse:

Paul Revere and the Lone Ranger would have been pedestrians.

A man could only lose his shirt in a laundry.

The Northwest Mounted Police would have calluses elsewhere.

The horsefly would have no objective; horseflies would have to buzz around and sting each other.

Longfellow would never have written *The Village Blacksmith;* the blacksmith would have been in some other racket, hence no Anvil Chorus in music.

Horse-radish would have another name, perhaps boy-radish.

Lady Godiva's hair would have dragged on the ground.

A centaur would be half something else.

We wouldn't have milk; the cow first gave milk, but it took the horse to get it around.

Kreisler, having no bow, would have to slap his fiddle.

The champion horseshoe pitcher of America would be angry.

Rodeos would look pretty silly—cowboys just jumping around with nothing under them.

This should give the reader a working knowledge of the horse. If you now have a desire to know more about the horse I suggest you place your index finger on your tongue, dampen well, and turn this page.

FRED ALLEN.

So, there is the vagabond preface.

If you feel kindly toward it, I have a suggestion to make. Go out and find a book about horses and glue it onto the back of this book, then it will have a preface. Anything but *Black Beauty*.